The Parental Tool Box for Parents & Clinicians

Dayna Guido

Jim Guido

Global Heart Books

Published in the United States by Global Heart Books, a division of the Global Heart Group, Asheville, 2018.

www.globalheartbooks.com

www.globalheartgroup.com

Printed in the United States of America

ISBN: 978-1-7321218-0-5

Library of Congress Control Number: 2018904411

This book is dedicated
to the loving parent
inside us all.

Table of Contents

Acknowledgements

We want to thank all of the children, adolescents, and families who have shared with us a privileged view of their private lives and personal experiences. The learning experience has always been a two-way street.

To our supervisors, mentors, and colleagues we thank you for the insight and perspectives which allowed our interventions to be effective and rewarding.

Gratitude goes to Dr. Brooke Judkins who provided us guidance on the selection of the book contents from the early days of our process.

We are appreciative of the judicious scrutiny of Donna Limperes' editing skills. Her dedicated support helped keep our focus sharp.

We are indebted to our son, Lucio, who from an early age made us look good as parents, and whose formatting and production skills have greatly added to the visual comfort of ***The Parental Tool Box***.

The Parental Tool Box for Parents & Clinicians

Introduction

In its earliest form the motivation for writing this book was to help support and expand the after care services for children and adolescents in out-of-home placements. Experience and data amply demonstrate that long term retention of therapeutic gains acquired through placements, programs, short term therapy, and interventions was less than impressive, to say the least.

During our discussions it became apparent that a "tool box" was not only needed upon termination of therapeutic services (such as when a child or young adult returns home after placement) but also in any significant transition. This might include a child moving to a less structured program; or to a higher level of care; or from one therapist to another.

Parents struggle with a therapeutic demand to be "consistent" while attempting to adapt to the various philosophies and practices of each facility and service provided. The transition problem is all the more magnified with the trend in human services to shorten the length of stay at a placement and the similar emphasis on short term therapy and intervention.

Yet, the more we thought about it, the need for a pragmatic, versatile, and comprehensive tool box for parents went even further than just in transitions and termination of a specific service or intervention. It would also be helpful for parents wanting to learn skills to improve their parenting and clinicians wanting to help parents implement effective relationship and communication skills with their children and adolescents.

Our vision of this book is for it to be a resource guide for parents and clinicians to find and maintain a common language throughout all interventions and stages of development. Therefore, the book's mission statement is:

> *The Parental Tool Box for Parents & Clinicians is a compilation of strategies, perspectives, and skills to be used by parents and clinicians which effectively promote*

personal development and improved relationship functioning in children and families.

The recommended list of target audiences for this book includes anyone interested in the change process for children, adolescents, parents, and families. This includes parents, grandparents, guardians, clinicians, and other professionals. ***The Parental Tool Box*** is designed to be the thread that connects and maintains the best intentions of clinicians and parents in coordinating their efforts in the best interest of the child.

A clinician could use this book to help transfer gains made at an out-of-home placement to the family home. Similarly, a therapist could use the skills and strategies in the book on either side of a transition. A clinician releasing a resident to another program could use it as a way to help the child retain and transfer gains and changes to their next situation. A program taking on a child from a previous placement could use ***The Parental Tool Box*** to help in a smooth transition, continuing the skills learned previously and finding a common language the child can understand to assist in their learning and consistency.

Parents of children receiving services could use the book as a way of understanding professional interventions and practically transferring these skills and perspectives into the home and school environment. The book's rich and varied description of skills and techniques could be used by any parent wishing to improve or expand on their parenting skills, even if their child has never been identified as being in need of an intervention.

The collection of skills, strategies, techniques, and perspectives contained in ***The Parental Tool Box*** are intended to be presented in a relatively neutral manner, not steeped in any specific school, model, or ideology. While some sections and exercises will be more at home with a specific model than others, every treatment modality should find ample skills and strategies which are harmonious with their style and objectives.

You will find at the end of each chapter numerous **Home Improvement Exercises**. These exercises are intended to give you an opportunity to put into practice what you are learning. Research shows us that repetition is the key to make a desired change in life.

Feel free to adapt the **Home Improvement Exercises** in a way which is comfortable for you, such as writing out the answers to the questions, if writing is your preferred method for processing. It helps to dedicate a journal, notebook, or digital file to keep your writing in one place so you can refer to earlier exercises. Write out the question before you answer it as that will help center your focus of attention. If you prefer to process by talking it out, try the method of recording the question and then speak out your answer. Recording is simple on smartphones and other handheld devices. The advantage to this method is that you can do the "work" while you are doing your daily walk or drive to work, or even while doing the dishes. The **Home Improvement Exercises** can be done on an individual basis or with the support of a therapist. They are also useful tools to use with groups in training, or in a webinar.

In putting together this tool box the authors have drawn upon their practical experience with children, adolescents, and families in a variety of settings and functions. We have provided therapeutic services as staff, therapist, trainers, teachers, and consultants since the 1970's. While the therapeutic profession continues to evolve and change, and cycles have come and gone and often come again, we have strived to find the common threads that successfully stood the test of time. We sincerely hope that you find ways to include and incorporate ***The Parental Tool Box*** into your personal and professional lives.

This brings us to a final observation before moving on to **The Power of Words** and the other sections of ***The Parental Tool Box***. Obsessing over picking the right tool is not necessary since there is seldom a job that can be successfully completed with only one tool.

The strategies, skills, and perspectives that comprise the tool kit you will be assembling in this book are tools and not magic wands. Some of the tools will work for a long time, some might need to be replaced and updated as you and your kids grow, age, and develop.

While some tools may be more effective in a given situation than another, there are no inherently right or wrong tools. You will never find the perfect words to say in a given situation which will therapeutically transform your children, yourself, or others. If the tool used was ineffective at resolving the problem or issue, then the problem will still be there tomorrow or some time in the future. This means you will have plenty more opportunities to find or choose a better tool for the job.

Frequent use of the same tool in similar situations creates consistency and aids in the learning process by making things predictable. The frequent and consistent use of the same tool allows healthy habits to form, thus making it easier for you and others to engage in desired actions and responses naturally and effortlessly. Yet, variety is the spice of life, and sometimes varying the tools at your disposal allows people to see things in a new light or appreciate the situation from a fresh perspective. Trying out new tools enables you to be flexible to the inherent changes in the lives of your children as they grow and develop.

We know that in your busy lives repetition may seem like a daunting task. It would be dishonest for us to imply that new healthy skills and habits can be developed instantaneously. Research has shown that it takes four to six weeks to replace an old habit with a new one and indicates that it takes a minimum of 20 hours of actual practice to make a new skill into a habit (Lally, Van Jaarsveld, Potts, & Wardle, 2010). The more frequently your child has an opportunity to practice a new skill the quicker it can be mastered. The more frequently you practice the implementation and monitoring of these skills the quicker you will enjoy a mutually respectful home.

So, gather up your tool box and let's add to the skills you already possess. You are on your way to build the relationship you desire with your child and become more of the parent you want to be.

Reframe, Replace, and Rewire

In the introduction we stated the **Goal** and **Purpose** of *The Parental Tool Box* as:

> ***The Parental Tool Box for Parents & Clinicians***
> *is a compilation of strategies, perspectives, and skills to be used by parents and clinicians which effectively promote personal development and improved relationship functioning in children and families.*

In order to accomplish this goal we have assembled a comprehensive and thorough parenting book. While many of you will find its diversity helpful others might find the sheer volume of its suggestions, strategies, and interventions a tad overwhelming or intimidating.

It might be helpful to keep in mind that all of the parental "tools" to be identified and described fall into three basic categories. Each tool will use **Reframing**, **Replacing**, and **Rewiring (The 3 Rs)** as a point of emphasis. We've developed and used **The 3 Rs** for over a decade which fit nicely into the current research on brain studies and the treatment of trauma.

The following descriptions should help you group strategies together so you can find them easier to understand and implement.

Reframe, Replace, and Rewire:

Reframe: Many of the strategies and interventions in this book will be geared towards giving you the means to teach your child how to see and feel things from a new perspective. These alternative ways of thinking and feeling will help your child be less defensive, defiant, and reactive. Their new found ability to reframe their feelings and perceptions will allow them to become more compassionate, open minded, and appreciative of the love, care, and concern that you show on a daily basis.

Replace: Another goal of many of the tools to which you will be introduced is to replace troublesome, unhealthy, alienating, or self-sabotaging behavior with those which will be more respectful of self and others. On many occasions we will discuss the benefits that the replacing of disruptive habits, attitudes, and behaviors have over the usually futile attempts to control, ignore, or extinguish them.

Rewire: On almost a daily basis information regarding the vital roles that biochemistry and neurology play in how we feel, think, and act is increasing. This knowledge forms the basis of the entire realm of interventions by the medical field to aid in areas such as depression, anxiety, and the ability to focus and be attentive. In ***The Parental Tool Box*** we will explore other means such as diet, exercise, and activities which can assist in the improved functioning and attitude of your child.

The tools in ***The Parental Tool Box*** are designed to have a positive impact on not only your child's habits and behaviors, but also on their emotional and psychological well being. In the section **Maximizing Therapeutic Growth** we will discuss the ways the habitual/behavioral, emotional/psychological, and neurological/biochemical elements interrelate and are interdependent.

Each time you choose to introduce, teach, and use a tool presented in this book will be an opportunity to improve the relationship between you and your child. While reading this book remember that every tool will help both parent/child, teacher/student, and therapist/client to grow and develop by having them **Reframe**, **Replace**, and **Rewire**.

The Power of Words

The Power of Words

It is almost impossible to overstate the importance and power of words. Words make up the skeletons of most everything in our lives. They are the structural foundation of our self-esteem, all of our **Relationships**, and how we feel and think about the world in which we live. We believe words to be the foundation of building positive, healthy **Relationships** so we start with **The Power of Words** as the first skills to place in our tool box.

In the following chapters we will explore (through various skills, strategies, and **Home Improvement Exercises**) ways to increase your comfort and control over the words you choose as well as the influence your words have on yourself and others. The words we speak and which comprise our thoughts, not only express who we are but help create who we will become.

Often problems, conflicts, and unsuccessful **Relationships** can be resolved or improved by the simple process of becoming increasingly conscious of the words we choose and the effects they have on others and ourselves. Words are often very instrumental in the creation of a healthy self-concept and in our ability to have people appreciate and understand us. Therefore, we start with **The Power of Words**.

The attitudes and judgments inherent in the words we choose to articulate and describe our experiences, desires, and reactions have a powerful influence over how we are perceived and how others will be inclined to react to us. There are many skills and exercises we can engage in which will have us gain more control and awareness of the words we choose.

The roles and functions of words are too numerous to list but some of the more predominate roles are to express, describe, articulate, question, investigate, inform, educate, and stimulate. Words are a major way in which we gain access to the world of others and let them into others into our own rich internal world of thoughts and feelings.

The **Relationships** between words, feelings, and experiences are very complex and interlinked. Words also create, alter, modify, color, and redirect our thoughts and feelings.

> The Power of Words *can be used to create love, support, and care or can be used to hurt, betray, or destroy one's sense of pride and dignity. Words can be building blocks or tear down* Relationships.

In this section on **The Power of Words** we will provide you with the tools necessary to build and maintain the home environment you desire. The verbal techniques and strategies which follow focus on creating caring, supportive, and mutually respectful **Relationships**. You will be introduced to a host of communication skills which can be used to help you enforce **Family Rules** and guidelines in a manner which minimizes conflicts and **Avoids Power Struggles**, while also engendering cooperation and familial pride.

In each chapter we will present a topic or skill which can become an essential element in the structure of your home and be added to ***The Parental Tool Box***. Each topic and strategy will contain its general format, procedure, mechanics, and hints of things you might want to be aware of to maximize its benefits. When appropriate, we also cross reference topics which can be found in other chapters.

The words we consciously choose can help us create family habits, traditions, and guidelines which promote the functioning of a caring home. It is through these healthy communication patterns that we are able to ensure every member of the household feels safe and appreciated. Just as there is a tool for almost any task, there are word patterns and strategies for almost any familial situation.

Every person and every family is unique, so the ways in which you use and modify the tools presented will vary. Yet, despite being unique, all people and all families have much in common. It is this simple fact that allows us to find a relatively small array of communication and verbal strategies which can be counted upon to benefit every family. Verbal techniques which promote qualities such as respect, care, recognition, appreciation, love, and harmony are valuable to every family. The exact manner in which they are implemented may vary but their basics remain the same. *In other words, we have the final "say" in the functional and emotional tenor of our family home.*

Chapter One

Framing

The skill of **Framing** is one of the most basic but powerful language tools you can employ. This skill is central to any discussion regarding a person's options and ability to choose their words (Burnett & Evans, 2016).

Most people are familiar with the concept of **Framing** in both photography and painting. The visual mood, impact, and message of a photo or drawing is highly influenced by how the scene is framed. Likewise, the words you choose to "frame" your experience, feelings, or thoughts have a great impact on what they mean to you and how you will remember them and incorporate them into your life.

An example of word frames with which most of us are familiar are the concepts of optimism and pessimism. We have all heard that an optimist views the glass as half full and the pessimist as half empty. This frame means that an optimist anticipates the glass filling further and becoming complete, while the pessimist predicts or warns that the glass is on its way to becoming empty and unfit to nourish or refresh us.

The above **Frame** is often used to **Advocate** a person adopt a "positive" optimistic frame over the "negative" pessimistic viewpoint. Yet, the tenor of this manual is not to **Advocate** one viewpoint while prohibiting another. The glass half empty or half full frame is more about alerting us to the potential impact such a habitual perspective could have on our life.

This is not to say that optimism is superior or more desirable in all situations than pessimism, but only that one be aware of what impact their choice of words and viewpoints has on their emotions and **Relationships**. The more aware a person becomes of the way they frame their experiences in word and thought, the more conscious control they can have of the choices they make.

Two professions which are very aware of the power of verbal

frames are novelists and advertisers. Both of these professions choose words designed to elicit a specific response in the reader/listener. An ad man understands that the words he chooses to describe a product can greatly impact sales numbers. The novelist carefully chooses his words to describe a setting or scene to elicit a desired mood or emotional response from the audience. The description of identical scenes would vary greatly in a romantic, suspense, or horror novel.

Your experience would be quite different if you described a mountain as being majestic and awesome as opposed to ominous and foreboding. Likewise you would be more willing to go into the ocean tomorrow if you described today's dip as invigorating and stimulating rather than freezing or shocking.

Even when not in the throes of a specific emotion we all have basic moods and attitudes which color most of our perceptions and experiences. These styles and common responses are what make up our basic personality and character type.

Conscious awareness of our most common frames help us understand ourselves and the effects we have on those around us. Becoming aware of our children's most common frames helps us identify some of our strong emotional reactions to their verbal presentations and attitudes.

In this manner we can begin to change the ways we interact with our children. *We can reframe our statements which most elicit negative responses from our children. We also can have them reframe statements to which we find ourselves or others having an adverse reaction* (Pozatek, 2011).

Significant changes in people's verbal frames alter the way they feel about and experience the world, themselves, and their **Relationships**. This can be accomplished by frequently offering an alternative frame to the person, or by having them reframe many of their statements, descriptions and judgements.

We have witnessed many children and adults who suffered from severe performance anxiety in sports, tests, and peer interaction make substantial progress by learning how to reframe. Often this was accomplished by choosing words that describe the situation as an opportunity, rather than an expectation or necessity. In this manner they were able to build on their successes and be patient with the errors that are part of any growth process.

As a parent we can help our children make shifts in basic attitudes and stances which are reflected in their verbal habits by reframing some of their statements and having them restate things in a more positive or healthy light. New verbal habits will slowly give rise to new ways of feeling, viewing, and interacting with their world.

Over time the way a person frames things shows up in patterns of thought and action. An example is one's preferred frames are often structured in a diagnosis or personality type. The frames of a person with depression are often filled with hopelessness, futility, and emptiness. An anxious person frames their experiences in words filled with worry, fear, and mistrust. A defiant person frames things as a battle, competition, and power struggle. In essence, people's verbal frames reflect how they feel about themselves and their role in the world.

A diagnosis could be viewed in the following manner. *A diagnosis is a constellation of behaviors which are indicative of a specific style and manner of interacting with others and responding to one's environment.*

Framing can be done in a supportive manner in which your child will not feel highly criticized or judged. **Framing**, when offered as a guiding or expanding tool, can often prevent your child from reacting in a defensive manner, especially if done in one-on-one situations in which they won't feel embarrassed or shamed.

Framing is a tool for you to address your child's remarks which you or others could find insulting, harsh, threatening, vulgar, or offensive in a way which is non-confrontational or emotionally charged. Having your child practice a socially acceptable reframe of an "inappropriate" remark can often successfully **Replace** the old habit with a more acceptable alternative without the need for a power struggle or "consequences."

Summary of Framing

What it is:

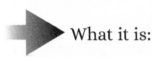

Framing is the conscious choice of words which present an alternate or desired way of viewing and internalizing an experience, situation, or interpersonal interaction, such as a conversation.

Reframing is when you reword a statement or thought soon after you have said or thought it, allowing you to see and feel the same situation from a more desirable or effective perspective.

Why use it:

Framing is a very valuable verbal tool with the following two general uses.

First, **Framing** can be used to broaden and expand your way of seeing and feeling, thereby preventing becoming stuck, frozen, or stagnant. It allows you an opportunity to see and experience the world in a manner different from your habitual way of being.

The second general purpose is to assist you in altering or **Replacing** a way of viewing or experiencing the world with a stance you no longer desire. Through frequent frames and reframes you can replace anxiety with anticipation; worry with care and concern; demands with guidance and support; dependence with connection; selfishness with self-reliance (autonomy); and need for appreciation with gratitude.

In sum, **Framing** is a versatile tool that can be used to improve self-esteem, develop a new perspective, and become less argumentative.

Reframe, Replace, and Rewire:

Framing allows you to help your child see things from a new and healthier perspective. Through frequent repetition and practice of the skill of **Reframing** you can have your child **Replace** an old habitual defensive, anxious, or disrespectful perspective with a new frame showing curiosity, adaptability, or confidence. The emotional tenor of these new frames will slowly impact your child's neurology and biochemistry by successfully **Rewiring** them.

Framing
Home Improvement Projects

1. Describe a recent interaction you had with a stranger (a cashier or waitress). Example: *The waitress spilled the tea all over me and the table at the restaurant.*

2. Now describe the same interaction from a different emotional perspective. Using dramatic or strong emotions will make this exercise easier for you. Describe the interaction from "negative" emotions such as anger, disgust, irritation, or conceit. Example: *The waitress banged down my tea on the table and it spilled over onto my hand. I was filled with hot resentment and irritation.*

3. Try describing this same interaction from a "positive" emotion such as kindness, joy or humor. Notice how different the experience of the interaction becomes depending on the emotional frame. Example: *The waitress was very apologetic after spilling the tea all over the table.*

4. Identify a quality you possess. Example: *I am loyal.*

5. **Frame** this quality in a positive manner. Example: *People know they can depend on me in hard times.*

6. **Frame** this quality in a negative manner. Example: *I sometimes defend friends when they have done something hurtful to others.*

7. Identify a quality your child possesses. Example: *My child is honest.*

8. **Frame** this quality in a positive manner. Example: *My child tells people what he is feeling.*

9. **Frame** this quality in a negative manner. Example: *My child often bluntly expresses his feelings in an angry and aggressive way.*

10. Identify a quality you and your child share. Example: *We both have a great sense of humor.*

11. **Frame** this quality in a positive manner for your child. Example:

My son loves to tell jokes and make people laugh.

12. **Frame** this quality in a negative manner for your child. Example: *My son is very sarcastic with his put downs.*

13. Can you think of a time in the last week when you might have used the tool of **Framing** with your child which would have made your interaction more pleasant?

Chapter Two

Scripts and Dress Rehearsals

Scripts and **Dress Rehearsals** are highly related and similar to the skill of **Framing**. The major difference is that **Scripts** and **Dress Rehearsals** involve planning and being prepared while **Framing** is something you do in the moment.

If we have repeatedly performed badly in a given situation, such as **Giving Criticism** to a colleague, we may want to **Script** and plan our next opportunity to express concerns. By thinking out what we want to say (**Script**) and practicing delivering the message in a relatively calm and cogent manner, we may be able to avoid the verbal and emotional pitfalls which have plagued previous attempts at providing **Constructive Criticism** and expressing feelings.

The fear and anxiety involved at the prospect of engaging in a historically difficult scenario such as a job interview, can be greatly reduced by using **Scripts** and **Dress Rehearsals** as a way to prepare for the upcoming event. While **Scripts** and practice rehearsals do not promise complete success, they are almost bound to improve performance and social functioning.

Scripts and **Dress Rehearsals** can be very detailed or fairly general depending on the need or situation (Sohn & Grayson, 2005). Effective **Scripts** can be composed of some simple reminders such as, "*Take a deep breath*," "*Keep my voice volume down*," and, "*Be sure to say thank you*."

Parents can use **Scripts** and **Dress Rehearsals** to help support, guide, and instruct their children on how to relax and succeed in a number of situations. Children often flounder in new or more formal social situations because they don't know what to do or say. Having your child practice **Scripts** and **Rehearsals** in advance, in a calm supportive and relaxed environment, has a far greater chance of success than a last minute tutorial done in the car on the way to the event.

Detailed **Scripts** are often needed in situations with a long history of personal pain and perceived failure. Many parents of children and young adults with high functioning autism know that preparation for transitions and new situations is often vital to their child not having a meltdown or freezing (Myles & Southwick, 1999). Numerous **Dress Rehearsals** and practices are often needed for their child to feel comfortable enough to perform during highly stressful times.

Since the goal of **Scripts** and **Dress Rehearsals** is to decrease anxiety and increase social functioning, it is important that all **Scripts** (whether for yourself or your child) are realistic in their scope and execution. **Scripts** and **Dress Rehearsals** are not the time to dream or be idealistic. A **Script** that doesn't boost confidence or reduce anxiety is not one to be written or practiced. While anxiety is expected to cause some resistance to new **Scripts**, one should see a reduction in the anxiety as the practices continue. If the anxiety increases it probably is a signal that a better and more realistic **Script** is in order.

The way to master any skill is through practice and repetition. When something becomes habit and second nature it is fully learned (Repetition & Learning, 2018). This is not to say that you have to memorize your **Scripts** but familiarity, especially done in a relaxed manner, breeds comfort and confidence.

When the goal of your **Script** is to express your feelings, voice a concern, or give criticism you may want to consider making it a monologue. Doing so will reduce the possibility of becoming flustered by unexpected dialogue, or reactive to the other person's words or viewpoints. If you choose a lengthy monologue, make sure you let that be known before starting your speech and be sure to allow the other person to respond once you are done.

Frequent use of these skills will likely end up with greatly improved performances in historically difficult situations. **Scripts** and **Dress Rehearsals**, like all skills, take time and practice, so make sure that you and your child focus on the improvements and not on perfect execution. While some **Scripts** will go without a hitch, it is likely that some will not go as planned because fears, anger, and anxiety may hinder the best of plans.

In order to reduce frustration and a sense of failure, it is advisable for you to build in an exit strategy to help your child leave the situation with as much grace as possible. If your child has worked on a great **Script** of how to explain to her teacher why her homework was not done, make sure she has practiced a sentence to utter if her anxiety gets to the point where she freezes, gets flustered, or angry. Maybe she learns to say something like, *"I'm having difficulty finding the words I want to say, can I talk to you a little later?"*

Whenever possible we try to build on progress by making sure a child has some success when first attempting the skill we are introducing. When it comes to **Scripts** and **Dress Rehearsals** this can easily be accomplished by giving them short and easy **Scripts** to use in relatively low stress situations. Maybe you can have them practice a **Script** to be used in the house shortly after dinner is done which will allow them to get their favorite dessert. After a few successful trial runs have them take on a more challenging **Script** which would cause them to have some performance anxiety, but would be relatively harmless if they stumbled or struggled.

When planning and reviewing **Scripts**, focus on the potential gains and benefits this skill offers your child. Put the possible missed opportunity in perspective during your **Dress Rehearsal** for your child before trying out the **Script** in real life. This often can be accomplished by reviewing previous successes and finding the humorous side of some of the less than stellar performances. In other words, Frame the success of the **Script** as an opportunity and not as an expectation.

Scripts and **Dress Rehearsals** are excellent tools for preventing potential dramas and tragedies. Their usage can be a blessing to any parent who is willing to spend the time proactively identifying potential problem situations for their child, whether that be a first day at school, dealing with a bully, how to speak with a peer with whom they are interested in having a deeper relationship, or how to interact and answer peer questions when returning home from hospitalization or placement.

Summary of Scripts and Dress Rehearsals

What it is:

Scripts and **Dress Rehearsals** are planned practices designed to reduce anxiety and raise confidence in one's ability to successfully act, speak, or navigate a new, potentially emotionally devastating, or historically problematic situation.

Why use it:

Scripts and **Dress Rehearsals** are a way to decrease the fear of the unknown through providing practical experience, making a plan and putting one's fears in perspective. Frequent use of **Scripts** and **Dress Rehearsals** foster confidence through skill development and the knowledge that most problems can be addressed by preparation and research.

Reframe, Replace, and Rewire:

Scripts and **Dress Rehearsals** give your child an opportunity to see things from a new perspective (**Reframe**). Their new words and actions allow them to see the possibilities and options in situations that once only produced failure and frustration. Repeated **Dress Rehearsals** allow your child an opportunity to **Replace** old words and actions with new more beneficial ones.

Dress Rehearsals and **Scripts** can be practiced in a safe environment where one learns how to breathe and remain calm when trying out new **Scripts**. Each practice and execution of the new **Script** done with calm and confidence will **Rewire** the thought process and also improve biochemistry while **Replacing** anxiety and fear with ease and comfort.

Scripts and Dress Rehearsals Home Improvement Projects

Let's assume your daughter, Nicole, is in an out-of-home placement for the remainder of the school year. While shopping at the grocery store you see the mother of a girl (Alexis) she has known since kindergarten. Here's an example of a **Script** you could write and practice so you are ready to answer another parent's likely question of the reason Nicole has not been at school for a month.

> *"We decided Nicole's needs were best served at a smaller school which addressed her particular learning styles while allowing her to take part in athletics on a less competitive basis. Nicole misses her friends from home but is fortunate to have found her place in her new setting. I hope Alexis is doing well. Thanks for asking, I've got a meeting to get to so I really must finish shopping. Say hello to Alexis for me."*

This **Script** could help you in an uncomfortable situation by giving you a tool to practice in advance to address inquiries of why your child has not been around. Taking the time to write it out and practice your **Script** in advance will lessen your concern of going out in public, for fear of seeing any of your child's friends, or their parents. Notice the brevity of this **Script**. It answers the question, is easy to memorize, and ends the dialogue quickly in an uncomfortable situation.

Here's another example, this time the **Script** is for letting your child, Aaron, know you will be monitoring the miles he is driving in the car each day.

> *"Aaron, can I talk to you for a few minutes? It's been wonderful to see how happy you are since you got your driver's license. It's another step on your road to adulthood. You know our relationship has been very important to me and I want to support you the best I can as you enter into this*

next phase of your life.

Some kids get swayed by the pull of freedom once they've gotten their license and I've been thinking of ways I can help you make good decisions when driving. I've decided that one way to help you remain honest about where you are going and what you are doing when you take the car out is for me to check the odometer each day. I want you to know I will be doing that so it doesn't seem like I am sneaking around behind your back. The reason I will be checking it is to support you and give you daily opportunities to show you are being truthful.

This will also help me as I learn how to parent you as a young adult. It will give me the opportunity to gradually let you go out into the world on your own, knowing I am supporting you the best I can.

I'd like you to think about this and let's talk in a few hours. Please hear that I am doing this as an opportunity to continue a good relationship and not as a punishment. Thanks for listening, Aaron. I appreciate your patience."

Can you see how planning this out in advance might help? It serves the purpose of keeping you focused and stating your objective in a positive manner without lecturing. As you read this you may be imagining your child blowing up in anger while you deliver this **Script**. We will address how to respond to angry outbursts and power struggles later in the book. Remember, the purpose of **Scripts** is to prepare in advance your words to maximize your success.

Now it's your turn. We'll start with an easy one.

1. Make a **Script** on the benefits of being prepared for a new situation.
2. Make a **Script** on letting your child know of a new rule you are going to put in place.
3. Help your child make a **Script** requesting their teacher change the seating in the classroom due to distracting influences (noise, a bully nearby, a window, etc).

Chapter Three

Visualization

Even though **Visualization** is a technique of the imagination and does not directly involve **The Power of Words**, we decided to include it here due to its strong similarity to **Scripts** and **Dress Rehearsals**. In **Scripts** and **Dress Rehearsals** we carefully select words and then rehearse the presentation as if it were a scene from a play until becoming comfortable performing the scene in real life. In **Visualization** we prepare for a situation by closing our eyes and imagining ourselves speaking and acting successfully.

Most of us are familiar with the technique of **Visualization** due to its popularity with athletes, actors, musicians and many other performance professionals (Hanson, 2013). Whether it be an Olympic skier imagining their next run down the slopes or a ballerina imaging each step of her dance, the power of visual rehearsals is well established.

The technique of **Visualization** can be used separately or in conjunction with **Scripts** and **Dress Rehearsals**. The choosing of which skills to use often depends on the learning style of the person and how they process information.

Dress Rehearsals involve more than just the words, they also include practicing and monitoring voice tone and volume, gestures, body language, spatial boundaries, and physical interaction with those involved in the practice. Many people find the actual real and alive nature of the practice helpful in both memorization and being able to later duplicate the **Scripts** in real time.

Parents involved in or observing the **Dress Rehearsals** are able to **Praise** and support the strongest aspects of the practice while also being able to guide and improve the entire performance and learning process. Parent's feedback and assistance are absent if their child is visualizing unless the child is willing to give a play-by-play commentary of what they are imagining.

Yet, there are children with specific temperaments and talents whose performance is enhanced more through **Visualization** than **Dress Rehearsals**. Children who are easily distracted or have sensorial sensitivities to their environment may find time spent visualizing more productive and beneficial than physical practices. Children with anxiety, Attention Deficit Disorder, or neural processing issues may experience a better focus and recall of Visualizations which are preformed in the mind's eye.

Even children who prefer visualizing often benefit from a few "walk throughs" with their parents after they have mastered their **Script** through **Visualizations**. In this way, parents can also verify that their child has actually engaged in the learning process and hasn't just chosen **Visualization** as a way of avoiding working on the issue.

Parents may also find it useful in remaining calm and grounded in difficult situations. Many parents **Visualize** the relationship they want to develop with their child which helps them in tough times. **Visualizing** how you want to relate to your child in two, five, ten, and twenty years sets the stage for how you interact with them in the present.

The quality components regarding voice tone and gestures, as well as, recalling all the details of the situation are often difficult to remember when doing a **Visualization**. Many individuals find that this can be adequately addressed by having a review sheet of important components to be aware of before beginning a **Visualization**. The list can be reviewed after each practice **Visualization** to assure that such components are being learned and incorporated into the mental rehearsals. Another option is to first audio tape your **Visualization** and then listen to it.

Many people who prefer physical practices and **Dress Rehearsals** often find that a **Visualization** in the car or in a quiet place shortly before the event in question often helps create a calm and focus leading to a successful execution of the **Script**. While **Visualization** can be a stand alone technique, it is often reinforced and made more powerful by being combined with **Dress Rehearsals** and **Scripts**.

Summary of Visualization

What it is:

A series of mental images in which a skill or event is played out and practiced to enhance your future performance.

Why use it:

Visualization can increase confidence, lower anxiety, and generally have you feel prepared to meet the challenges of upcoming events. **Visualization** is one of the best ways in which people can see themselves as if they were being filmed on a camera and see themselves and their gestures as others see them.

Reframe, Replace, and Rewire:

When you **Visualize** yourself executing a task or social skill correctly it allows you to **Frame** the event in a positive fashion. The **Clearer** and more precise the **Visualization** the easier it becomes for you to execute the task in real time, allowing you to **Replace** the old behavior with a new one. Frequent **Visualizations** enable you to not only **Rewire** how your brain functions during the task, but also lets you bring an added calm and confidence to the event positively impacting your biochemistry. When you are calm and confident you secrete hormones consistent with those feelings and in effect begin to **Rewire** your brain and nervous system.

Visualization
Home Improvement Projects

Find a place where you can be undisturbed for 15 minutes. You might want to play some favorite music in the background, or light a candle before you begin to practice **Visualization**. Relax in a comfortable position and take a few deep breaths. You might want to read this through once and then close your eyes as you practice the **Visualization** or audio tape and read the instructions out loud so you can play it back with your eyes closed.

Some of you may find setting the stage in this manner uncomfortable. **Visualizations** similar to daydreaming can be done while walking, taking a shower, or in any environment of your choosing.

1. Think about a pleasant time you have had with your child. What age was your child? What were you doing together? Where were you? What feelings does this invoke in you? What was special about this time you had together?

2. Imagine now it is 10 years in the future and you are with your child again. You are both 10 years older and are having a pleasant time together. What are you doing together? Where are you? What feelings does this invoke in you? What is special about this time together?

3. Open your eyes and write down what you **Visualized** if that is possible. If not, review in your mind what you envisioned.

4. How were those **Visualizations** for you?

5. **Visualize** giving your child feedback on how they did a chore you instructed them to do. Envision your ideal facial expression and voice tone while delivering compliments along with areas of improvement.

6. Teach your child the skill of **Visualization** and help them develop one for a situation in their life.

Chapter Four

Creating a Learning Environment

The primary responsibility of being a parent is to provide for your child's basic needs so that they not only survive, but are safe, healthy, and happy. Once basic needs are tended to, the next layer of parental responsibilities involves helping your child grow, develop, mature, and progress.

On so many levels our primary job is to teach and our child's job is to learn. Let's explore some of the ways we can create a productive **Learning Environment** and how we can establish a successful teaching relationship with our child.

If a parent is the teacher and the child is the student, what is the most important element to establish for successful learning to occur? Surprisingly, it isn't intelligence or even articulateness which insures a great teacher. There are many brilliant and articulate teachers who have failed to become successful. No matter what one knows or says, learning does not take place if the student isn't listening and paying attention.

If your child isn't listening then you as a parent cannot teach, you can still talk, but no learning is taking place. Therefore, a primary element of becoming a better teacher and a more effective parent is to get your child to listen and be attentive when you speak. Speaking to your child when they are not listening is generally a waste of both of your time.

Many parents choose to try to do their best teaching when their child is angry, defiant, frustrated, or currently feeling bad about themselves. The chances of the contents and substance of the teaching being heard and accepted during these times is near zero.

The belief that one can win a dispute or out logic a child having a tantrum does not die easily. While witnessing many arguments and conflicts between kids and parents, teachers, and health care professionals, we have never seen a single instance in which a child has ceased in mid fury and said anything resembling, "*Oh good point, I can now see that you are right and I am wrong*," (at least not without a whole lot of sarcasm).

Despite this fact, the tendency to try to out will and out argue a child into listening and learning when they are "*out of control*," is the norm and not the exception. When a child is acting out the goal is to get them to calm down and become respectful (Siegel, 2014).

Later we will review many useful techniques to help you be more successful in de-escalating your child and getting them to be more compliant. We will also present many strategies and skills which will help you **Avoid** getting into **Power Struggles** and heated conflicts with your child.

One of the ways to avoid your child reacting to your guidance and instructions with anger and tantrums is to spend a little more time consciously setting the parameters of a healthy **Learning Environment** and a pleasant teaching relationship.

Take a few moments to review the roles and responsibilities of both the parent/teacher and the child/student. Observations of successful parents/teachers and kids/students in **Learning Environments** reveal these essential job descriptions (figure 4.1):

Job Descriptions

The parent's job is to listen; show respect; model and teach; support and praise; and validate the child's feelings.

The child/student job is to listen; be attentive; be respectful; comply; and implement what they are being taught.

**figure 4.1*

Two of the shared tasks of parent and child are to listen and be respectful. Therefore, in any interaction with your child in which teaching is your goal, mutual respect and attentive listening is imperative. *An effective* **Learning Environment** *is a focused and mutually respectful one.*

This does not mean that both of you have to be in a serene and isolated room without any stimulation or potential distraction, though conducting potentially explosive interactions in such an environment is probably best.

Often conversations while in the car; on a walk; having dessert; playing a game; or engaged in a joint mindless activity such as doing the dishes can be very productive. Many children with anxiety or a high level of defensiveness can find a minor diversion calming and feel more comfortable disclosing when the conversation happens in the flow. Many children experience a form of stage fright when they feel forced to express feelings or **Accept Criticism** while in a room locked in their parent's gaze.

Yet, the diversions listed above must remain minimal enough to allow your child to stay relatively focused and attentive to the content of your discussion. While a calm and relatively quiet environment is helpful, the emotional comfort of both parent and child are even more important.

Emotional states such as anxiety, frustration, anger, and irritation are not conducive to effective teaching and learning. We will look to other more suitable outlets for these emotions and their conflictual counterparts such as debate, argumentation, and venting in later chapters, yet in the majority of learning situations these emotions are counterproductive.

A parent's own anger and anxiety are often triggered by their children's reactions to their corrections and criticism (McCurry, 2009). These reactions can be placed into three main categories:

1. *The child becomes defiant and begins interrupting and contesting what the parent is saying.*
2. *The child is physically reacting with sighs, rolling their eyes, or making sounds and gestures indicating*

that they are about to explode.

3. *The child stays silent and stares at the parent.*

Before discussing suggested ways of dealing with these resistive behaviors, let's take a moment to explore what we can do to help prevent these behaviors from occurring. Many of you reading this book will have had an extensive history of tense and conflictual interactions with your child. Therefore, it would be advisable to be proactive and create a new and well structured discussion format with your child. The new format should be introduced in a calm setting and include the parameters and behavioral expectations needed to engage in a productive and successful dialogue with your child.

A typical format for discussion with your child or adolescent may include the following (figure 4.2).

Discussion Skills

- ✓ Relaxed body language
- ✓ Listen attentively
- ✓ Wait turn to speak
- ✓ Respectful voice tone and volume
- ✓ Ask clarifying questions
- ✓ Stay on topic
- ✓ Remain open to suggestions

**figure 4.2*

The success of the new ritual can be maximized by having **Clear** boundaries and well established alternative means of interaction with your child. The discussion format will be contrasted and made separate from other formats such as your child being given an opportunity to express his concerns (see **Respectfully Disagree**), his feelings and frustrations (see **Venting**), and having input into **House Rules** and how it functions (see **Family Meeting**).

When you have **Clear** and separate formats of interaction it allows you to keep each interaction pure and gives you the opportunity to point out when your child is straying from the current format in a calm and respectful manner. If your child begins to argue a point just remind them of the goal and format of a discussion to get them back inside acceptable parameters.

Similarly, when your child interrupts, gets loud, swears, gets off topic, or tries to hijack the discussion to their own agenda, you can gently guide the conversation back by pointing out or reviewing the format. The better you tailor the format to the needs and habits of your child the easier it will be to create a new productive conversation ritual.

Take a look at the discussion skills presented above (figure 4.2) and notice that while addressing all our concerns it was done so in a positive frame. Stating the positive aspect of the goal models respectfulness and often helps in reducing your child's resistance to the format. *Each goal gives a specific positive behavior and not the negative framing of that behavior.*

A format stated in what not do, is more often resisted and can itself be a trigger with many adolescents. Therefore, it is advisable not to list parameters in the negative such as, "*Don't interrupt, yell, swear, or make threatening gestures.*"

Through your patient guidance and reminders to honor the components of discussion most resistive behaviors will dissipate and the conversation can continue. Yet, if the resistive behaviors do continue it is at this point in which you can identify them (see **Being Specific**).

To protect the sanctity and purity of discussion, it is important to stop the process if your efforts of persuading your child to be attentive and respectful fail. If you truly want new cooperative habits and patterns to take root it is important to not tolerate them becoming avenues for argument and debate. You will have other vehicles and formats to deal with such expressions.

One of the best ways to help the new discussion format be successful and accepted by your child is to start with easy topics that are not emotionally charged. Only after a few successful conversations would you then broach a more controversial subject matter. Maybe the first discussion is regarding minor changes due to work and school schedules; the care of a new pet; or the maintenance of an electronic device.

At the beginning it's often beneficial to officially introduce that you are about to start a discussion and have them review the components and format. It is often a nice touch to ask if they are ready or if they would like to set up a later time. Yet, obviously, they can't ask to delay the talk numerous times, one delay to a set agreed upon time is sufficient. Asking them if it's a good time helps them feel respected and a participant as well as modeling the skill of scheduling a time with you to discuss their concerns or disagreements (see **Respectfully Disagree**).

If you have had a history of contentious and conflictual discussions with your child it is only natural to approach these situations with a little anxiety or hesitancy. The reliance on the format and starting with some easy topics will help reduce your anxiety as well as your child's anxiety and resistance. Both you and your child can build off the successes of the early safer talks while giving the format a chance to become a new and appreciated ritual.

Once the format has been established it would be helpful to use the tool as early and often as possible. Bringing up topics before they become urgent is another way of keeping anxieties and tensions from becoming a problem or a distraction. The longer you wait the bigger the elephant in the room and the harder it is for you to keep your emotions from harming the reliability of the format.

As we mentioned earlier, *attentive listening is essential in the success of any discussion or teaching interaction* (McCurry, 2009). While your child's attention will likely be demonstrated through many common signals such as frequent eye contact, head nods, and relaxed body language, it is helpful to verify that they are listening by having them repeat back what they have heard you say. Make sure you do this often enough so that the content of what they have to repeat back is not too overwhelming.

If your child finds repeating things back irritating or annoying just assure them that it helps you determine if you've left anything out or need to explain something a little more **Clearly**. In other words, having them repeat things back is a tool you use to become a better and more efficient teacher, as well as checking to see if they are listening. Similarly, repeating back and summarizing what your child has said is a good way to demonstrate to your child that you are listening to them and value their input (see **Attunement**).

Earlier we mentioned that a parent's anxiety often climbs when their child is either completely silent, or is making sounds and gestures indicating escalating resistance to the conversation. In such situations parents often find themselves speaking increasingly faster due to their discomfort with the monologue, or in an effort to outrun the coming tantrum. The quickening monologue seldom works as it just adds to the tension in the room, often leading to the parent matching their child's anger and intimidating behavior. A child who is given to tantrums is very attuned to a parent's fear or anxiety and will escalate into a tantrum even if the parent does not become harsh or challenging.

The solution to this problem is often fairly simple. The first thing to do is to stop the monologue and ask them to repeat back what you have said, or to ask them a simple question to get them involved and invested in the conversation. If after speaking your child continues to exhibit anxiety or escalating resistant behavior, review the format and point out what they are doing which is contrary to attentive listening and learning. If they continue to escalate or become belligerent you may want to officially stop the discussion and just deal with their attitude and offensive behavior. Postponing the discussion is not a failure, but trying to force a discussion during a tantrum is seldom beneficial.

The components/steps of the skills listed in this chapter are just examples and are effective with many of the children we've known. *Whatever list you come up with make sure it is tailored to the needs and habits of your child.*

The guidelines you choose and skills you want to cultivate should be **Clearly** stated in the components. It is very helpful if you model the skills, guidelines, and parameters that you want your child to use and incorporate. As an example, to help model and reinforce the components we listed above, a parent may model attentive listening by referencing a positive point or contribution their child has made earlier in the conversation or in a previous conversation or by summarizing what they have said (see **Active Listening**). A parent can model mutual respect by using a calm and relaxed voice tone; avoid yelling or interrupting their child when they are speaking; or by summarizing and repeating back to your child what they have said. A parent may also model relaxed body language by asking that they both take a few deep breaths or do some head rolls to relieve neck tension.

If you and your child have had a long history of arguments and power struggles, we strongly recommend you begin anew and start a new ritual by a strict adherence to a discussion format as suggested above. Once the format and its guidelines begin to become habit and natural you can always back off the formality.

Summary of Creating a Learning Environment

What it is:

A formal conversation format which is designed to create an environment of mutual respect in which listening and focus are maximized.

Why do it:

The guidelines and parameters inherent in your structural design of the new discussion format will help create a more productive vehicle for your ability to guide, instruct, and **Constructively Criticize** your child. Having it be one of a number of formats you use for an exchange of thoughts and feelings will allow you to keep the teaching environment from becoming mired in debate, argumentation, and emotional venting.

Reframe, Replace, and Rewire:

When a formal structure is never used most emotional conversations can become battle zones or chaotic verbal free-for-alls in which your child feels that anything goes. Having certain guidelines and expectations for a discussion converts free-form conversation into mutually respectful discussion.

The **Reframing** of saying whatever is on one's mind into a respectful exchange of ideas helps in the creating of a healthy learning environment. In this way arguments and emotional venting can be **Replaced** by productive and respectful conversation. When the format of a conversation becomes habitual, our children learn (**Rewire**) to think rather than react, and the calm and respect of the new conversation skill allows every family member to be relaxed and cooperative.

Creating A Learning Environment Home Improvement Projects

1. Imagine you are preparing to learn something new. This could be a new sport, exercise routine, gourmet meal to prepare, hobby, or mastering a new technology. Describe the ideal environment for you to learn. Are you reading the instructions? Watching YouTube to follow along?

2. Remembering back to when you were young and your parent or a caregiver was trying to teach you something new. You may remember learning how to snap your fingers for the first time, or shuffling a deck of cards, or driving a car. Describe the method of teaching used. Was it effective? Would you have preferred a different style?

3. Skip to your late teens or early twenties and think of a time you were learning a new task of adulthood, such as filling out taxes for the first time or applying for a loan. Describe how you wanted to be taught this new task.

4. Remember a recent time when a boss, colleague, spouse, partner, or friend was trying to talk to you about something new, such as using a new office device, home appliance, or explaining how they want you to water their plants when they are on vacation. Describe the scene. Was it an effective way to communicate with you?

5. What do all of those descriptions have in common? What works in your **Learning Environment**? What are barriers of effective learning for you?

6. Think of something you want to teach your child, such as using good greeting skills when meeting one of your friends, establishing rules for the new pet in your home, or how to use the washing machine. How can you set up the **Learning**

Environment to be successful in your role as parent/teacher?

7. Now find someone you trust to practice teaching the above skill. Remember to teach *what* you *want* them to do/learn. Stay focused on the positive goal. Ask your trusted partner for feedback on how if felt to them, paying particular attention to your volume, tone, speed, and general affect. Practice feeling comfortable with this skill, if possible, before trying it with your child.

8. Now try teaching the above to your child.

Chapter Five

Being Specific: Say What You Mean

The goal of this chapter is to help parents develop communication patterns and habits which insure your child actually hears what you want them to hear. Much parental frustration is born from unintended vagueness, grey areas, wiggle room, or misinterpretation formed in the short distance from parent's mouths to their child's ears.

Since the following conceptual skills are intertwined we will try to address them all in this chapter. We will now address the importance and benefits of being:

- ✓ *Specific*
- ✓ *Concise*
- ✓ *Clear*
- ✓ *Descriptive*

while **Giving Directives**, **Instructions**, **Praise**, and **Constructive Criticism**.

Part 1: Directives and Instructions

Often parents make the mistake of sounding as if they are giving a suggestion or recommendation when they are, in fact, giving their child a directive. A child who hates mowing the lawn will likely interpret your observation that, "*You know you should trim the edges when you're done mowing*," as a possibility and not an instruction. This would likely result in the borders not being done and an argument in which you state you told them to trim and they argue that, "*You never told me to do it, you only said I could.*"

Similarly a parent who points out that, "*You've been watching too much TV today,*" will find that their child has interpreted this comment as a complaint and not as an instruction to turn off the TV. In many cases the TV will stay on until the parent specifically tells their child to turn off the TV, yells in anger, or turns it off themselves.

Many parents blow a fuse when they tell their child to clean their room and they walk in later to find its is still a mess. When the parent confronts the child on not doing what they were told, the child will often defensively swear that they did clean their room.

Whether the reasons for your child's lack of cooperation and hearing what you are saying are due to laziness, personal convenience, or willful defiance the solution will begin with increased clarity and specificity in your verbal instructions and criticisms.

Let's take a few moments to discuss some of the best communication habits to help insure that your instructions are heard and have the best chance of meeting your standards. If you want something done to your standards or done a certain way, then it is best you relay that information in the **Clearest** and most concise manner possible.

When telling you child to clean their room, organize the garage, mow the lawn, get ready for school, cook dinner, brush the dog, or any of the other tasks and chores that make up family life be as descriptive and specific as possible.

What does clean the room mean to you? Do they make the bed, put clothes in drawers, empty wastebaskets? Do they vacuum, dust, put things away on shelves, or clean the mirrors? It is our experience that child and parent definitions of the most basic of tasks from making toast to emptying the dishwasher vary with astounding differences.

We have found that making **Chore Cards** is the most effective way of having kids know what to do, and avoid any grey areas for debate or interpretation. The less motivated your child is to do the chore or do it well, the more specific and descriptive you need to be in your verbal or written instructions.

We have worked with kids who would use yards of paper towels, or half a bottle of windex to clean one small mirror in their room if we hadn't have written on the chore instruction card, "*Take one paper towel and three spritzes of windex at the top of the mirror and wipe until dry.*" While such specificity wasn't always needed, we found 'over description' had far better success and results than 'under description'.

The best way to overcome the selective hearing of your child is to be very **Clear** and **Specific** with all instructions. Yet, even when some kids try they still have a hard time remembering every step of a complex instruction. Even if a child isn't officially on the Autism Spectrum or have an Attention Deficit Disorder diagnosis they may legitimately struggle with remembering everything they were asked to do.

If you have a child with processing or attention issues it is best to break down a complex task into a few steps or sections at a time. Have them inform you when they have completed the first part of the task, and then give them the next digestible segment of the task. Obviously writing down the assignment is the best option if your child has auditory processing issues or is a visual learner. With visual learners, having pictures on **Chore Cards** depicting the task rather than written descriptions can be highly effective at improving your child's ability to do complex tasks with minimal guidance.

There are two very important steps or components which if emphasized will greatly contribute to your child's mastery of **Following Your Instructions** and executing your directives. The converting of these two steps into habits will increase both your child's ability to successfully complete the task and your ability to monitor their listening skills and performance (Dowd, Czyz, O'Kane & Elofson, 1994).

The two steps are:

1. *Have your child repeat back the directive or instruction.*
2. *Check in when the task is completed before they go on to something else.*

When you give your child a directive have them repeat back what you told them. This makes sure that your child was not only paying attention and listening, but they were processing what they heard. Often, children with auditory processing deficits finally hear what was said when they repeat it and it comes out of their own mouths.

The repeat step of any formal learning of the skill of **Following Instructions** also allows you an opportunity to catch any aspects that your child missed or might have mistranslated. The repeat back also decreases the possibility that your child will later debate with you what your instruction actually was (figure 5.1):

Following Instructions

1. Listen attentively
2. Say OK
3. Repeat back instructions
4. Do task
5. Check back

**figure 5.1*

Upon completion of the assignment or task your child should immediately report back and let you know that they are done. This checking back upon completion lets you see if your child is completing tasks in a timely manner. The parent is able to evaluate their job performance and allows you to make suggestions for the future, or have them redo or finish aspects that are below standard. This also prevents your child from sneaking out and having fun before they finished their responsibilities leaving the task undone. If life intervenes and you are not able to check out the assigned task or you are away from home when the task is completed, it is important to remember to check it as soon as possible.

When a child knows that every task and assignment given to them will be checked and evaluated in a timely manner they are much more likely not to limit test or do a shoddy job the first go-around. If you make their ability to **Follow Instructions** into a formal skill, you can always have them practice the skill a few additional times to better learn and master it. The average child of a parent teaching in this way will soon realize that doing the chore right on the first attempt will save them time in the long run. The doing of the chore on the first go-around will also be a time and energy saver for the parent.

With children who are particularly resistive to learning the skill, or truly struggle with auditory instructions, you may want to introduce the chore or task by modeling for them how you want it done. For example, you might show them the actual dusting motion, or fold a few socks and then have them do it with you watching until they get the hang of it. You may want to monitor certain aspects of the task with them and then have them check in with you before they complete the entire task.

While **Being Clear** and **Specific**, it is important to remain sensitive to your chid's age and maturity level. One can **Be Specific** without being insulting or demeaning.

Giving Directives or **Instructions** is just one of many forms of communication you have with your child. Making a **Clear** distinction between the various forms of communication and the skills involved in their execution will greatly assist in the quickness and consistency of their learning and their ability to recognize and interact with you in the appropriate manner in each situation.

Part 2: Praise and Giving Constructive Criticism

Probably the most frequent missed opportunity to be descriptive with our children is when we are praising them or giving them a compliment. Usually parents thank or Praise in the most general of terms. Most smiles and even hugs are accompanied by such gushes as, "*Good job!*" "*You were awesome!*" "*You rock!*" or "*Thanks, that is such a help!*"

While all of these heartfelt expressions of appreciation and gratitude have your child feel good about themselves, they do little to let them know specifically what they can do in the future to earn your praise. The general compliments listed above are definitely better than those given in sarcasm such as, "*Well, look at that! He cleaned his room; it's going to snow in July!*"

General compliments are not something to completely avoid, but descriptive ones teach, inform, and reinforce all at the same time. A great job on cleaning their room could continue on with, "*You put all your clothes in the drawer and you tucked in your sheets perfectly. Wow! Your entire room looks so cozy.*"

Most of us have an easier time listening to compliments than criticisms, therefore, one should take advantage of your child's attention by being descriptive and thorough. Obviously you don't want **Praise** to be too lengthy for then it could start to sound like a positive lecture. Yet, one or two sentences articulating what they specifically did which so pleased you will reward them and inform them how to replicate their wonderful feat in the future.

Few people in our culture embrace and welcome criticism even if it is constructive. We do not want to avoid using this term (or replace it with "feedback") with our children because it would be to their benefit to master the ability to handle being criticized by teachers, employers, and even peers.

We want to get in the habit of having our **Constructive Criticism** evolve into critiques, suggestions, assessments, and supportive evaluations of how their behavior impacts the perception others have of them. *When* **Giving Criticism** *which might be difficult for your child to hear, it is good to remind them that you are on their side and even when you are frustrated your observations are motivated by care and concern* (Pozatek, 2011).

When receiving **Constructive Criticism** it is often hard not to feel attacked or threatened, yet having a parent say, "*I'm on your side,*" or "*I'm only saying this out of care and concern,*" truly helps to melt away resistance. We've often witnessed kids initially rebuffing or even responding in anger to a parent saying, "*I'm on your side.*" In the end it was obvious the child heard and appreciated the words of care.

If you want your child to become comfortable with receiving **Constructive Criticism**, then you want to become comfortable giving it. There are many potential practical drawbacks caused when a parent hesitates or refrains from giving their children immediate **Constructive Criticism** which include:

- *Your child may not be aware that their behavior is asocial, bothersome, or potentially alienating to others;*
- *Unspoken criticism often festers until it gets expressed in anger and urgency;*
- *Criticism then given in anger and urgency become a big deal and a negative event having your child fear and resist future criticism;*
- *Infrequent criticism makes it difficult for the child to master the ability to receive criticism and master the skill; and*
- *The parent does not develop the skill of how to give* Constructive Criticism.

Let's look at the mechanics of **Giving Criticism** and how it can be a constructive and productive parenting and teaching tool (figure 5.2). Inherent in the term **Constructive Criticism** is the feeling that criticism can be unconstructive or even destructive. The fact that many people, probably even a majority, are fearful or resistant to giving and/or receiving criticism seems to support the idea that criticism can be destructive or be a trigger for hurt and destruction.

Giving Constructrutive Criticism

✓ Eye Contact
✓ Positive Voice Tone
✓ Be Descriptive of Your Observation
✓ "Thank You for Listening"

figure 5.2

Constructive Criticism enables one to grow, develop, learn, and become a more respectful, compassionate, happy, and enjoyable person. Healthy **Constructive Criticism** is imparted with relative calm in which your child learns specific ways to conduct themselves in the world. This will foster interpersonal and social success which raises self-esteem and confidence.

The goal of **Constructive Criticism** *given by a parent is to educate, inform, and support your child to understand family and social rules, protocols, and conventions which will benefit their ability to create and maintain enduring friendships and loving* **Relationships**.

A good portion of **Constructive Criticism** will be warranted when your child is acting or speaking in selfish, mean, defiant ways, or when their actions and mannerisms could alienate or hurt those with whom they interact. While respect, compassion, trust, loyalty, kindness, patience, and understanding are valued in almost every human society, they are not usually inherent instinctual qualities. Children learn these valued social skills through the teaching and guidance of parents and other adults in the community. **Constructive Criticism** is the standard means by which parents teach politeness, empathy and all the other valued interpersonal skills of family and community.

> *Probably the most important element of healthy criticism is that it is descriptive and not vague or general. Descriptive criticism concisely informs the child what they specifically need to do to show the desired quality, be it respect, kindness, etc.*

The beauty of describing what the child is doing, is that it separates the behavior, gestures, and the words of your child from who they are. When you describe what you see, you avoid labeling, insulting, putting down, categorizing, or making negative assumptions about the intentions of your child.

When you categorize rather than describe it is hard not to sound harsh or imply that they are bad. It also opens you up to a debate in which your child points out that you can't read their mind. Non-descriptive criticism minimizes instruction and maximizes potential hurt feelings and lowered self-esteem.

The choice is not between being highly tolerant and ignoring, minimizing, understating, or rationalizing your child's social indiscretions and selfishness and being brutally honest by being harsh, insulting, or shaming. As parents it isn't a choice between handling with kid gloves or angrily "putting reality" in their face. **Constructive Criticism** is an honest description of the gestures, words, and actions of your child which could result in their harming, angering, or alienating others. Healthy criticism given often and before you become extremely frustrated or angry is more a process of FYI than an attack on their character.

We are all familiar with the vague criticism and orders given by parents:

- *"Don't be so rude!"*
- *"Don't you dare speak to me like that!"*
- *"You are so selfish!"*
- *"I'll give you something to cry about!"*
- *"You're not listening!"*
- *"What is your problem?!?!"*
- *"Now look what you did!"*
- *"Don't be a smart ass!"*
- *"You disgust me!"*
- *"You're just like your father/mother!"*
- *"Hey, who taught you to act like that?!?"*
- *"You're lying!"*
- *"Stop that!"*

Most of us remember hearing some of the above being said to us when we were young. I doubt any of us found such criticism helpful nor informative, and many of us felt the sting of those words for years to come resulting in cognitive distortions (Stallard, 2002). The negative impact such criticisms had on our self-esteem is a big reason most of us are uncomfortable giving or receiving criticism.

When **Giving Constructive Criticism** you observe and then you describe. Focus on the individual particular event and not on the general/habitual. Refrain from using the statements, "*You never,*" or "*You always,*" and instead describe what you observed. In essence, when **Giving Constructive Criticism** you become a talking camera, just relating what you're seeing and how that can and will be perceived by both you and others.

The bulk of the vague criticisms involve the terms, "*You are,*" or "*You're being,*" as a part of the proclamation. These are words that label, insult, categorize, and characterize. Most frequently they are expressed only after the parent has reached their breaking point and the harshness and sting is amplified by shouting, yelling, additional name calling, and sometimes physical threats or corporeal punishment.

In the above list of typical general criticisms there were a couple that did contain some positive elements. It is better for a parent to focus on the current event and say, "*You're lying,*" then make a proclamation of their kid's character by saying, "*You're a liar.*" Yet, what would be preferable is to describe what the child is doing or did which has one perceive that they are not telling the truth. Here's an example: "*When I spoke to Tommy's mother, she said that you weren't at their house this afternoon.*"

In the other partially descriptive example when a parent says, "*You're not listening,*" one is sticking to the particular singular event, yet making a conclusion and pronouncement which: the child could debate and lacks a teaching element.

A more specific and instructive criticism would go something like, "*When your head is down and you mumble under your breath, it does not show respect to the person talking to you.*"

A parent can avoid "*You always,*" inflammatory statements by using **"I Feel," Statements** such as, "*I feel disrespected when you mumble.*" Yet, at times of conflict your child doesn't so much care about your feelings and the "*I,*" part of the statement personalizes the issue. Therefore, it is usually beneficial to use general rather than personal statements such as "*When you swear and speak loudly people are less likely to listen to what you have to say.*"

Praise and **Giving Constructive Criticism** are important skills to master as a parent. Remember to **Be Specific**, **Concise**, **Clear**, and **Descriptive** when using these skills.

Summary of Being Specific: Say What You Mean

What it is:

It is the ability to **Be Specific**, **Concise**, **Clear**, and **Descriptive** in the verbal interactions of **Giving Directives**, **Instructions**, **Praise**, and **Giving Constructive Criticism**.

Why Use it:

Using and mastering the skills outlined in this chapter will increase **Familial Harmony**, lessen your child's conflicts with all authority figures, and greatly improve the functional **Relationships** with your children. The use and mastery of the above skills will have both you and your child feel better about yourselves and in your abilities to create and sustain mutually respectful and loving **Relationships**.

Reframe, Replace, and Rewire:

Framing criticism, guidance, and directives in a **Specific**, **Concise**, **Clear**, and **Descriptive** manner prevents grey areas that could cause your child to misunderstand or misperceive what you want. **Replacing** vague or emotional statements with descriptive ones allows us to **Clearly** state goals and intentions without using insulting or demeaning judgmental language. **Being Clear** and **Specific** makes it possible for your child to both repeat back to you what you've said and to do it in a timely manner. Tasks done with **Clear** and concise instructions are easier to execute and become habitual, and soon the neural **Rewiring** will make future instruction on the desired task unnecessary

Being Specific: Say What You Mean Home Improvement Projects

1. **Chore Cards** are an excellent way to practice being descriptive in your directives and instructions. These are written instructions or "cheat sheets" which explain all the steps to a task clearly and specifically. Think of a chore or task you want to teach someone else in your life and write down the steps.

2. Gather the members of your household together and teach everyone the importance of **Chore Cards**. This is a great opportunity to work in **Praise** and **Giving Directives**. Have everyone identify someone in the household for whom they want to write a **Chore Card**. (Every person will get ONE **Chore Card**.) Explain that this will be a chore which is not punitive and only takes 5 to 10 minutes to complete. We want this project to be light hearted and fun while teaching the idea of **Chore Cards**. Set a time limit for when you want the **Chore Cards** to be completed (right away, in 30 minutes or 24 hours). Then, gather again and have each person read out their written **Chore Card** and present it to whomever will complete the chore.

3. After completing the above assignment, Praise each individual who participated in the exercise. Remember to **Be Specific**, **Concise**, **Clear**, and **Descriptive** in your **Praise**.

4. Now that you have had some practice, think about the household tasks for which you would like to create **Chore Cards** and make them. You can make as many as you think will help your household run smoothly. Depending on the ages of your child you might want to enlist their ideas on the chores and specific tasks.

5. Since learning how to describe and **Be Specific** is an acquired

talent and it is hard to stay calm and patient when **Giving Constructive Criticism** or in potentially emotionally charged situations, it is beneficial to prepare for and practice this skill often. Sit quietly for awhile and imagine the behaviors and habits in which your child engages that most irritate, frustrate, or anger you. Then, in this relaxed atmosphere write the descriptive words to say to your child which inform and guide them into an acceptable alternative.

6. You may find it helpful to practice saying the **Script** numerous times in practice by yourself or with another adult in **Role Plays** before trying to **Give** the **Constructive Criticism** to your child in an actual situation.

Chapter Six

Being Firm: Mean What You Say

Whether you embrace or even acknowledge it, the responsibility of parenting is tremendous. Each word you say or don't say, and every action you do or don't do in the presence of your child influences who they are and who they will become. In other words, as a parent you have nowhere to hide, for avoiding and hiding are just passive and often harmful ways of parenting.

You would have to go a long way to find a single clinician, psychologist, or parenting instructor who would say that children do not need structure or consistency. The emphasis in this chapter on **Being Firm: Mean What You Say** is designed to help parents develop verbal skills and habits which will provide your child's family life with healthy structure and consistency.

In the previous chapter we explored the benefits of **Being Specific** and descriptive when **Praising**, **Instructing**, and **Giving Constructive Criticism** with your child. Yet, all of that clarity and specificity will not result in your child learning and mastering skills unless you are consistent in your teaching and expectations. The adoption of new communication skills and habits such as **Following Instructions** are dependent on consistent and frequent identification and practice.

If you want a limit to be respected, it cannot change day-to-day. Consistent standards and expectations will quicken your child's learning and allow the skill to become habitual and natural. One of the skills most dependent on being firm and remaining consistent is that of **Saying No**. Your child's ability to learn and master the social skill of **Accepting No** is highly dependent on you, the parent, being firm and consistent.

As we said in the opening paragraph your child is going to learn by your every word and action. A parent who initially says no, but for one reason or another gives in, has taught skills they probably would prefer their child not master. In most cases a child having difficulty **Accepting No** has a parent with difficulty sticking to their word.

A typical scene we've seen played out time after time is when a parent is with their children at a pool. The parent announces that it's time to go and the child needs to get out of the pool. The child pleads with the parent until the parent finally gives in with the standard, "*One more time*," or "*You've got two minutes*." Each limit set or time limit expired is met with an encore performance usually resulting in a new limit being set. We have witnessed this scene go on for up to an hour and usually only ends with the parent finally getting frustrated or angry enough to punish the child.

Children with different personality types have various ways of getting parents to remove a set limit. A short list of methods employed by kids would include pleading, performing, debating, promising, cajoling, begging, or even cutting deals. Yet, there are other kids who use more defiant means such as ignoring, pouting, crying, shouting, threatening, or having a full fledged tantrum to successfully get the parent to back down off of their limit.

In every situation we've observed over 40 years, teaching did occur, yet probably not the teaching the parent intended. The child learned that they can manipulate, badger, outlast or wear down their parents to get their way. They learned that their persistence pays off. A child who cries for candy at the supermarket counter, who gets scolded, threatened, and even paddled and whose tantrum lasts ten minutes before mom finally caves in, has just learned that it takes ten minutes to get the candy. This child will likely be prepared to give at least ten minutes of an intense tantrum to get the candy the next time they go grocery shopping.

While "no means no" is an important lesson for people to learn about dating and sexual **Relationships**, it should be a lesson all children learn from their parents at a young age. This has become even more critical in modern times with the pervasiveness of technology at our fingertips. The question becomes how can we teach our children to respect the limits we set and to learn how to **Accept No**? This in turn will teach our child how to make healthy choices of setting personal limits. Making **Accepting No** into a formal skill to be practiced and mastered is one tool you can use (Dowd, Czyz, O'Kane & Elofson, 1994).

The skill of **Accepting No** can be broken down to 3 easy steps

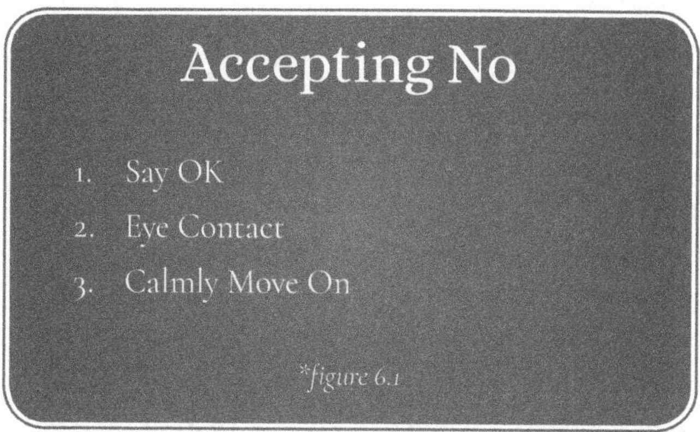

Accepting No
1. Say OK
2. Eye Contact
3. Calmly Move On
*figure 6.1

(figure 6.1):

The **Purpose** and **Goals** of each step are:

1. Eye Contact - *your child does not have to lock in on you as your speak. Glaring and staring would be inappropriate uses of eye contact. This just means that they are showing respect by facing and occasionally looking at you.*
2. Say OK - *this is to show that they are listening and accepting your answer. This is also to emphasize that when* Accepting No *there is no need to explain or defend actions. Such behavior, even when done calmly, can be perceived by others as not accepting the answer.*
3. Calmly move on - *this is to demonstrate that the resistance to the acceptance hasn't gone underground or continue to smolder. A child who can* Accept No *and calmly move on is one who understands the care and concern behind your limit setting.*

Introducing any new skill during a relaxed time is always helpful. So is practicing the skill with your child during a calm time in the car or during a mindless task. Make sure your initial practices are about non-important or fictional issues.

First you could role model how to do the steps, by having your child be the adult and you ask them questions like, "*Can I go to Mars?*" or "*Can you lend me a million dollars?*" You would then say, "*OK*," when your child denied your request. After a few practices review the steps with them and then have them ask you a couple of similar outrageous requests to which you say, "*No*," and they practice the skill.

You may want to be proactive and verbally identify the skill the first few times you use it with your child. You could say something like, "*Now would be a good time to practice* **Accepting No**," or "*Could you tell me the steps of* **Accepting No**?" and then reply "*No*," to the question they put forward, or set a limit for them to acknowledge and accept.

Another strategy to help your child **Accept No** while you are able to remain firm in keeping high standards is to offer other options when you **Say No**. This allows you to not just be the bad guy and helps divert your child's attention away from their original request. As an example, if your child asks to have a huge sugar snack right before bed, you might **Say No** to the ice cream sundae but offer instead some sweet fruits like watermelon, peach, or banana. Likewise, if they wanted a snack too close to dinner, you could accompany your no with a reminder of what they could have for dessert after they finish their dinner.

Saying No with Options is an excellent way to lighten the blow of their request being denied while allowing you to **Stay Firm** and not bend your principles. If you use this skill regularly you will begin to identify many acceptable alternatives to their requests regarding activities, media usage, and plans with peers, often with the adjustment being as small as a time delay.

Children react to parent's limit setting because their immediate focus is on what they are losing or not getting. **Saying No with Options** is just one way that you can show your child what they are getting and not just of what they are being deprived. Giving options is just one method you can use to help prevent your child from stubbornly obsessing on a specific goal of theirs (see **Redirection**).

The best way to get your children to accept limits and accept being told no is to have them see and feel how their cooperation benefits them in the long run. A child who is **Accepting No** and your limits is a more pleasant child to be around. Therefore, when your child has **Accepted No** or a limit you have set, find a reward that shows your appreciation and that they enjoy. Being **Praised**, validated, and rewarded for one's efforts are integral to learning and a positive self-esteem.

An example could be:

> *"Erik I know it was hard for you when I said you couldn't go over to Tim's house because I needed you to stay with your little sister while I did errands. I really appreciate your handling the situation with maturity, it was an awful big help. How about we go out and pick up whatever you want for dinner tonight?"*

Another strategy you can use to reward their usage of the skill of **Accepting No** is to initially **Say No** to something you are actually fine with them doing. The moment they accept your denial of the request, thank them for their growing mastery of the skill and then tell them that since they were so mature you've changed your mind and they can now do what they requested. Doing this on occasion will motivate them to master the skill while concretely showing them that they get more when they comply than when they battle.

When possible point out to your child how their cooperation and maturity inspired you to do something special for them, or motivated you to reward them. Most adolescents want freedom, privacy, and trust and it is easy to equate their respectful cooperation to your decisions and limits. This increases your trust in them which results in greater freedom, trust, and autonomy. In other words, their mature cooperation allows you to start to treat them in a more adult manner. This will be covered more in depth later in the book (see **Rationals, Cooperation and Avoiding Power Struggles**).

One of the strategies you can employ to once again help you **Stay Firm**, and at the same time encourage your child to comply with the least amount of resistance is the use of "**When/Then," Statements**. If your child is refusing to take out the garbage, instead of arguing, threatening, or backing down you would simply say, "When *you take out the garbage,* then *I'll take you to the soccer field.*"

"**When/Then," Statements** *allow you to* **Stay Firm** *and set limits and expectations without needing additional dialogue.* In fact, once you have made the "**When/Then," Statement**, there is no need for any further discussion. We will talk more about "**When/Then," Statements** in the next chapter dealing with **Avoiding Power Struggles**.

Before addressing the final recommendation on how to help you **Stay Firm** and motivate your child to accept your decisions and limits, a quick review of what we've already covered would be beneficial. We've talked about the benefits of remaining firm and to be wary that our children will often try to make exceptions to the standard procedure by attempting to wear us down through tantrums and attitudes, or by pleading and begging.

We discussed how making immediate acceptance of being denied what they want into a formal skill can help our children develop habits that show respect and cooperation. T*he new skill becomes something for them to do and puts their focus on the skill and not what they are being denied.*

Just as important in having them master skills which show cooperation, respect, and maturity is the parents' growing ability to show the child that they get more when they comply and are respectful then when they badger, whine, or pout. *It is the parents' job to make sure that the child feels better and gets more when they comply then when they battle.* This is an art form and while this book can make a few suggestions, it is up to parents to make their child's world of cooperation more attractive than their world of wearing us down.

While incentives, rewards, **Praise**, and improved parent/child **Relationships** are the best and most efficient ways of getting your child to accept and respect your rules and decisions, sometimes it is necessary to administer consequences for your child to truly appreciate that you **Mean What You Say**. A consequence is a bottom line and will be discussed more thoroughly later in the book.

Summary of Being Firm: Mean What You Say

What it is:

It is the ability to set limits and establish boundaries in a firm and calm manner.

Why use it:

Saying what you mean allows parents to follow their heart in setting limits by remaining firm in their decisions. This helps the house run smoothly while keeping the best interests of their child in mind. It allows the children to appreciate the benefits of behaving in a respectful manner and in the long run feel good about themselves.

Reframe, Replace, and Rewire:

Focusing on the skill **Reframes** the situation, thereby avoiding a battle over the topic. The repetition of the skill **Replaces** old defiant ways and the positive feelings gained by mutual respect dissolve anger by demonstrating the benefits of using the skills. The positive feeling gained through mutual respect and cooperation biochemically and neurologically **Rewire** your child having them feel better about themselves as well as improving their attitude towards tasks and responsibilities.

Being Firm: Saying What You Mean
Home Improvement Exercises

1. Think back on a time you said, 'no' to your child initially and then backed down and gave in to their request. Can you recall what happened to have you change your mind? How did you feel after you relented to their request? What was the outcome?
2. Describe how your child reacts when you **Say No**.
3. Describe how you feel when your child reacts in this manner.
4. **Saying No** is often hard for parents. What makes it particularly hard for you to **Stay Firm** and **Mean What You Say**?
5. What support do you need to **Stay Firm**? Do you have people in your life to whom you can call on for support in your decision to **Stay Firm**?
6. Make a **Script** of how you will teach your child the skill of **Accepting No**.
7. Think of a recurring situation in which your child has difficulty **Accepting No** (bedtime, curfew, media time, seeing friends). Compose a **Script** which you can teach your child regarding this recurring situation to use in the future. Refer to this when **Staying Firm** to avoid debate with your child and to help them **Accept No**. Here's an example:

   Your son Dylan asks to go out with his friend after dinner. You remind him the rule of completing homework before seeing friends on a school night. He begins to argue you with you. Remaining calm you ask him what are the steps to Accepting No. *Now you can* Stay Firm *and remain on the topic at hand which is the household rule of completing homework and the skill of* Accepting No.

8. Using the situation above, can you think of a way to use it in **Saying No with Options**?

Chapter Seven

Cooperation and Avoiding Power Struggles

The vast majority of the skills, strategies, perspectives, and attitudes covered in this book will go a long way in ensuring that power struggles and tantrums become a very rare occurrence in your home. Parent and child **Relationships** grounded in cooperation and mutual trust find many ways to use all the good times to help them weather conflicts with grace and dignity. In this chapter we will highlight some of the most essential tools that when used in concert with each other have a great history of minimizing, if not making extinct, parent and child power struggles.

Accepting Criticism

Making **Accepting Criticism** into a formal skill will both help you in your improved delivery and in your child's ability to accept your critiques and suggestions. When a parent focuses on the use and mastery of a skill they are able to avoid debates on who is right or wrong regarding the details of what was actually said (Dowd, Czyz, O'Kane & Elofson, 1994).

The steps are the same as **Accepting No** which we covered in the previous chapter (figure 7.1).

Please refer to the previous chapter on **Accepting No** for a short description of each step.

Keep in mind and remind your child that mastery of the skill of **Accepting Criticism** does not mean that they are to become subservient to anyone in authority. You will be teaching them other

Accepting Criticism

1. Say OK
2. Eye Contact
3. Calmly Move On

*figure 7.1

formats of **Self-Advocacy** in which ideas are expressed and rules questioned (see **Respectfully Disagree**, **Self-Advocacy**, and **Problem Solving**).

"*Stop arguing!*" or "*You're not listening,*" could become, "*Your voice is too loud for me to understand what you're saying,*" or "*Please let me finish speaking before you respond.*" If you have identified the 3 steps of **Accepting Criticism** you could simply say, "*Would you just say OK?*"

Identifying and practicing the skill of **Accepting Criticism** will assist you in depersonalizing your critiques and observations while being able to have your child focus on using and mastering the skill. Doing daily practices in non-threatening situations regarding hypothetical minor issues will help both you and your child become increasingly comfortable with the process.

In the long run you and your child will find that frequent, immediate, and early criticism is easier to give and receive than criticism that is stored and only given with a sense of anger, frustration, or urgency. While there is no magic wand to have your child become compliant and appreciative of your guidance and instruction, the mastery of the skill of **Accepting Criticism** will go a long way to creating a mutually respectful and battle free home environment.

Finally, here are a few suggestions regarding how to help your child identify opportunities to use the skill of **Accepting Criticism**. One is to ask your child to review the steps of **Accepting Criticism** before giving the criticism. A second tool is to ask your child if they are ready to use the skill of **Accepting Criticism**. A third strategy is to have a **Visual Cue** you give before you begin your observation. This could be something as simple of touching your nose, giving the peace sign, or any number of gestures your child could suggest.

A skill that is practiced regularly and frequently has the best chance of being mastered and retained. The learning and mastery of a social skill such as **Accepting Criticism** *takes weeks to become habitual and reflexive. While your child is mastering how to* **Accept Criticism** *you are mastering the skill of how to give criticism.*

We have presented the components of three very vital skills which foster cooperation. A child who has mastered the skills of **Following Instructions**, **Accepting Criticism**, and **Accepting No** is a child who will seldom resort to trying to bully or wear down a parent. The beauty of identifying these formal skills and working on their becoming habitual is that they are an excellent way to depersonalize a potentially explosive situation by having both the parent and child focus on performance of the skill rather than on the debate or argument inherent in the topic.

Focus on Skill Usage

It is easy for a power struggle to ensue when perceptions and opinions become the focus (Hughes, 1997). Debates over who said what and when, who is right, or the definition of fairness are potentially endless and very ripe for a power struggle. In such situations children feel mistreated and bullied, and parents feel disrespected and attacked. The feelings and viewpoints of both parent and child are heading towards an emotionally charged power struggle.

When a parent, instead of trying to out-logic or out-will their child, asks the child to use the skill of **Accepting Criticism** or to review the components of **Accepting No**, they are depersonalizing the conflict and avoiding taking the bait for a heated debate. Parents who role model and request their child calm down and say OK and who refuse to escalate the situation by allowing their child to make the situation into a debate, soon find that their persistent and relaxed request to calm down succeeds.

Reassuring your child that once calm is restored they could

use the skill of **Respectfully Disagreeing** is often helpful (this will be covered in a later chapter). Yet, the firm but calm expectation that nothing moves forward until voice tone, volume, and language become respectful will win out. If a child refuses to calm down, the parent could postpone the conversation while not backing down from their standards and use a "**When/Then**," **Statement** such as, "*When you calm down and show respect, then we can continue our conversation, but now I'm going to go back to the work I was doing.*"

In such a situation it might be nice to add something like, "*We've gotten through these situations in the past, and I appreciate the growth in maturity and cooperation that you have been showing of late. Just remember I'm on your side and am your biggest fan.*" Another example of the type of verbal you can use to encourage your child to calm down is to say something like, "*It seems like you have something important to say, but I can't understand a word you're saying when you're speaking so loud.*"

The important thing is that by focusing on their usage of skills you can avoid getting into heated debates and power struggles. Every power struggle you side step and every argument you refuse to engage in is a step in the right direction. The less successful your child's challenges and threats are in provoking a battle or in your caving in to their demands, the less often they will use such methods.

Catch them Being Good

If a parent only mentions or focuses on their child using a skill such as **Accepting Criticism** in times of conflict, then it will be hard for the child to master the skill or be motivated to use the skill. The seeds for using the basic social skills of cooperation need to be planted in calm times, in successful times. A skill frequently identified, practiced, and recognized in relatively harmonious times will have a better chance of being quickly demonstrated during emotionally charged times (McCurry, 2009).

A child who is praised often or recognized for the times they are **Accepting Criticism** or **Following Instructions** is able to draw on these emotional reservoirs when they are being asked to say OK or repeat the steps of a skill during times of stress or strong criticism. As the old saying goes, "*A spoonful of sugar helps the medicine go down.*"

Even the most defiant child **Follows Instructions**, **Accepts No**, and **Accepts Criticism** sometimes. In fact, each and every day our children do so a number of times. It is often about things they are not very invested in, yet they are listening to us, respecting us, and accepting our authority.

In homes that have become conflict ridden, it is easy for a parent to focus on defiance and take the time between battles for granted or avoid any contact with their child when the arguing stops. We also pointed out that praise is often doled out in general terms while the list of a child's defiant actions is often repeated and specifically emphasized during times of conflict.

The majority of the most defiant children we've worked with over the years had at least one of these three viewpoints: 1) "*My parents never recognize the good things I do, only the bad;*" 2) "*Adults are against everything that is fun;*" and 3) "*I get more when I argue, lie, cheat and steal then when I obey.*"

While working with these children it was often found extremely beneficial to balance criticism with **Praise** and with examples of when they didn't follow directives correctly with **Praise** of the times they did. We find that catching the kids being good and building on their successes quickened the process of their mastering skills of cooperation and respect for authority.

During the average day even the most defiant child can be found being compliant to a number of directives, denials, and criticisms such as: "*Pass the remote;*" "*Let me know when the water is boiling;*" "*Tuck in your shirt;*" "*Use a pen;*" "*Hush, the baby's sleeping;*" "*Remember your soccer ball;*" "*Wait for me at the counter;*" "*We can only get pepperoni on one pizza.*"

All of these are excellent opportunities to **Catch Them Being Good**, and each time you recognize and praise their cooperation you are tending to their perception that you focus and only recognize the bad things. While you're working on getting better at identifying all the times they are being compliant and respectful, you may want to help yourself in your improvement through the application of a few techniques.

One, is to review an interaction with your child when it's

over to see if you can think of any directive they followed, denial they accepted, or criticism they accepted, and then go back and thank them for their cooperation. For example, "I was just thinking of our time in the kitchen, and I wanted to tell you how much I appreciated your putting the dishes in the dishwasher rather than leaving them on the table."

A second similar strategy is to take notice of something they have done in the past such as, "*I just came out of the bathroom, and I noticed that your towel was hung up, thanks for implementing the feedback I've been giving you. I realize its not important to you, and so I truly appreciate the effort.*"

Increasing your ability to recognize the times your kids are being considerate, polite, and helpful may take awhile. A third strategy which you can use which will also help you notice things in the moment is to preplan a few easy positive interactions with your child. Maybe before sitting down for dinner at a restaurant think of 3 instructions you can give your child that they most likely do, such as, "*Please hand me the menu;*" "*Pass the salt please;*" and "*Tell me what you want for dinner.*"

The more **Praise** and **Recognition** your child receives regarding skills you have targeted for them to work on such as **Following Instructions**, **Accepting No**, **Accepting Criticism**, **Implementing Feedback**, **Sibling and Family Harmony**, **Asking Permission**, etc., the more likely they will be motivated to use and master the skills during difficult times. **Praise** and **Recognition** of times in which your children are using desired skills regarding cooperation and respect will definitely help reduce their need to get into power struggles.

On numerous occasions we have pointed out that the more a skill is identified and practiced, the easier and quicker that skill can be mastered and became habitual. Each time you give specific **Praise** tied into a formal behavior identified for improvement, you are getting closer to the goal of your child's mastery of that skill.

Earlier we mentioned that years of data have established that it takes a number of weeks for a new skill to be learned and mastered. *Mastery takes both time and frequent repetition.* While recognizing the skill in the moment is the most powerful means of having your child learn the skill, reviews after the event or recalls are never to be avoided.

In other words, any opportunity you have to identify and work on the skill should be utilized, including practices and the preplanned interactions like the restaurant example above.

Learning Theory

Educational theorists long ago recognized that optimal learning often follows the so called 80/20 rule (Cline & Fay, 2006). This rule states that in a given class at least 80% of the material should be review of material already known and mastered and less than 20% of the material should be new and unknown. *When more than 20% of the material being covered is new the student becomes overwhelmed, lost, or disoriented and learning is minimal at best.* Yet, if almost all the material is known there is no challenge for the student and they become bored and inattentive to any new material contained.

Learning social skills is a form of learning and experts in the field note that the 80/20 rule also applies in this realm. If a child is criticized or told they are not succeeding at a skill more than 20% of the time, then they will likely feel like a failure and overwhelmed at the task before them. This usually results in resistance, temper tantrums, and battles. Similarly, If the child is complimented regularly and only criticized once or twice a week they will not see any reason to change.

With these clinical observations regarding learning in place, it is advisable to keep your **Praise** and identification of positive exhibitions of the desired skill with a ratio of four or five for every time you point out a misuse of the skill. *The goal of learning is 4 or 5 positive recognitions per every correction or criticism* (Gottman, 2011).

We noted previously that when it comes to having your kids handle your limits, expectations, and criticisms in a respectful manner that a spoonful of sugar does indeed help the medicine go down. Your frequent descriptive **Praise** and positive identification of when they are being compliant and respectful will motivate them to not react so strongly to your observations of when they are not being respectful and cooperative.

While parents often don't recognize when their children are being cooperative and polite, kids often miss how often they are being thanked, praised, or recognized by their parents. This is why it is so important to **Be Specific** and descriptive with your **Praise**. A simple thank you is often missed or quickly forgotten, so it wise to make an effort to have your **Praise** be personal and emphatic. In general, *we want* **Giving Constructive Criticism** *to be depersonalized and focused on performance of the skill, and our* **Praise** *to be personal and highly validating of your child's abilities and efforts.*

Receiving recognition for each time they use the skills of cooperation and respect will have them look forward to listening to you and begin to see and feel the benefits of mastering the skills. Coupling this with making sure that your child is rewarded and gets more when being good than when they wear you down or lie will go a long way towards your child choosing compliance over defiance.

Kid-Oriented Rationales

Another tool to help motivate your child to master skills of cooperation is by pointing out the payoffs through **Kid-Oriented Rationales**. Rationales are your answers to your child's questions of why they should listen to you or master the skills. Many parents often answer the why questions with payoffs that either mean more to the parent or aren't particularly exciting for the kid.

Kid-Oriented Rationales are those which reflect what your child desires or provide them with a payoff they would enjoy. Adolescent rationales often revolve around areas such as time, freedom, peer acceptance, success, privacy, and trust. Adolescents will be more responsible when they learn that with increased responsibility comes more freedom and autonomy.

We have highlighted some examples (figure 7.2):

Using **Kid-Oriented Rationales** is just another way in which your child begins to see the benefits and wisdom of cooperating with and listening to you. Finely worded rationales have your child see that in exchange for their cooperation that they will earn free time, trust, privacy, and that you will be more open to their engaging in activities that they want to do. In other words, they will hear and begin to see that they get more of what they want and desire then if they choose to

Kid-Oriented Rationales

When you come home at the agreed upon time after seeing friends...

- ✓ I will be much more likely to say yes the next time you ask
- ✓ I won't feel a need to have you check in so often
- ✓ I will be more open to your staying out later for special occasions

When you do what I ask without arguing...

- ✓ The task will get done quicker giving you more free time
- ✓ I'm likely to give you less things to do
- ✓ I'll be more open to your having some say in when the chores are scheduled

figure 7.2

engage in battles and power struggles.

Consequences that Promote Good Behavior

A good consequence is one that teaches a lesson while supporting or setting a limit. Consequences often reinforce and stress the importance of a limit by enacting a restriction based on the violation of a known rule or expectation.

The goal of the consequence is to teach the importance of

the breached expectation and have your child engage in some form of emotional or practical restitution for the violation. Consequences are also excellent opportunities to have your child review and practice the skills they could have used to avoid the breach initially (Hughes, 1997).

During the time of restriction parents often desire their child to apologize or show remorse for the behavior which resulted in the consequence. The child is also expected to make verbal commitments to not repeat the breach and describe what they will do in the future to prevent a reoccurrence.

The above distinguishes a consequence from a punishment. The goal of a punishment is to inflict emotional and/or physical pain. While it may share the same desire for the violator to show remorse, it is geared more towards instilling fear than educating or teaching competing appropriate behaviors.

While punishments can at times succeed, data clearly shows that consequences are a far more effective method of changing behavior and fostering improved values regarding trust, compassion, and a desire to rebuild a positive relationship with their parents. Children who are punished often desire to retaliate against their parents resulting in increased rebellion and violation of additional rules and expectations.

Let's take a look at the type of consequences a parent could administer to their child who has repeatedly come home later than expected. A standard consequence for such behavior is in parents informing their child that they are "grounded" and will not be able to go out at night or leave the house for a designated length of time. Let's explore the ways in which our consequence is different from a punishment, and how to maximize its effectiveness.

A punishment for this event would begin by a late night verbal assault on your child accompanied by a host of additional warnings and threats while emphasizing the restrictive nature of the grounding, basically promising that you will make them suffer for their gross violation and betrayal of your trust.

A consequence would begin by emphasizing the damage that the violation has had on your trust of them. The goal of the grounding consequence is to have your child understand the damage it has done to your relationship and an opportunity to slowly earn back your trust.

It is very difficult for sizable restrictions such as an extended grounding to not escalate into a full fledged power struggle. Yet, there are many measures you can take which will allow you to firmly keep the highest of standards while reducing the likelihood that your child will look to punish you with endless attitudes and arguments.

Many parents find it helpful to take some notes and do some **Dress Rehearsals** before their child comes in the door. Some parents find it near impossible to control their anger when they first see their child. In this situation it is preferable to inform their child that they are too angry to talk, setting a time to talk in 20 minutes or the following morning.

One important element is to make sure that the care and concern underlying your hurt doesn't get lost in lengthy emotional tirades. While it is only natural to have your hurt and fears be expressed with a sense of urgency, it is also very possible to make sure your message of care and concern gets demonstrated in word and action.

Let's take a deeper look into the difference between a punishment and a consequence. A punishment for curfew violation would likely involve much isolation where your child sits and is restricted from most, if not all, social interaction. In essence, your child would be doing time and their isolation would show the damage done and the intensity of your anger.

In a consequence the emphasis would be on teaching them the importance of following curfews, the review of skills pertinent to the situation, and the things they need to do to earn back your trust. While you might isolate them from some fun activities, you will still want to interact with them to give assignments and practice skills to show they are learning and making retribution for damage done.

Again, it is important for both you and your child to realize that you haven't given up on them and they are still deserving of an opportunity to earn back your trust. *Your child needs to know that they can make amends and that despite the hurt and anger you are still their* **Advocate** *and you are on their side.*

A consequence of this magnitude would probably involve a number of tasks, exercises, practices, and assignments to make amends and regain your trust. Skill review and practices around communication, cooperation, and mutual respect should occur many times throughout the day. Written assignments/journaling regarding what they did that night and why they stayed out could be tied into restoring trust. Having them do a number of tasks which demonstrate their care and respect for the family would also be in order. These tasks and practices should be positive and not punitive in nature to help foster positive family feelings.

During the latter stages of the process of earning back your trust you may want to have them do a few daytime outings with friends with a set curfew. Only after succeeding with those would you try a nighttime curfew and the first one of those could be set for an earlier curfew. This slow progression shows that trust is earned and lets them know how important it is for them to honor all curfews in the future.

When a child feels they are being punished and just doing time, they very often decide to make their parents suffer. Many children say to themselves, "*Well, if I'm being punished for two weeks, then I'm going to punish you for two weeks.*" In such a situation the child figures they have little to lose and much to gain by making their jailer's life miserable.

The methods above which emphasize the teaching, making amends, restoring trust, and relationship restoration all help reduce your child's desire to punish you or engage in endless power struggles during their grounding. Yet, as we said earlier it is very hard for a child receiving a sizable consequence to not become belligerent or resistive.

Therefore, it is strongly recommended that you include incentives for good behavior in addition to the methods covered above. When giving a harsh, severe, or lengthy consequence it is extremely beneficial to find a way to reward good behavior. A standard rule is to have the original consequence be larger and longer than you feel is necessary with the option for your child to be rewarded for accepting the consequence (known as earning "half back"), thus making it more reasonable. The recommended doubling of the consequences serves two distinct purposes.

One, it allows you an opportunity to explain to your child that if they accept the consequence that they will earn 'time off' of the consequence. This allows you to reward their efforts and compliance while making sure that the consequence served reflects the severity of the offense and doesn't lose its effectiveness by making the consequence too short or easy.

The second advantage of doubling the consequence is that the length and severity of the consequence will still be appropriate if they refuse to take advantage of the opportunities you offer, and they decide to try to make you miserable and continue to make the entire consequence into a power struggle. Yet, it is our experience that parents who **Stay Firm** in this method soon find that their child will be sufficiently motivated to comply by the prospects of getting time off for good behavior.

Laying Down the Blankets

In the proactive strategy of building into a hefty consequence the prospect of earning half back, you can highly incentivize a child's willingness to remain respectful and work hard during the restriction period. **Laying Down the Blankets** is the term we give to another proactive strategy you can use when administering large consequences, restrictive limits, or delivering any news which you anticipate your child will have a difficult time accepting in a non-reactive manner.

The purpose of **Laying Down the Blankets** is to soften the blow while presenting you with an opportunity to show your care and concern by demonstrating confidence in their abilities and actively being their support system. Your role as teacher and **Advocate** is highlighted in this technique even at the very moment you are delivering difficult news or administering a consequence. **Laying Down the Blankets** is an excellent way of showing you are on your kid's side even when you are frustrated or angry with their recent actions and decisions.

As an example, let's say you find out that your child shoplifted the two new pairs of jeans you found in their closet. In response to this you come up with a thorough plan of consequences involving bringing the pants back; increased money monitoring including receipts for all purchases; and a restriction from going to the mall unattended for up to a month. While planning to enlarge the consequence to allow for earn back, you also anticipate that your child will have a particularly difficult time not becoming defensive and aggressive when you administer the consequence.

Let's assume that you have been working on a number of formal skills with your child and they have shown significant improvement in the way they show respect and handle your criticism. Let' s also assume that you've been using a number of the other tools that we've covered so far in this manual. When **Laying Down the Blankets** you review their recent success and improvement in skill mastery as a way of encouraging them to continue on their path of increasing maturity, cooperation, and effort.

You could begin the process by letting them know that you have something important to talk to them about, and, while you know they can handle it, you're aware that it may be difficult for them. At this time their anxiety will probably escalate and they will try to rush you into telling them, "*What this is all about*," or begin to fidget, badger, or become increasingly non-compliant.

At this point it is important for you to remain as calm and confident as possible. Your child, though anxious, is reading you to decide how anxious or angry they should be. This process is similar to the process of **Attunement** which we will soon discuss in depth in the section on **Relationships**.

Rather than matching their mounting anxiety by speaking faster or louder, make a concerted effort to model and/or practice relaxation techniques. While reassuring them that everything will be OK, you may want to have them take a few deep breaths or use some other calming technique.

You would continue the process of **Laying Down the Blankets** by reviewing their recent success and how well they have dealt with difficult situations. Having them review the steps to **Accepting No** or **Accepting Criticisms** and doing a few practices are often very important at reducing their sense of urgency and beginning to accept and feel that they will survive whatever is coming. Your confidence and belief in their abilities is paramount to the success of this technique. *We have been amazed throughout the years of how infectious a parent's calm can be even when a child is angry, frustrated, or highly anxious.*

When they appear relatively stable and you feel they have heard and felt at least a portion of your support and belief in them, you could then ask if they think they are ready for you to talk about the central issue. If they say, or show, any signs of not being ready you may want to do more reviews, relaxation exercises, or practices to better prepare them to move on.

Each moment your child sits through and engages in the process of **Laying Down the Blankets** is a success to build on, both in the present and in the future. Even if your child does explode or becomes defiant when you give them the consequence, you still have their earlier maturity to reference as you try to have them regain their composure.

We've been in the room using this process with kids who are being told such things as they are going to a more restrictive placement, to jail, or that their recent behavior will result in the cancellation of their entire summer plans, and watched in amazement as they accepted their consequence while appreciating our support. While **Laying Down the Blankets** does not always prevent explosions or retaliatory behavior towards the person administering the consequence, if used with calm and care, it almost always has a great impact on your child's overall ability to accept the consequence and in their willingness to learn the lesson being taught.

Redirection

Anytime you are guiding your child away from a combative or aggressive thought or feeling you are using the skill of **Redirection**. Throughout ***The Parental Tool Box*** we will provide many skills and techniques you can use to diffuse potential arguments and power struggles by **Redirecting** your child away from the topic they want to debate, shifting their focus instead onto another less contentious area. In the previous section, we discussed how providing acceptable options and alternatives when **Saying No** to your child will often shift their attention to what they can get and away from what they can't.

In this section we discussed the benefits of having your child focus on the demonstration of skills such as **Accepting Criticism** and thereby avoiding getting into a debate on the topic or area of conflict. In this way, we are not avoiding or skirting the issue, but redirecting their attention to their maturity and ability to be respectful. Short recounts of previous successes of skill usage and the benefits it has provided them is another great redirect which can diffuse anger and our child's desire for a power struggle.

Asking them reflective questions on their feelings and how they can best deal with them (see **Active Listening**, and **Attunement**) can also be effective means of **Avoiding Power Struggles** through having your child see that you care and are on their side. The longer you look the more tools in your ***Parental Tool Box*** you will be able to use as a form of **Redirection** (see **Problem Solving** and **Framing**).

Summary of Cooperation and Avoiding Power Struggles

What it is:

Fostering **Cooperation** and **Avoiding Power Struggles** is an ever evolving parental talent which is developed by the use of many different tools. It involves the identification of skills for your child to master and the repetition and patience needed for the skills to become habit.

The ability to **Avoid Power Struggles** is dependent on being able to raise your child's self-esteem through descriptive praise and recognition of their efforts and admirable qualities. By building on your child's successes your are able to instruct and challenge them to do better and become respectful of other's needs, including yours. You show them you are on their side and have their best interests at heart.

Why use it:

A home in which power struggles are rare is a happier and more intimate home in which all members feel supported, appreciated, and validated. It is a safe and mutually respectful environment where people can grow and in which healthy **Relationships** are modeled and able to be replicated in your child's future friendships and personal and professional **Relationships**.

Reframe, Replace, and Rewire:

The skills and strategies discussed in this section help you **Reframe** conflicts in your home from power struggles and a battle of wills into the ability to use skills that promote respect and being heard. A parent can **Replace** arguments and debates with cooperation and respect by focusing on skill usage and not get embroiled on the topic at hand, focusing on respectful behavior rather than trying to ascertain who is right or being more logical. Making basic social skill usage a priority and predecessor to any discussion **Rewires** all participants in the discussion away from anger and self-righteousness and towards cooperation and harmony.

Cooperation and Avoiding Power Struggles Home Improvement Projects

1. How can you set the stage to teach your child the steps of **Accepting Criticism**? With young children it is helpful to teach this skill using fantasy or exaggerated examples.

   "We're going to practice Accepting Criticism. *First, tell me the steps to* Accepting Criticism*... Ok, great. Now I'll give you some criticism and you can practice. When you fly around inside the house in your space ship you have been knocking all the pictures off the wall. From now on you can fly in your space ship in the basement and garage. I really love how you are listening and said, "OK." Thank you."*

   With adolescents it is helpful to teach this skill and practice it on a situation which is humorous or unimportant.

   "I know you think it's silly when I spend time going over skills with you and I want to thank you for indulging me. My intention is for us to have more positive communication so I want to go over the steps to Accepting Criticism *and then practice it a bit before we are in the heat of an argument. Review the steps with me...*

   "Great. Thanks. So here it goes, let's try it out."

   'You know the rule is to feed your pet gorilla before you leave for school. Yesterday you forgot to feed him and he ate up all the bananas I was saving to make banana splits for dessert. Thanks for saying OK and not giving an excuse.'"

   Make a list of non-threatening examples of teaching your child the skill to **Accepting Criticism**.

2. Think of a directive you have given your child in the last couple of days which they followed. Plan a time to compliment them on their good behavior.

3. Name some ways you can pay attention to **Catch Them Being Good. Be Specific** in how you can identify the times your child does listen, complete a chore, is pleasant, or does something kind for another person.

4. **Kid-Oriented Rationales** are often focused on incentives, time, freedom, peer acceptance, success, and trust or a combination of these. Name some rationales which would work for your child regarding:

   Incentives *or* Payoffs: *"When you put your dishes in the dishwasher, I am much more likely to let you watch TV after dinner."*

   Time: *"When you call me at the agreed upon time, I know you are safe and am more comfortable letting you go out without me around."*

   Trust: *"When you tell me the truth like you did about knocking over my favorite vase, my trust in you increases. The more I trust you to tell me the truth, the more I will trust you to be safe and have more freedoms."*

5. Name a few times with your child that **Laying Down the Blankets** might have resulted in less of an eruption and more of a positive outcome.

6. What are some practical ways you manage **Laying Down the Blankets?**

Chapter Eight

Respectfully Disagreeing

A common complaint among parents is that their child doesn't listen to them, by either tuning them out or constantly arguing with them. Since a parent's desire to have their child listen to them is fairly universal, it makes sense for parents to model the behavior they desire and listen to their children. This is why we have stated numerous times that mutual respect is a fundamental goal of this book.

Parents whose homes have become verbal battlefields of non-compliance often cringe at the thought of encouraging their children to speak. For many parents the thought of teaching and providing a forum for their child to disagree with them is like giving a blow torch to an arsonist, and to make matters worse, you are the one about to be burned.

Yet, when it comes down to it, almost every parent wants their children to learn how to stand up for themselves. Parents want their children to be able to **Say No** to friends and peers who try to lead them into illegal or dangerous activities. Parents want their children to be able to stand up for what they believe, but to do so in a manner which does not get them in trouble or render them friendless and isolated.

The benefits of your child learning to **Respectfully Disagree** are numerous, benefiting the parent as well as the child. Teaching and practicing it as a formal skill gives a parent an opportunity to foster not only cooperation but maturity.

When **Respectfully Disagreeing** is made into a formal skill it gives a parent the opportunity to monitor and guide their child into its proper usage. It allows the parent to teach them when, how, and where it is appropriate for them to express their concerns and disagreements.

The timing of when your child attempts to use the skill of **Respectfully Disagreeing** is very important. Choosing to frequently disagree at the moment they are receiving your criticism would be a sign of being defensive and argumentative, and the parent should gently state that now would be a time to use the skill of **Accepting Criticism**. Usually it is beneficial to make sure your child understands that **Respectfully Disagreeing** involves making a request as to whether it is a good time to talk. It is a separate occasion from a conversation about a different topic such as their receiving criticism or being denied something (see **Accepting No**).

Most parents find that making this request the first step in the formal skill highly beneficial, while also helping their child see that immediate comebacks are disrespectful and gives one the impression that they are not listening or accepting the criticism they are receiving. This shows that they have listened and have thought over what was said, and gives them an opportunity to get their emotions back under control before using the skill (figure 8.1):

A good rule of thumb is for a person to wait at least 15 minutes after being told **No** or receiving a criticism before expressing a related or unrelated concern.

**figure 8.1*

In the instances where your child is disagreeing after they have **Accepted Criticism** or **Accepted No**, the 15 minute waiting period is needed for them to demonstrate the final step of these two skills and they show they have been successful in "calmly moving on." Yet, even if they wait 15 minutes they still need to show respect and composure before being allowed to express their concerns.

Built into the format of the skill should be steps which address and monitor how your child expresses disagreement and concern. The term respectful is important because it implies that your child's voice tone and volume are non combative, and that they are not insulting you or being aggressive and challenging. A sentiment we've often heard expressed to a defiant child is that it is not what they are saying that is the problem but *how* they are saying it.

One component you can include which will help your child begin their disagreement in a respectful manner is to make sure they begin their presentation with a statement of understanding which demonstrates both that they were listening and that what you said to them had value.

A child wishing to have a later curfew might begin with, "*I understand that coming home early on a Sunday evening insures that I get enough sleep before getting up for school, but...*" Another beginning could be, "*I see the benefit of my doing homework before evening practice, yet...*"

An additional skill that your child can use to help their presentations not appear to be complaining and blaming is the use of **"I," Statements**. Many parents feel less blamed or attacked when the child says, "*I feel,*" rather than "*You make me feel,*" or when they say, "*When I,*" as opposed to focusing on what the parent does by saying, "*When you tell me what to do...*"

While children can still turn **"I," Statements** into guilt trips or indirect insults and accusations, it is still less confrontative and blaming than "*you*" statements. If your child focuses on their feelings and behavior they sound more like they are asking their parent for assistance or for compassion and less as if their parent is doing something wrong or ruining their life.

Addressing **Respectfully Disagreeing** as a formal skill also makes it easier to teach the many environments and situations in which you would want them to refrain from using the skill. Most parents do not want to engage in the process in public, in front of other adults, or when their child is with peers. It is also an important skill to practice for school and work environments (Dowd, Czyz, O'Kane & Elofson, 1994).

The use of the formal skill of **Respectfully Disagreeing** is also a tangible way for you to demonstrate to your child that you do indeed listen to them when they are respectful. Listening to your child does not necessarily mean agreeing with your child, and they should learn that the skill does not mean they will always get what they want. Yet, be aware that the skill will become ineffective if the child's requests, concerns, and desires are never acted upon or adopted into new family rituals. Even with fairly immature children a parent must find a way to **Reframe** some of their concerns in a manner which shows that the child's ideas and concerns do matter and that you value them. Repeating back or summarizing what you heard them saying is a concrete way of demonstrating to your child that you have heard what they are saying.

When you give your final decision, let your child know how much you appreciate them using a format which promotes mutual respect. When possible, if you deny their requests provide a short explanation of why the original decision stands or of its overall advantages (**Rationales**). Similarly when you adopt the suggestions of your child, do a quick review of their potential benefits.

Since **Respectfully Disagreeing** is a complex skill there is always the possibility of having too many or too few steps to it. One recommended format that most children find learnable and parents find complete is (figure 8.2):

Respectfully Disagreeing

1. Ask if it's a good time to talk
2. Statement of understanding
3. Express concerns/feeling (**"I," statements**)
4. Present case
5. Use **Rationales**
6. Listen to reply
7. **Accept Decision**

**figure 8.2*

The 5th step of **Rationals** in this case means that your child states the specific benefits of their proposed change or idea. We noted earlier that it is helpful for parents to use rationales that stress benefits the child will experience. Likewise, the child who is **Respectfully Disagreeing** will highlight benefits for parent, family, and household in their reasons for desired change.

As in the case of social skills a sufficient amount of repetition is needed for the child to master the skill. While many kids will want to use this skill multiple times a day, others will be extremely reluctant to ever use it. Therefore, you will be responsible for making sure your child uses it enough where it becomes part of their tool box, but infrequent enough for it to remain respectful and impactful. The skill of **Respectfully Disagreeing** is one that becomes ineffective and bothersome (for listeners) if it is used too often.

It is recommended that a child use the skill about two to three times a day during the learning process. Children wishing to use it more frequently should be taught the practical and perceptual drawbacks of overuse, such as just being seen as uncooperative, selfish, and controlling as well as taking up far too much time and interrupting the flow of the day. Let them know that the skill is one that becomes more powerful and effective when used sparingly.

Parents of kids who want to use the skill too frequently may want to devise some form of documentation to regulate its use. Give the child a small number of tangible objects (such as a sticker, printed emoji, or a small card) which they show to you each time they want to **Respectfully Disagree**. In this manner the child learns to become more selective of when they want to use the skill.

Yet, especially with older and more mature kids, you may find your child very reluctant to learn and use the skill. In such cases the parent is advised to set up situations, real or fictional, for your child to practice the skill. Having your child practice the skill regarding issues they aren't emotionally invested in is a great way to have your child learn and become comfortable with the format and process.

One of the potential goals of having your child practice the **Respectfully Disagree** skill is to have them begin to see and appreciate other people's point of view. If they want to be listened to, they need to listen to others. Proper use of the statement of understanding should demonstrate that they are understanding the content and intention of what has been said.

A way to dramatically improve your child's ability to understand your viewpoint is to have them present your case as well as theirs. At times it is even helpful to completely switch roles and have them present your case while you present theirs. Your child will see things from the perspective of others and gain a greater appreciation of the other person's feelings.

Summary of Respectfully Disagreeing

What it is:

Respectfully Disagreeing is a formal skill with a format which provides an opportunity for your child to voice their concerns and to disagree with your viewpoint in a mature and respectful fashion.

Why use it:

By providing your child with a formal way of expressing their concerns you are able to identify and tend to all of your child's inappropriate arguments and debates using more suitable skills, such as **Accepting Criticism** and **Accepting No**. At the same time you get to funnel their legitimate concerns and disagreements into a respectful structure at a time of your choosing.

The use of this formal skill allows you to help your child say and present things in a relatively calm and mature manner. The use of this skill is an excellent vehicle for parents to help their child learn that the substance of what they say and the manner in which they say it are both pivotal in having people be open to and appreciative of their viewpoints. Finally, the formal skill demonstrates to your child that you become a vested listener when they present their ideas, feelings, and concerns in a respectful manner.

Reframe, Replace, and Rewire:

The teaching and mastery of the skill of **Respectfully Disagreeing** is a great way to reduce the frequency and amount of arguing that occurs in the home. Many battles and arguments can be **Reframed** into an opportunity for your child to **Self-Advocate** or maturely present their viewpoint. Endless volatile discussions can be **Replaced** with a platform for your child to present his case and viewpoint and then allow the parent to make a final decision. The more often a child can be praised for their maturity, and sometimes have their viewpoint alter a previous decision, the quicker they will be **Rewired** to trust in their parent's decision making and be able to accept when things don't go their way.

Respectfully Disagreeing Home Improvement Projects

1. What are some of the **Rationales** you can think of to have your child learn the skill of **Respectfully Disagreeing**?

2. Can you think of a time recently that if your child used **Respectfully Disagreeing** appropriately you might have changed your mind about a decision?

3. Is there anything about this skill which makes you uncomfortable?

4. Do you have any reluctance to teaching your child the skill of **Respectfully Disagreeing**? If so, explain your reluctance.

5. Keeping your answers to the above questions in mind, plan out a **Script** for teaching the skill of **Appropriately Disagreeing** to your child.

6. Think of a recent situation when you were angry with someone and made an accusatory statement of how you wanted them to change or stop a behavior. How can you **Reframe** that accusation into an **"I," Statement**?

Chapter Nine

Three Voices

There are many verbal styles and voices you can use when parenting and speaking with your child. We will discuss and explore below the benefits and potential drawbacks of **Three** basic **Voices**: **Demander**, **Stimulator**, and **Soother** (Vorrath & Brendtro, 1974).

The **Demander** is a person who makes sure that things get done in an orderly and efficient manner. They accomplish this through a variety of strategies and techniques including teaching, guiding, delegating, ordering, demonstrating, and monitoring. The **Demander** is firm and consistent in making sure that tasks are completed, standards are met, and all home rules and policies are enforced and maintained.

A gifted **Demander** is quite comfortable mastering the skills and tools in two previous chapters, **Say What You Mean** and **Mean What You Say**. They are **Clear** and firm in letting their children know what the expectations are while demonstrating and teaching their children how to execute each social task and functional chore assigned to them.

The following instruction is a common way that parents use the **Demander** role with their children.

> *"Bobby, we have to leave for school in a few minutes. I want you to go to your room right now and make sure it's clean before we leave. Go make your bed, put your dirty clothes in the hamper, and make sure nothing is left lying on the floor. Check back with me when you're done, so we can be sure your room is clean before we leave."*

A **Stimulator** asks their child questions in order to have them learn how to think things through, plan, make healthy decisions and choices, as well as learn how to be independent, autonomous, and self-directed. A **Stimulator** wants their child to be able to think for themselves and not be totally reliant on others to get things done. The child of a good **Stimulator** feels competent and confident in their own abilities and is comfortable asking for help when they need it.

In the above scenario regarding doing chores before leaving for school, a **Stimulator** would handle it in the following manner. "*Bobby we are leaving for school in a few minutes. What responsibilities do you need to handle and check in with me before we get in the car?*"

A **Soother Praises**, compliments, nurtures, and provides an emotional sanctuary for their child. A **Soother** is generally affectionate and is quick to provide solace when their child is emotionally distraught, confused, or anxious.

In order to make sure the child's room is clean before going to school the **Soother** may say, "*Bobby I know how much you like to have time to play video games before we have dinner. Let's make sure your room is clean before you go to school so that you have time to play before dinner.*"

In its most basic form a **Demander** tells, a **Stimulator** asks, and a **Soother** comforts and **Praises**. All **Three Voices** recognize past successes and use them as motivators and resources for their child to draw upon. A **Demander** would point out how much free time their child gets when they clean their room quickly and efficiently. The **Stimulator** would ask their child how they felt yesterday when they had all that free time due to getting all their chores done before school. And the **Soother** would **Praise** them for how well they've been cleaning their room, give them a hug, and tell them how much they appreciate their cooperation and effort.

Good Voice, Bad Voice

While each voice has its own beauty and potential effectiveness, they all can be be over and misused. The organized and compassionate **Demander** creates a safe and secure living environment in which everyone knows what is expected of them. The consistency and specificity of the well run home makes it easy for everyone to be respectful and considerate of each other.

Yet, a harsh and controlling **Demander** can alienate and intimidate everyone in the home. They can create a tense and conflictual home environment in which some people feel crushed and overwhelmed while others feel a constant need to fight and argue. One who **Demands** too often or too strongly can foster power struggles and a house which seems to go from one crisis to another. Some parents feel that using any other voice than a **Demander** is a sign of weakness or an invitation to rebellion, yet children of these individuals often themselves feel that compliance is a sign of weakness and that defiance is the only way to salvage one's pride.

The child of a gifted and caring **Stimulator** feels listened to, appreciated, valued, and respected. The parents frequent asking of questions has them view themselves as being competent and worthy of others attention, and emotionally and psychologically validated. Children of parents who frequently use the **Stimulator** voice are able to think for themselves and, therefore, are able to withstand peer pressure and take pride in their own critical thinking.

A parent who overly relies on the **Stimulator** role can often be viewed by their child as being indecisive, lacking in personal confidence, and somewhat emotionally uninvested. Too many questions make a parent look weak and may result in their child feeling unsafe, vulnerable, and isolated.

Some children become irritable, anxious, angry, or defiant when asked a lot of questions. Many children feel pestered and invaded by a **Stimulator's** inquiries, or that the questions are some sort of test. While some children feel empowered by being asked questions, others just wish their parents would just get to the point or tell them what they want them to do.

The child of a **Soother** generally feels emotionally validated and understood. They feel safe, supported, and emotionally close to their parents. Children usually feel comfortable sharing and disclosing with a parent who soothes. **Soothers** strive to create a non-conflictual living environment and make relationship building a major factor in their parenting.

A child of a **Soother** parent may become overly dependent on their parent's emotional support and lack the emotional resources and practical skills to solve problems or deal with setbacks, conflicts, or crises on their own. A chid accustomed to a **Soother's** constant emotional support may often view themselves as a victim during trying times, and have a tendency to blame others or view them as insensitive to their needs.

The More Voices the Better

Most parents can quickly identify which of the **Three Voices** they use most often. We strongly recommend that you become comfortable being able to use and master all **Three Voices**. Each voice is a great tool to have in your tool box, and through time you will improve your ability to decide which voice to use in a given situation, or with a specific child.

As we noted above your child's basic temperament and personality may make them more receptive to specific parenting styles and their related voices. This may go a long way in explaining why parents often find it easier to parent one of their children over another, or why the same words and demeanor often have different results with different children. Parents often find that as their children age, they may begin to prefer and respond more favorably to a different voice. A young child who craved your using a **Soother** voice, may feel insulted or being treated like a baby as they become a teenager, and prefer your talking to them in a **Stimulator** voice.

Your ability to feel comfortable with and master all **Three Voices** will have many benefits for both you and your children. Not only will you be able to gauge which voice to use at a given time and situation, but it will also teach your child how to best utilize and respond to each verbal strategy and parenting style. Your child's ability to interact respectfully and maturely to a variety of voices will increase their ability to succeed with the various authority figures they will encounter throughout their lives. Their comfort level and ability to respond to all **Three Voices** will help them succeed with teachers, coaches, and employers in their developmental years as well as coworkers, employees, friends, and partners during throughout their adult lives.

From a clinical perspective, use of the **Three Voices** is often influenced by the mental health issues of your child, the situation and their personality type. At times an anxious child will respond positively to a **Soothing** voice, while at other times the **Demanding** perspective will help them to feel safe and secure and the **Stimulator** might escalate their anxiety. Conversely, at times a child with ADHD needs the structure of a **Demanding** voice from their parent while in other situations the use of the **Stimulator** voice will motivate them to make a good choice.

Summary of the Three Voices

What it is:

The **Three Voices** of **Demander**, **Stimulator**, and **Soother** are very basic and common ways in which we can verbally interact with and parent our child.

Why use it:

The conscious and intentional use of the **Three Voices** allows us to better meet the needs of our children and find the right verbal style to best motivate and guide them to be more respectful and appreciative of all our efforts to have them be successful and happy individuals and family members. Each voice has its own beauty and effectiveness and when used in concert with each other, the **Three Voices** provides our parenting with a great deal of diversity and range. This allows us to impart our highest standards and expectations for our children in the most loving and supportive manner.

Reframe, Replace, and Rewire:

Each voice has its own emotional tenor and perspective. An underlying parenting goal is **Framed** and, therefore, experienced quite differently by the child depending on the voice in which it is given. Repeated use of a selected preferred voice can have us **Replace** an undesirable voice with a more desirable one. The mastery of all **Three**

Voices will help **Rewire** both ourselves as speakers and our children as listeners creating emotional, biochemical, and neurological pathways steeped in comfort, confidence, and adaptability.

Three Voices
Home Improvement Projects

1. Think of a time when you wanted your child to interact with you and put away their phone or device. Come up with a sentence or two to state this to your child using each of the **Three Voices**:

    - ✓ Demander
    - ✓ Stimulator
    - ✓ Soother

2. Which of the **Three Voices** are you most comfortable using?
3. What are some ways in which you could practice using the voice(s) which are less comfortable for you?
4. Can you think of internal messages to give yourself using each one of the **Three Voices**?

The Parental Tool Box Inventory Update

This seems like an excellent juncture to pause and to review some of the skills, strategies, and attitudes we've **Advocated** for you to add to your ***Parental Tool Box***. We have come far enough to begin to cast a better light on the book's general style and goals.

We began this book by highlighting **The Power of Words**, both in words we speak and the words we say to ourselves. Our choice of words greatly influences how we see and experience the world, ourselves, and our children.

Words are the basic building blocks we use to create a productive **Learning Environment** based on cooperation and mutual respect. We observed that all the positive qualities we wish our kids to possess such as being kind, courteous, respectful, and trustworthy are not inbred and have to be learned.

Parents, we noted, are the most important monitors and teachers of all these socially valued traits and qualities. *Parents who use specific and descriptive language generally have an easier time successfully having their children see the benefits of mastering these social skills.* We've recommended that parents teach these desired qualities as formal skills to make them habitual and natural.

The learning and the mastery of these skills will help create a mutually respectful environment in which cooperation and teamwork **Replace** areas which were previously a source of conflict. We have **Advocated** ways of addressing sensitive issues such as giving **Constructive Criticism** and setting limits which will help your child see and feel the care and concern that underlies your standards and expectations.

We have discussed the need for parents to find a way for their children to get more attention and more of what they want when they comply, as compared to when they pout, argue, or manipulate. We will continue to present tools which parents can use which will assist in having your children see and feel the benefits of respect, compliance, and cooperation.

Our successful guidance and instruction of our children is enhanced when they feel that we are on their side and that we have their best interests at heart. In the previous chapters we have presented multiple skills and strategies which will have your child tangibly feel your care and concern even when it is expressed through **Constructive Criticism** or denying their requests. We discussed the importance of staying firm in your resolve to honor the long term best interests of your child, and how to do this in a supportive and not adversarial manner.

We all want our children to grow, develop, and become good people. Growth always involves change and one seldom grows without being challenged. Parents challenge children to be and do better, and conflict is itself inherent in growth and progress. Therefore, our goal is not to remove all conflict between parents and children, that would be unrealistic and opposed to some of their developmental needs. *Our goal is to provide parents with the tools necessary to address the conflicts inherent in growth and development and to* **Avoid Power Struggles**.

The authors do not believe that there is an ideal parent or that in each parenting situation there is only one right and many wrong things to say or do. This is why we are attempting to fill your ***Parental Tool Box*** with a host of skills, strategies, techniques, and parental voices which will help you construct the type of relationship that you want with your child.

If we do have a bias it is that we believe while every parent, child, and family is different and unique, there are general principles that can be shared to assist families in becoming more harmonious. When parents teach, inform, guide, and challenge in a supportive manner, conflicts and resistance can be heard and resolved while an air of mutual respect is maintained. One does not have to completely agree to be agreeable.

The authors are offering parents the tools necessary to establish control without being controlling. *Respect is something learned by your child seeing you as being on their side and their biggest* **Advocate**.

We hope to provide every parent with the tools necessary to create a home environment in which your children feel that cooperating and listening to you is the best option available to them. This leads us to the next section on **Relationships**.

Relationships

Relationships

Early in the section on **The Power of Words** we noted that everything you say, as well as everything you don't say, affects your children, influencing who they are and who they will become. We could also say that everything you do and don't do influences and molds your child. Yet, no matter what your intentions are and how much you strive to actively manage the relationship with your child they will grow and develop in ways which will surprise you.

While parenting is a huge responsibility, it is also an incredible opportunity and privilege. Parenting is not an exact science, and, therefore, it is an ever evolving work. This is why we have stressed the importance and benefits of adding various tools to your ***Parental Tool Box***. A strategy or activity which proved so successful and pleasurable with one of your children may feel empty or be a nightmare with another.

The goal of ***The Parental Tool Box*** is not to become the perfect parent, but to be a parent who can eventually find a tool that works in a given situation. Every person is unique and we can best respect that uniqueness by adapting our **Relationships** to our child's individual needs, talents, and emotional constitution.

Our children are not only unique, but ever changing and developing. Therefore, our parenting style and even the tools we use must be tweaked and honed on a daily basis. With all that being said, there are basic needs which never change such as security, safety, support, recognition, validation, and guidance. The only thing that changes is how these needs are addressed as our children age and mature.

We are forever relating and responding to our children's personality, needs, and interests. The essence of all **Relationships** is in the act of relating and responding. Each day we reassess and modify our **Relationships** with our children based on their responses to our previous guidance, interventions, and interactions.

Any parent who looks backward can be filled with regret and

guilt focusing on everything they did and said which could have been done differently. Yet, as we learned in the very first section on **Framing**, that while the above **Frame** is true it is also not the only one available to us. If your regrets and guilt motivate you to make things better, then these feelings could be helpful. Yet, if such feelings paralyze you or injure your self-esteem then it probably would be best to adopt another **Frame**.

The important thing to realize in every relationship you have with others is that their uniqueness makes their relationship needs different from yours. Finding a balance between getting your needs met and identifying and respecting the needs of others is crucial to the overall success of a relationship. This is especially true as a parent, where respecting our child's needs and preferred relationship style needs to be balanced by our responsibility to teach them how to be respectful and sensitive to others.

We have known many parents who have struggled with the fact that while their children are respectful of others, they do not seem to have many friends and/or seem too isolated. This is especially true of parents of children on the Autism Spectrum, but often includes parents of children who are more introverted than the parent. There is no hard and fast rule of deciding what a parent in such a situation should do. We have seen parents who eventually accepted that their child is happiest with minimal social interaction which centers on their interests and activities. We have also seen parents who helped their child work through their "inhibitions" with the result of finding increased joy in the presence of friends.

The important thing is for the parent to be open to their child being different from them and to let their child's happiness be their guide. A caring parent who feels their child is too social or too isolated might act on these concerns by gently modifying their level of social interaction and then note the changes in their child's quality of life. We caution all parents not to project too strongly their preferences onto their child and to consider following the stated preference of their child.

Obviously if your child's actions betray their word, or their health and safety is at stake, then bending to their stated wishes would be inadvisable. An example of this would be a child who states a preference for a high level of social interaction which repeatedly results in episodes of self-harm or depression.

This book can help make your **Relationships** with your child stronger in the following ways (figure R.1):

Improved Relationships

1. Developing new skills fostering mutual respect.
2. Helping reduce conflict and tension in the home.
3. Encouraging you to find and engage in shared interests.
4. Helping you recognize and celebrate family values and rituals.
5. Helping you **Attune** to each others needs, talents, and viewpoints.
6. Helping you see opportunity where you previously saw none.
7. Providing you with information regarding stages of development.
8. Informing you of the mechanics of bonding, autonomy, and dependence.
9. Helping your care and concern find expression in your words and actions.

**figure R.1*

A parent only knows the validity and benefit of their actions and decisions by the results. The best way to monitor the effectiveness of your parenting decisions is by watching the effect they have on the functional success of your child and on their emotional well being. Keep in mind your child is not you, and their happiness may lie in interacting with others and the world in a way which would not work for you or would not provide you with a sense of contentment.

In the previous section we discussed many verbal skills you can employ to help create an environment of mutual respect. The development of mutual respect will most assuredly have a positive effect on your overall relationship with your child. Similarly, a child who has a good relationship with their parent will be more willing to learn and master skills dealing with compliance and cooperation. Therefore, growth in one area will aid growth in the other.

Most books and professional discourse on **Relationships** focus on conversation and verbal sharing. Yet, human **Relationships** involve a whole lot more than just words. Joint activities, shared interests, and time spent together are all vital aspects of a relationship. One can form very close bonds to another with a minimal amount of verbal interaction. The intimate bonds of many successful parent child **Relationships** are activity based and involve very little discourse.

In the following chapters we hope to provide information regarding **Relationships** which will help you see things in a broader perspective. We hope this information both reduces your anxiety regarding the changing needs of your child as well as increases your knowledge of your child through each stage of their development.

We can help heal old wounds that were created from conflict and endless power struggle, or from a lack of self-esteem and an outlet for personal expression. Yet, the one vital ingredient we cannot teach is the level of care and concern for and emotional investment you have in your child. We know for many of you and your children it has been a very difficult and emotionally painful, exhausting journey. We truly appreciate all the efforts you have made, and encourage you to continue to fill your toolbox with the tools necessary to create the relationship you desire with your child.

Chapter Ten

Give What You've Got

Working and living with children with emotional, behavioral, and mental health issues can be exhausting. In many instances the combination of worry, frustration, and conflict can take up the majority of a parent's waking hours and at times some of their sleeping hours. While this is especially true for single parents with no extended family, it still can ring true as well for couples or parents with available extended family.

Even parents of children with mild to moderate emotional and behavioral issues can find their personal time diminished and their energy level near zero. It can be difficult to find time alone for themselves or time with their partner or friends.

While some find it admirable for parents to sacrifice so much for their children, and some others deem it a parental duty to do so, the reality is one can only **Give What You've Got**. Parents who take care of themselves often have greater and stronger reserves to give to their child.

Parents who sacrifice all their time for their children are not role modeling self-care. Some children become intoxicated and dependent on getting all of their parents' time and attention. This becomes a family problem, especially if siblings are being denied the care and concern they require.

Children with emotional and behavioral problems have just as much a need for age appropriate autonomy as any other child. Those who are emotionally regressed will have a different time table than a mature child, but their need for growing self-sufficiency and autonomy is still vitally important. The most common progression for mammals who give birth and care for their young is to bond, teach, and eventually launch their child into the world as an autonomous adult.

This bears testimony to the importance of parents finding the time to get their emotional and physical batteries recharged (Hanson,

2013). *We strongly recommend that parents make time for themselves and take care of themselves. A rested and self-nourished parent is better prepared to engage in the quantity and quality of teaching required for new habits and mastered skills to occur.*

While the majority of parents we worked with initially stated that it would be impossible for them to take time for themselves, in the long run we always found ways for each parent to make time for themselves. We are also still waiting for a parent to later decide that this was a bad idea for themselves or for their child.

Parents who make time for themselves and develop interests, hobbies, and recreational activities find it easier to get their children to begin to engage and stay consistent in similar activities. This then provides parents with more free time and their child with increased independence and improved behavior and attitude. When one considers how frequently boredom is a common thread with children who have emotional, behavioral, and mental health issues, it is very helpful to find ways to stimulate them to engage in activities they enjoy. We have found the role modeling of interests and hobbies an excellent means of getting your child to get active and involved.

Our job description as parents is to be a care giver. The first person you need to give care to is yourself, because as we've said earlier you can only **Give What You've Got**. Well, to be a good care giver, what exactly do we need?

While everyone's needs are different, there are some general recommendations which seem to benefit a majority of people. A person who feels better about themselves is usually a more pleasant person. We generally gravitate towards and want to have a relationship with pleasant people. A happy pleasant parent is usually going to have an easier time cultivating a close and strong relationship with their child. The closer our children feel to us and the more they want to be around us the easier it is for us to be a good care giver.

A beneficial care giver is, therefore, a person who feels good and has their children feel better about themselves. This does not mean that a good care giver is a push over and never is critical or does not have high expectations. Children do like to have fun, but they also want and need to feel safe, secure, and worthy of other's respect.

A parent who feels good about themselves and draws others to them is one who feels good in their own skin and enjoys life. Parents who do not give care to themselves have a difficult time meeting these requirements.

When our basic needs are met, it is easier for us to satisfy the needs of others. A person who has ways to relieve stress has a better chance of feeling good and have an improved mood. When we aren't stressed and engage in activities which we enjoy, we usually find ourselves feeling relaxed and energized.

While being selfish and ignoring your children is a genuine concern, being a grumpy task driven martyr is just as unhealthy or even destructive to the general welfare and well-being of your children. *Having a good relationship with yourself and having a good relationship with your child are not mutually exclusive, they are interdependent.*

Here are some suggestions (figure 10.1):

Healthy Activities

- ✓ exercise
- ✓ play
- ✓ healthy and enjoyable food
- ✓ sensual/sexual activity
- ✓ hobbies
- ✓ spa activities
- ✓ pampering moments
- ✓ laughing and finding humor
- ✓ getting restful sleep
- ✓ personal development
- ✓ time in nature

**figure 10.1*

With all of this in mind we've provided a general menu of activities and things to incorporate into your lives which will have you feel better and keep your batteries charged (figure 10.1). Please put things that make you feel better high on your priority list. Be creative in how you find time to give care to yourself. Much of the menu has more to do with perspective (see **Framing**) and approach than in drastically altering the way you live.

Rarely is anyone shocked by the above list. We all know what we can do to feel better and be a more enjoyable person to be around. The key is to stop making excuses and do what we can. The above list isn't all or nothing. Each moment that we smile, have a pleasant thought, or go for a walk is a step in the right direction. Postponing doing something because you can't do it in its fullest form is just an excuse.

> *You owe it to yourself and your children to do whatever you can, whenever you can, to enjoy yourself and life.*

Every animal with a higher form of intelligence or complex life learns most if not all of their skill set from play. Tigers, dolphins, monkeys, cats, dogs, otters, birds, and squirrels learn all of their survival skills through play (Kuczaj, & Eskelinen, 2014).

Humans have the ability to learn their entire lives, and much data supports that the more fun we have while learning, the easier it is to learn (Dewar, 2014). Animals and humans deprived of play, exercise, and activity can become listless, depressed, or aggressive.

So, as we noted before, that while parenting is a responsibility it is also an opportunity and a privilege. We are relatively free to see and feel it as a burdensome and stifling responsibility, or we can see it as an amazing gift.

No one is discounting the trials and tribulations you have encountered, or blaming you, or saying it is your fault. We are suggesting that as you expand your ***Parental Tool Box*** with additional parenting skills, strategies and perspectives you also add relaxing and enjoyable activities, attitudes, and habits to your life.

Summary of Give What You've Got

What it is:

It is the recognition and acceptance as a parent that one's physical and emotional well being and energy level affect their potential positive influence on their child. Using this observation can help insure that we, as parents, get our needs met and find ways to improve our self-image and comfort in our own skin.

Why do it:

Our ability to effectively parent and do so in a personally enjoyable and rewarding way is immensely affected by the quality of the relationship we have with our child. The relationship we have with our children which has many variables, including verbal discourse, time spent together, and shared interests, is something that we can cultivate and improve. Parents who have developed strong **Relationships** with their kids are generally happier people whose home environment is a source of pride and satisfaction.

Reframe, Replace, and Rewire:

Realizing that you can only **Give What You've Got** is an important **Reframe** for many parents who feel that taking care of themselves is just being selfish. When one creates an atmosphere of mutual trust and joy in what you do and share as a family, it can **Replace** an atmosphere of conflict and a feeling of always being on duty. The more that you find and cultivate the joy in your life, the more **Rewired** you will be to find solutions to problems and keep them in perspective.

Give What You've Got Home Improvement Projects

Giving care to your self is an opportunity for you to practice many of the skills in the previous section on **The Power of Words**. Use the suggested menu in this chapter, add to it, and personalize it to your taste. Think big and small, 1 to 5 minute activities, 30 minutes to an hour activities, and even an entire day activity. Here are some ways to help you along:

1. Remember **Framing**? Choose one activity which you would like to do for yourself that you haven't done in a while. Verbally **Frame** it in a way with a **Rationale** of why it is important for you to do. After you have created the **Frame** use your voice and tell someone, maybe call a trusted friend or tell a colleague. We want you to use your **Power of Words** to say it out loud to someone.

2. Think of another activity from your menu and **Script** out a scenario of how you can accomplish it. **Be Specific** yet realistic. Another way of thinking of this is to set an intention of engaging in an activity which will bring you good feelings and specifically make a **Script** of how to make that happen.

3. We have been emphasizing the importance of teaching your child what you want them to do rather than focusing on what they do wrong. The same is true for the messages you give yourself. What is it you want to do? Choose another activity from your menu and **Visualize** it.

4. A way to **Create a Learning Environment** for yourself is by setting the time and place to do something for yourself. Right now go to your calendar and schedule in two quick activities you can do for yourself in the next 24 hours. Maybe set a timer to remind you. By quick, we mean real quick.

Here are some examples:

- ✓ *Go outside and take a deep breath and look up at the sky*
- ✓ *Close your eyes and smile for 60 seconds*
- ✓ *Sing a favorite song out loud*
- ✓ *Rub your hands and/or your feet for 2 minutes*

5. Create a **Visual Cue** to remind you of the importance of taking care of yourself. You can simply draw a star on a scrap of paper and put it somewhere you will see it often to remind you of the importance of getting your own needs met. Or, how about taking a few moments right now to set the wallpaper on your computer or smartphone with a picture to remind you of something you love to do. These visual reminders help your brain to focus on what is good. It's a way of turning around **Catch Them Being Good** on yourself.

Chapter Eleven

Embracing Ambivalence

We say a person is ambivalent when they have mixed or contrary feelings towards something or someone. Ambivalence is often viewed as a negative experience or as something to resolve or solve. Yet, from a psychological perspective ambivalence is a common mental and emotional occurrence and can be looked at as a basic and fundamental human condition.

Every child has a basic need to belong and be accepted while also wanting to feel and be viewed by others as a unique human being. The ambivalent desire to be both socially accepted and loved while at the same time be a unique independent person lasts throughout our entire lifetime.

Many of the hormonal changes that occur during adolescence speed up and heighten emotional swings. This biochemical roller coaster is often accompanied by grandiose feelings of social success being quickly followed by feelings of social failure. One sentence by a peer can send an adolescent's ego into the stratosphere and another comment, or even a look, can send their ego crashing into the pavement.

Even though adolescence epitomizes this emotional and intellectual process, children and adult lives are pervaded by various ambivalent feelings and thoughts.

> *The desire to be separate and unique as well as to belong is central to much of the ambivalence we experience in all* Relationships. *The basic tension between these two poles dominates both social and internal life.*

Parents often find it difficult to stay grounded and calm when their adolescent subjects them to their emotional ambivalence and turmoil. A child may complain that you ignore them and don't support them one moment and demand that you leave them alone or that you are suffocating them the next.

The hormonal roller coaster is amplified by the fact that the desire for autonomy increases during adolescence. While the desire for autonomy is increasing so is the recognition of how vulnerable they are and their pronounced fears of rejection and failure.

A parent who lets their child know they are on their side and who calmly reminds their child to use skills of mutual respect and cooperation has the best chance of keeping these emotional tidal waves from ending in volatile conflicts and power struggles. Your child's crusades for independence and their attacks and complaints of your lack of support are just part of their process of becoming an adult. The more one does not personalize the complaints of their child the better.

Pointing out to your child how inconsistent and unrealistic their emotional demands are is usually futile and only enflames the situation. Making their ambivalence into a topic of debate or logical discourse is also seldom fruitful. The best thing for the parent to do is to make themselves available, not react and take things personally, and continue to have their child separate **Venting** and emotional processing from being disrespectful and noncompliant.

Since the bulk of your adolescent's furor is often hormonal and a natural phase of the transition into adulthood, it is fine to reassure them that their feelings are normal. When they assert, "*You are not me and you have no idea what I am feeling!*" do not argue the point but only offer your support. One of the greatest things you can provide your child during these heightened states of ambivalence is calm, patience, and the confidence in their abilities to get through all of this successfully.

Though being an understanding and supportive parent is a good thing, allowing your child to use their emotional turmoil as an excuse to be verbally abusive or to engage in tantrums is generally unacceptable. A parent can validate their child's feelings and emotions without lowering standards regarding what they tolerate in terms of voice tone and volume, language, physical aggression, or destructive behavior.

While a parent doesn't want to stifle their child or prevent them from expressing their emotions, they do want their child to learn how to express and channel their emotions in a therapeutic and productive manner. In most situations it is relatively easy to guide your child away from personal attacks, power struggles, non-compliance, and complaints regarding **House Rules** and parental decisions by redirecting your child from their agenda to their use of skills of cooperation (see **Follow Instructions**, **Accepting No**, **Accepting Criticism**, and **Respectfully Disagree**).

Yet, when a child's expression is more about ambivalent feelings than defiance and non-compliance it may prove to be a more difficult task. If a parent senses that their child is truly overwhelmed by emotional confusion regarding contrasting emotions involving some form of ambivalence, it is best to encourage respect while not demanding total adherence to skills.

The goal is to allow your child to **Vent** and articulate their confusion and emotional conflict while making sure they do not become destructive or self-destructive. The best approach is often to combine attentive listening with sparse statements of support, understanding, and validation. Most children will have short respites between waves of verbal expression providing opportunities for the parent to validate their child's feelings and make reassuring statements showing confidence, belief, and pride in their abilities and the normality of what they are feeling.

During these times a child might find it helpful if their parent identifies this as an opportunity to **Vent** or to work through the kind of thoughts and feelings that lead from adolescence to adulthood. In this way your child will understand what is permissible in this situation without mistakingly thinking they will be able to speak in the same manner at other times where strict adherence to respect are foremost.

One of the ways to help insure that your child is able to articulate "their" emotions and feelings of ambivalence is to encourage them to use **"I Feel," Statements** and to avoid making statements about "you" or anyone else. In this manner your child may be able to avoid attacking, even if their ambivalence is centered on their desire to be more autonomous. As long as your child is able to stay focused on their feelings and not on how others "make" them feel, then they will likely be able to remain relatively respectful and mature during their emotional expression and processing. An easy way to learn how to use "**I Feel**," **Statements** is to use the following formula.

Using "**I Feel**," **Statements** in this manner allows you and your child to focus on emotions "**I Feel**," beliefs or thoughts "about"; and actions "*I Choose to*," (figure 11.1).

"I Feel," Statements

I Feel: ____________________

About: ____________________

I Feel this way because I Believe/Think: ____________________

____

I Choose to: ____________________

figure 11.1

Another strategy you can use to help your child identify and respectfully work through feelings of ambivalence is to have a casual talk about the nature of ambivalence during relaxed free time. Informing and educating your child on the role, function, and developmental inevitability of ambivalence will make future identifications of these feelings easier and less threatening. In this manner one can reference the previous talk as away to help your child understand how to proceed and best use your assistance at helping them process feelings of ambivalence as they occur.

Many children are often paralyzed by the feelings of ambivalence and instead of lashing out or complaining, become sullen, sad, or depressed. You may notice your child becoming moody and see them hover about or become clingy and/or later become isolated, irritable, or even weepy for no reason that they can identify.

One can help them through these hormonal shifts by being

patient, supportive, and letting them know that their feelings are normal. The empathetic labeling and identification of ambivalence is often the swiftest means of having your child move past being overwhelmed by emotional confusion, allowing them to process these feelings in a productive manner.

While ambivalence is a hallmark of adolescence, it is also present in every stage of your child's development. In instances where a child is too young or immature to identify or process these emotions parents often find that calm support, **Praise**, review of good times and successes, and humor are all that is needed to get their child through their emotional rough patch. Many children find their emotional confusion dissolved when their parent engages in a fun activity with them (often of their choosing), or just is affectionate and gives them full attention.

The younger a child is the more frequent their conflicts between dependency and autonomy will be played out in feelings of loving and hating their parents, and wanting to be around them and wanting to be away from them. This is a good time to use **Praise** of the unique talents and personality of your child. Once they feel connected, you can tend to their needs for individuality by having them do something on their own, later **Praising** their maturity and growing self-sufficiency.

Ambivalence: Relationship and Autonomy

Most of us are familiar with the studies which demonstrate the importance of touch, affection, and invested interaction on the health and survival of infants (Harmon, 2010). Infants deprived of love and care quickly begin to waste away, become isolated, and depressed and many will eventually die even when an ample supply of food is available. Man is a social animal and without connection to others his mental and physical welfare is endangered.

A parent or care giver's words, smiles, tender caresses, and focused attention have their child feel special and unique, as well as bonded. In this way we can see how both the desire to belong yet be unique is intertwined in earliest development and is crucial to not only our just surviving but thriving (Kaufman, 1992).

The emotional impulses to be a unique individual yet also part of the group can sometimes be experienced as contrary forces leading to ambivalence. Taken together they help a person thrive. An individual with no validation and acceptance by others is seldom happy, and a person overly dependent on the group is usually anxious, vulnerable, and insecure.

> *A healthy relationship with your child is one that satisfies their needs and aids in their development and overall happiness. Since the need for connection and the need for individuation are both vital to the overall happiness of your child, it is generally advisable to foster both.*

The parent child bond in which your child feels safe and enveloped in your love, care, and concern is an important and rewarding component of parenthood. Yet, so is having your child feel themselves to be a competent, unique, and a special human being. Therefore, it seems safe to say that a healthy relationship with your child would involve a balance between bonding and independence, between connection and individuation.

A healthy loving relationship is when two people feel close to one another. Too much distance and the relationship does not provide enough warmth and connection; too close and the relationship smothers, suffocates, and the over-dependent child struggles to become a self-functioning adult.

The relationship we form with our child should be one which we feel comfortable with them replicating with others throughout their lives. Though a parent child relationship can be close and special, it is potentially harmful if it is an exclusive relationship. Such exclusionary ties are what is called an enmeshed relationship in which the forming of significant **Relationships** to any person other than the parent is felt to be tacitly prohibited and emotionally experienced as an act of betrayal (Pozatek, 2011).

Such **Relationships** are often not willfully or intentionally formed by the parent or the child but arise from the situational and emotional needs of either one or both. In some instances, the child has some form of mental or social disability, and the parent feels a need to protect them from social stigmas or predatory behavior of peers. In other cases, a single parent may find themselves spending all their time with their child and over a span of time find themselves in a very tight mutually dependent relationship with their child.

Parents involved in a very contentious divorce or separation may find themselves vying for their child's love and respect. In many instances one parent will feel the other unfit to be a responsible or healthy parent and seek to protect their child through dominating the child's time to insure their own **Values**, principles, and parenting style are adopted.

The examples in the two paragraphs above only scratches the surface of the potential scenarios and life situations which could cause the formation of an enmeshed relationship between parent and child. The initial impulse could be an event such as an accident or disease, or be an overreaction to one's own upbringing. An enmeshed relationship could occur in coupled **Relationships** as well as single parent households.

There are many excellent books written about enmeshed **Relationships** of all kinds, including parent and child. If you have any concerns regarding the possibility that your child is involved in an enmeshed relationship with you, your partner, or any other significant person in their life, please seek professional help to assess if your concerns are clinically based and in acquiring some assistance in how to proceed.

The point we are emphasizing in this section on ambivalence is that *healthy* **Relationships** *between child and parent are ones in which the child feels connected and cared for and is also encouraged and assisted in becoming a self-loving person.* As a caring parent we want to help our child become an adult who is capable of giving and receiving love, and forming bonds with others that respect and cultivate their friend's or loved one's privacy and uniqueness.

Even if you have no concerns about being enmeshed it is always good to do self-appraisals on how well you are balancing your bond with your child with fostering their autonomy. One of the best ways you can help your child with their ambivalence between healthy dependence and independence is to model it. Balance your affection and attention to them with keeping generational boundaries and privacy.

The balancing of independence and connection to others is a life long dance. In each stage of life this balance looks different. During adolescence the emotional confusion caused by the tug of these drives can become both dramatic and pronounced. *Helping your child identify the roots of their ambivalence and assuring them that their feelings are natural and normal will help calm them and give them much needed perspective.* As parents, identifying these feelings for our child will help them stay respectful and connected to us and encourage them to see us as a support system and not an obstacle to their growing independence.

Summary of Embracing Ambivalence

What it is:

Embracing Ambivalence is the ability to identify and accept that our children will be spending their entire lives struggling to find a balance between their need to connect and bond with others with their desire to be unique individuals. As parents we can help identify these feelings and remain a support system even during their most emotionally difficult times.

Why use it:

Guiding our children to identify and accept their feelings of ambivalence allows us to help them through difficult times without using these feelings as a forum for all out rebellion or frequent impassioned power struggles. A child who successfully deals with these powerful feelings is better prepared to find a healthy balance between autonomy and rewarding interpersonal **Relationships**.

Reframe, Replace, and Rewire:

Poor self-esteem, anxiety, anger, aggression, and mild depression can occur when your child has unrealistic or rigid expectations regarding what they feel and think. Reassuring them by **Framing** that ambivalence is natural and healthy not only normalizes and validates their feelings, but also allows them to **Replace** defensiveness and self-hatred with positive feelings of acceptance and understanding. Through frequent reassurance regarding the role of ambivalence, your child will be **Rewired** to naturally become calmer and better equipped to deal with stress and internal conflict.

Embracing Ambivalence Home Improvement Projects

1. Healthy parents create healthy boundaries with their children. List some of the similarities between you and your child. In what ways is it important for you to be connected emotionally to your child?

2. Now think of ways in which you are very separate from your child. What are your different interests? How can you support the differences in your relationship? Name some areas in which you want to support their independence and autonomy.

3. **Embracing Ambivalence** requires us to tolerate accepting our negative thoughts and feelings and those of our children. This is more difficult than it sounds. Think of the times you silence your child when they are expressing a negative thought or feeling. How can you model expressing these thoughts and feelings in an acceptable manner?

4. The use of "**I Feel**," **Statements** is a useful tool in parenting as well as in all **Relationships**. Think of a situation in your life currently in which you are frustrated or angry with another person. Write a few sentences about that situation.

5. Now it's time to **Reframe** that situation by using an "**I Feel**," **Statement** (figure 11.1).

Chapter Twelve

Attunement

Attunement is a relatively new term which is being used in various schools of psychology and neurology to articulate a way in which people relate, bond, and attach to one another which is beyond the scope of intellectual understanding or knowledge. One who **Attunes** feels and senses what the other needs or is experiencing by "placing themselves in the other's shoes" or "entering into their skin." What this essentially is saying is that **Attunement** is the process by which we feel what the other is experiencing or that we become in harmony with their experience (Siegel & Bryson, 2014).

Often times **Attunement** can occur without conscious effort. When an infant lies with their mother (or care giver) their vital signs begin to get in sync with mom (Butcher, 2013). Soon mom and baby's heart rate and breathing pace become the same.

Young children often look to their parents to learn how to respond in a given situation. When a child falls down they look to their parent to see how they should respond. If the parent gets up quickly and begins to run to the child, the child is very likely to respond to this rescue attempt by crying. Yet, if the parent smiles and reassures them that they are OK, the child usually smiles, gets back up, and continues their adventure.

In previous chapters we discussed the importance of remaining calm when **Giving Constructive Criticism**, **Saying No**, giving consequences or delivering difficult news. Our calm is not only role modeling how we want our child to react, but is also emotionally and kinesthetically (physically) pulling them towards remaining composed. No matter how old our child is, a part of them will always be using our reactions as **Cues** of how they are to respond. If our goal is for them to be respectful and feel OK, then from an **Attunement** level and a modeling level it is beneficial for us to feel OK and remain calm (see **Laying Down the Blankets**).

If you ever have had to sit in a waiting room next to someone who is anxious and fidgety, you know how hard it is to stay calm and resist the natural tendency to **Attune** yourself to those in your immediate environment. The process of **Attunement** testifies to the power and influence our emotions and feelings have on each other.

Generally, **Attunement** involves the reading of or sensing another and physiologically and emotionally synching with them. In some instances we may be unaware of the process as in the cases of the heart rate, breathing, or gait synchronization in the examples above. Yet, while we may be peripherally aware of the positive impact staying calm will have in helping our child not react to our setting limits and giving consequences, we are not consciously making them **Attune** to us.

If our calm is fostered by care, concern, and our belief in them they will likely stay cooperative, yet if they instead interpret our calm as emotionally detached or uninvested they will likely act out. Our calm without care and concern will not be successful in creating **Attunement**, but instead have our child feel unsafe or alienated and could inflame their fear and anger. Our care and emotional investment into what they are feeling is the very core of **Attunement**.

A detached adult can still teach skills of cooperation and respect to a child, but it will be a more difficult road if done without **Attunement**. The care and concern inherent in **Attunement** tends to many of your child's basic psychological and relational needs which we will list later in this chapter.

One of our goals as parents is for our child to become sensitive to others. Social skills such as sharing, not excluding or abandoning friends, and being polite to and respectful of others all involve teaching our children to be caring and sensitive. Just as in the case of being cooperative and compliant, these skills can be taught and learned as habits devoid of internal connection to others. Many parents hope to instill in their child a genuine appreciation and connection to the people they interact with or with whom they befriend. The care we hope they show to others and the emotional bond they feel to family and friends is a form of **Attunement**.

As we mentioned earlier the parent child relationship is

literally how you relate to your child. If you relate to your child mainly on a cognitive intellectual level, then it will lack emotional richness. If you relate to them only from your emotional world, then they may feel misunderstood or alone and rebel against you and blame you for basing the relationship all on your feelings and perceptions. Even if they don't rebel, your relationship with your child will lack the beauty that comes from feeling and appreciating their unique way of feeling and being in the world.

Often times our children adopt many of our basic mannerisms. They may smile like us, visually resemble us, and even say things in the same way as we do. While this is often comforting in its familiarity, it is often deceiving in helping us understand and appreciate our children. It is difficult for a parent to understand that when their child smiles, gets angry, or stands like us that they may not have the same feelings as we do when we do those same things or look that way.

The only way we can appreciate and understand what our child truly feels and thinks is by caring enough to listen to and enter their world. Care based **Attunement** allows us to begin to piece together and feel their world through their eyes and their bodies. While no one can fully understand another or feel the world in the exact way, we are capable of listening, asking questions, and being sensitive to another's emotions.

Being **Attuned** *to your child is more than an intellectual task, it is an emotional receptivity to their inner world. The more you focus on their world and experiences, the richer your appreciation, support, and guidance can become.* Human emotion and experience are very complex and this causes the road to **Attunement** to be filled with many detours and mistaken routes. Yet, a parent who remains sensitive, caring, and open to the inner world of their child will feel progress over the long run and feel closer to their child.

On many occasions in this book we have mentioned that the parent child relationship will involve different types of verbal interactions. At times you will be giving them directives, other times you will be setting limits, giving them criticism, or denying their requests. There will be times when you help them problem solve, provide them an opportunity to express their feelings, or even to **Vent** their frustrations. While **Attuning** to your child can become a very useful and beneficial tool, it will probably not be necessary or useful in every situation or conversation.

Yet, since **Attunement** is grounded in a parent's care and concern it should always remain within arm's reach and be a fundamental way in which you listen and share. **Attunement** is a relationship skill and, therefore, is something that your child learns and adds to their toolbox. Just as they were taught to share, they must also be guided to listen to and try to feel what their family and friends are saying and experiencing.

For the skills regarding mutual respect and cooperation we noted that often the problem is not in what your children are saying, but how they are saying it. Likewise when our child is expressing themselves, it is not so much what we hear as how we are listening. *Hearing what our child is saying is important, but being* **Attuned** *to what they are feeling and experiencing is often even more important.* So while we might want to assist our children in expressing themselves in a more respectful manner by having them focus and master skills of cooperation, we also do not want to ignore or discount the feelings behind the words.

Children whose needs are being met and who feel that their parent cares for them and is **Attuned** to them are more likely to be respectful and cooperative. All of the basic internal and social (relationship and attachment) needs of your child can be addressed through the process of **Attunement**.

Throughout this book we've been discussing the importance of tending to basic needs as well as recommending various strategies and skills you can use and teach which will help meet those needs. **Attunement** is just one more tool that can be used in concert with many of the other tools to help your child feel good about themselves and their relationship with you.

In the previous chapter on **Embracing Ambivalence** we spoke of every person's need to belong and feel connected as well as their need to be recognized and valued as a unique individual. A short list of this type of basic needs shared by children and adults includes the following.

Basic Needs:

Here is a list of some of our most basic needs (figure 12.1):

Basic Needs

- ✓ Safety and security
- ✓ Feeling respected and valued
- ✓ Having feelings and perceptions validated
- ✓ Having feelings viewed as normal
- ✓ Having a positive impact on others and the world
- ✓ Feeling accepted
- ✓ Feeling cared for and loved
- ✓ Feeling worthy
- ✓ Feeling heard and paid attention to
- ✓ Receiving structure and consistency
- ✓ Having someone to depend on

**figure 12.1*

A parent who tends to the above needs of their child is fulfilling the highest function of being a parent. It is hard to imagine meeting the above needs without having a strong relationship with your child (Kaufman, 1992). In many ways one could view the meeting of these needs as the very definition of a healthy relationship between child and parent.

Attunement is a parenting style and perspective which helps in meeting our child's relationship needs in a mutually rewarding way.

Attunement is a way of insuring that your care for your child stays centered on their needs and not your own.

An **Attuned** parent is one who combines intellectual insights and practical instruction with emotional empathy. An **Attuned** parent is not seeing the child through their own eyes, but attempting to feel their child's world arising from inside their body. An **Attuned** parent is not just hearing what they are saying, but is feeling how they are saying it. The goal of **Attunement** is to try to understand what your child's world means to them, and how their emotional world feels to them.

Care and concern are probably the two most important qualities of being an effective and beneficial parent. A parent's care makes every tool in their tool box more effective. A person can be a wonderful parent even if they are not particularly intelligent or insightful, as long as they care and are willing to find tools which help their child become a self-loving and respectful young adult.

Many parents often feel themselves incapable of or not having the right emotional constitution to sufficiently develop the skill of **Attunement**. This may be due to factors such as personality type, clinical depression, anxiety, a diagnosis such as Autism Spectrum, or the emotional damage they have suffered over the last number of years trying to parent their child. While any of the above could potentially impact the use of the skill of **Attunement**, it does not prohibit you from learning and using the skill in a beneficial manner.

The simple addition of a few strategies and skills can help you develop the ability to **Attune** to your child and have your child feel **Attuned** to by you. Skills such as **Active Listening** can be used to **Attune** to your child by giving you an opportunity to ask them reflective questions regarding their feelings. **Active Listening** also involves the skill of repeating back or summarizing what your child has said.

Reflective questions and repeating back what you hear your child saying both validates their feelings while demonstrating your interest in what they feel. As an example, if your child relates a story regarding how they are being mistreated by a peer, rather than saying something like, "*It will be okay*," or offering a solution, you could show empathy by asking how it makes them feel and how they are coping.

If for any reason you feel uncomfortable or incapable or using any of the skills in this book it would be wise to consult a professional to see if and in what ways your concerns are valid. Each parent will find certain tools presented in this book easier to use and master than other strategies and skills. The goal is for you to find the right mix of tools to have in your ***Parental Tool Box***, allowing you to feel comfortable and relatively successful in any given situation.

As we noted earlier in this chapter, **Attunement** is often a physiological process that occurs without any conscious effort. A parent can **Attune** to a child and have the child **Attune** to them just by doing activities together or spending time in close proximity. When you are near your child just your positive physiology or emotional state can have a positive impact on your child. Science has proven that a parent's positive mood, confidence, optimism, and care are infectious and will have a stabilizing impact on their child's attitude and self-esteem.

Summary of Attunement

What it is:

Attunement is the process by which parent and child become physiologically or emotionally in sync with each other. Through attentive listening and empathetic dialogue a parent who is **Attuned** to their child is able to not just hear what their child is saying, but feel their inner world which is at the root of what they are expressing. An **Attuned** relationship is more than intellectually relating to another, it is a sensing and appreciation of each other's uniqueness and individual experience.

Why use it:

Attuning to your child successfully addresses many of their basic personal and relationship needs. A child who feels **Attuned** to is one who feels listened to and understood and is, therefore, better able to listen to and see their parents' viewpoints. A child who feels **Attuned** to is more likely to be able to **Attune** to their parents, making them much more sensitive and supportive and reducing the need to use verbal battles as a way of becoming more autonomous.

Reframe, Replace, and Rewire:

Understanding that **Attunement** is a natural bond in any relationship, especially that between parent and child, can be a helpful **Reframe** and guiding force to help parents stay the course during difficult times. Confidence, patience, and calm are often the most influential tools we have in a given situation. When parents **Replace** anxiety, frustration, and fear with a firm belief that everything will turn out well, they often find their children are far more cooperative and able to **Attune** to your positive energy. Through the use of many of the skills and strategies in the ***Parental Tool Box***, you will be able to **Rewire** both your way and your child's way of interacting and relating to each other.

Attunement Home Improvement Projects

1. Before being **Attuned** to another it is important to practice attuning to our own selves. Performing a body scan allows you to focus on the interior of your body, to become aware of your own "self." There are many free body scans you can find on the internet which will lead you through this exercise. Try doing one.
2. After completing your body scan describe what you noticed happening during the exercise. Did you make any useful discoveries?
3. Think of a time when you were very connected to your own feelings and had a felt sense of really knowing what you wanted. When you are **Attuned** to your own needs, when you really know what you want, where do you feel that in your body? Is it in your head, your heart, your gut? Each of us has our own way of our body knowing when we are **Attuned** to ourselves. What's yours?
4. Think of a recent situation in which you felt connected to another person. Maybe you felt as if you really understood them or they were **Attuned** to you. Describe this situation in detail.
5. Think of a difficult interaction you have had with your child. Describe what you were feeling and thinking at the time.
6. Do you remember what was your intention in the above difficult interaction with your child? What did you want to have happen at the time?
7. Try describing this difficult interaction from your child's perspective. This is hard to do, so take a deep breath and allow yourself to try to see and feel what they might have been feeling and thinking at the time.

8. Now, consider the perspective of a casual observer and pretend that this person was observing the difficult interaction with your child and describe it from their perspective.

9. Considering the three perspectives above (yours, your child's, a casual observer's), how could you have **Attuned** to your child without losing your own integrity and original intention in the interaction?

Chapter Thirteen

Family and Personal Values

When a person says they **Value** something they usually mean that the thing is important to them, has personal significance, or gives meaning to their lives. Your **Personal Values** are those qualities and ideas which are meaningful to you and guide you in the decisions you make and the activities you choose. In many ways your **Values** are the basis of your priorities and those qualities you **Value** pervade your self-image, influencing how you interact with others (McCurry, 2009).

As a person you have your own **Individual** set of **Values** and almost any social group you are a part of also has a set of **Values**, even if never vocalized. Every family has a combination of each **Individual's Values** and their **Shared Values** as a group. Cultures, religious groups, and nations often stake a claim to a specific set of **Values**. While an **Individual's Personal Values** may differ from others, they often take pride in those of the larger group. This is usually the case in **Family Values**.

Before we go on to discuss the role **Family and Personal Values** play in your relationship to your children and family, let's take a minute to name a few common **Values** (figure 13.1).

While our children may be born with inherent personality traits which will likely later express themselves in specific **Values** (neatness, enthusiasm, etc.), they learn the bulk of their initial **Values** from their parents. This is the parental responsibility often stated as "instilling good **Values**" into your child.

The older your child becomes the more likely they will develop their own set of **Values** as well as deepen many that they learned from you. Those which have the greatest power and influence over us are labeled our **Core Values**. These **Core Values** are often the ones in which we are highly invested in our children learning and keeping throughout their lives.

Values:

Here are some examples of common **Values** (figure 13.1):

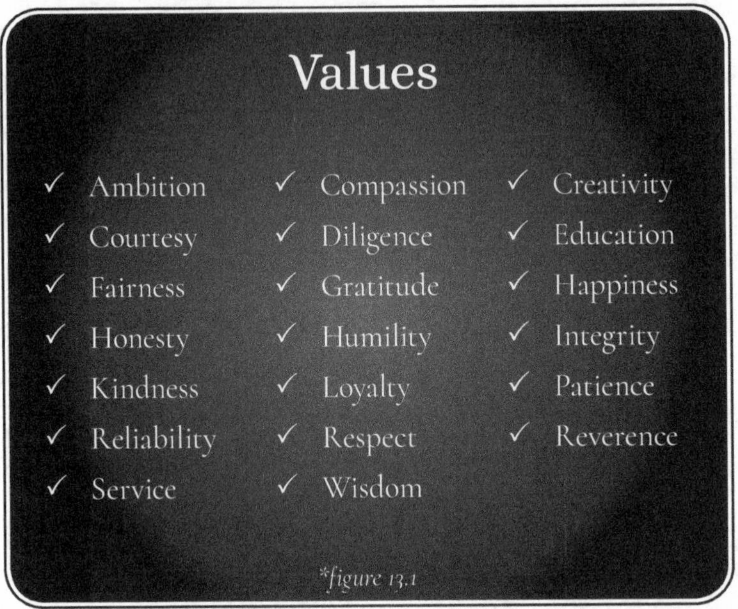

Values
✓ Ambition
✓ Compassion
✓ Creativity
✓ Courtesy
✓ Diligence
✓ Education
✓ Fairness
✓ Gratitude
✓ Happiness
✓ Honesty
✓ Humility
✓ Integrity
✓ Kindness
✓ Loyalty
✓ Patience
✓ Reliability
✓ Respect
✓ Reverence
✓ Service
✓ Wisdom

*figure 13.1

Our overall satisfaction with the relationship we have with our child is often dominated by three areas. The first area, which the bulk of the early part of this book dealt with, is the level of respect and cooperation they demonstrate towards us. The second area has to do with all that we have in common with them such as personality traits and shared interests. The third area is the **Values** which we share with them or admire in them which fill us with a sense of pride.

While we sometimes do not live up to the **Values** we would like to have, we cannot help but act according to those we actually do possess. Yet, while we and our children live our **Values**, we often have not taken the time to identify them or understand the role they have in our ethics, morals, and interpersonal **Relationships**.

There are many benefits to a parent identifying, learning,

and committing the most cherished **Values** of each family member to memory. A parent aware of each child's **Values** can use this information to strengthen and improve their relationship to them.

A parent who is aware of their child's **Values** has not only a better handle on their child's interests but also on what is behind and motivating the interest. In this way, you can approach a discussion from their inner emotional world much in the way discussed in the previous chapter on **Attunement**. This will assist you in avoiding the possibility of alienating them by talking about their interests from your perspective. It allows you access to seeing the interest from their perspective and emotional tenor.

Understanding your child's **Value System** may help you gain a better understanding or appreciation of the source of some of your conflicts or rough areas. If organization is near the top of your list and creativity is at the top of theirs, then the fact that they never meet your standards in how they keep their room might be a little more than laziness. While you still may decide that you want them to meet your standards, it may be helpful to see that their "messiness" is not totally structured in laziness or resistance, but a natural outcome of their view of a creative environment. In such a situation, you may be able to find an acceptable negotiation in which they meet certain standards of neatness while being allowed to have an unregulated designated space for creative exploration.

You can also incorporate your child's **Values** into the reasons they should follow your directives or heed your guidance. If you recall in the chapter on **Cooperation and Avoiding Power Struggles**, we recommended using **Kid-Oriented Rationales** to help make your teaching more relevant to your kids. Each of the concept areas for **Rationales** we suggested (which included trust, peer acceptance, freedom, and time) are all typical **Values** of most adolescents. Your personalized knowledge of your child's **Values** will help you **Frame** much of your guidance and teaching in language reflecting their interests, emotional pay offs, and principles.

A common perception among parents is that their adolescent does not share their basic **Value System** and that their child's **Value System** is in conflict with or opposed to their own. Many of the parents we have worked with have expressed the concern that their children will never adopt their **Value System**.

In most cases, we help the parents see that their children do indeed share many of the **Family Values**. Additionally, it has been our experience that the bulk of the **Family Values** absent in adolescence begin to reappear around the age of twenty-five or so. It is the rare child whose **Value System** does not reflect many of the **Values** of their upbringing by the time they become thirty.

Yet, for any parent who is disappointed or frustrated with their child's **Value System** differing from their own, we suggest they compare their own **Value System** with the **Value System** of their family of origin. While most of us recognize many **Values** that have been handed down to us or that we have embraced, we usually identify some that we adopted on our own or through marriage or other significant **Relationships**.

While developing the initial **Value System** of your child is a parental responsibility, it is also your responsibility to support their efforts to become a unique individual with their own **Personal Values**. It is only natural for any person to feel their **Value System** important and, therefore, not unusual for a person to feel that their **Value System** is the best one available. Although it may be the best one for you, it may not be the best one for others. In most cases there is no right or wrong set of **Values**, and if your child chooses a **Value** different from yours it isn't necessarily an insult or a bad choice for them.

Caring parents hope that their children will grow up to be good people, and that their **Values** will speak well of them. It makes sense that they hope their children follow in their footsteps and treasure some of the **Values** they learned while growing up. Yet, it is important to not allow this desire to prevent us from embracing our children's individual gifts and **Values**.

We hope each family household takes pride in and celebrates the **Values** which sculpt the beauty in their lives and have a positive impact on the people they know and the community in which they live. Taking pride in **Family Values** helps unite a family and deepens and enriches the **Relationships** we have with our children.

The term **Value** judgment is often used to identify when you feel your **Values** are superior to another or when you are unhappy with one of your own **Values**. In many cases a person prone to making **Value** judgments can become intolerant to the **Values** of others or view them as lacking in "good" or "healthy" **Values**.

The authors of this book have been trained to develop a rather neutral stance towards **Personal and Family Values**. We have worked with hundreds of families from different cultural, spiritual, and socio-economic backgrounds which has uncovered extreme variances in **Personal and Family Value Systems**. Generally, our job has been to honor and respect the **Value Systems** of the families we have worked with, and have only questioned or intervened when the **Values** have caused demonstrable harm to self or others. We **Advocate** that you take the same stance whenever possible.

An appreciation and acceptance of the **Values** of others becomes difficult for many parents when they view outside **Values** and priorities to be in competition with the **Values** they want their child to adopt. In some cases the outside **Values** seem to be short sighted and seductive and appear detrimental to or not in the best interest of our children.

More often then not we don't even equate these potentially harmful forces as **Values** but only as dangerous outside influences. These dangerous influences which seen to undermine or compete with the **Values** we hope to instill in our child can be found in the media, technology, consumerism, pop culture, peer groups, or in drugs and alcohol. All of our efforts to have our child be safe and a good person seem at a disadvantage to the short term rewards and easy outs offered by many of these factors. In these situations parents often feel that they are forced to be the bad guy and their long term internal good feelings can't compete with the short term seductions and thrills offered through these other outlets and mediums.

We will address some of the specific challenges posed by technology and the media in a later chapter (see **Parenting in the 21st Century**). Yet, at this point we can offer some perspective and suggestions to help you address these concerns regarding your child adopting a healthy set of **Values**.

Your first duty is obviously to keep your child safe. All of your actions of care and concern should be to insure that your child remains safe and healthy. It is helpful to be proactive and find ways of making your time with your child fun and enjoyable while still maintaining your high standards. Finding outlets for your shared interests and making sure you spend enjoyable moments with your child will strengthen your relationship with your child and reduce the perception of you being the bad guy.

As mentioned above we will have an entire chapter on parenting and technology, offering suggestions of how to deal with many of these outside factors. Yet, we want to emphasize that the cultivation of a strong, healthy relationship with your child is the best defense against potentially detrimental societal influences.

The above stance is far easier said than done. It is very hard to trust both yourself and your child and that your relationship built on care and concern will win out over the temptations, seductions, and instant gratification offered by others. Yet, if the powers of seduction were so superior to your set of **Values**, you yourself would not have chosen your set of **Values** and instead given in to the seduction.

We also want to strongly caution you against going into an all out battle with the outside influences. The mentality of perpetual battle and its accompanying emotions such as anger, mistrust, frustration, and over protectiveness will not enamor you to your child and often make the other side look all the more attractive. While a parent's fear might be justified, a battling mentality seldom helps in having your child see you as being on their side or wanting them to have fun and be happy.

A parent who becomes entrenched in winning the battle against the **Values**, or lack of **Values**, of others will have a difficult time maintaining a healthy relationship with their child or remaining a positive role model. When it comes to building a strong and healthy relationship with your child, it is usually better to be proactive than reactive. This means it is usually preferable and more beneficial to create good times with your child in harmony with your **Value System** than try to defeat or prohibit your child from outside influences.

The hypervigilant parent always on the look out for potential harm will often develop enmeshed 'us-versus-them' **Relationships** with their child, or stunt their child's developmental growth by being rigid and over controlling. A weak, excessively dependent child will seldom be able to live up to the **Values** you envision them having. Therefore, we balance our protective concern for them by giving our children the freedom to become healthy independent adults.

In the next chapter we will address the dynamics and intricacies of shared parenting. Yet, conflicts in parenting style can sometimes become less of an issue when there is a consensus of agreed upon **Values**. In a two parent or a multi-generational household it is beneficial to have discussions on the underlying **Values** each want instilled in the children. In such a way, even when there are differences, each adult's priorities and **Values** can be honored and respected.

While consensus can often be reached or at least differences in **Values** can be minimized in a household, it is much more difficult to accomplish **Value** consistency when your child lives or spends a great deal of time in other households (with your ex, step-parents, etc.). Though efforts to reach consensus or compromise are **Valuable** and potentially highly beneficial it is usually unrealistic to think your household **Values** will be adopted by other households, even when they are family.

We previously noted that doing battle with competing **Value Systems** is seldom productive or a benefit to your child or to your relationship with your child. The best a parent can do is to **Advocate** for the **Values** they want their child to adopt by informing others, such as, their ex, teachers, and friends, of their wishes and preferences and encourage them to honor and respect those goals.

> *The* Values *you hold dear have the best chance of being successfully transferred to your child if they permeate your relationship with your child in your decisions, teaching, and shared activities.*

Trying to manage and control the **Values** and actions of all others interacting with your child is unrealistic and in most cases counterproductive.

Celebrating and enjoying your **Core Values** and showing the benefits they have on your life will have a great impact on your child.

Providing them with ample opportunities to see and feel the benefits and personal rewards of your **Values** is often more successful than mere words or logic.

Family Traditions, Rituals, and Activities

One of the best ways to instill positive **Values** in your child is though time spent together as a family engaging in activities, **Traditions**, and rituals which support and exemplify those **Values**. The range of activities and **Traditions** are truly endless. While it is best if many of these family activities are enjoyable for all, it is not essential that the **Family Traditions** and **Rituals** are fun. It is not unusual for some **Family Traditions** to center on obligation and responsibility and that their significance and rewards aren't recognized until later in life.

A **Family Value** of giving to others or providing service to the unfortunate may not seem very fun to an eight year old, but can later become a cherished, rewarding, and uplifting **Value** and **Tradition** passed on to future generations. Many times we can be unaware of the precise **Value** we are passing on through the **Family Tradition** or weekly activity we share with our children, but we can feel good in the time we are sharing with our children.

Time spent together creates bonds. Spending the time in identifiable and frequently engaged in activities creates memories that **Frame** those ties, and make them easy to recreate later in life. The ties we forge with our children deepen and enrich our **Relationships** with them. *A child who has a positive relationship with their parent is more likely* *to continue and cherish the* **Values** *of their parent and family.*

Family Activities

Family Activities

- Watching TV and movies
- Playing games
- Attending weekly worship
- Eating dinner together
- Sports
- Arts and crafts
- Holiday celebrations
- Preparing traditional foods, meals, and desserts
- Visiting relatives
- Reading out loud
- Gardening
- Family conversation
- Attending events of family members
- Camping, hiking, and vacations
- Cultural rites, rituals, and ceremonies

**figure 13.2*

Here is a list of activities in which families frequently engage (figure 13.2):

Many of these activities can be done with a subset of the family members with shared interests or a desire to solidify that specific relationship. A child's need to be recognized as an individual often requires that they have special "one on one" time with a parent or with each individual family member.

Any activity done frequently can become a treasured memory and cherished **Tradition**. Even if we are not conscious of it, we express our **Values** in the activities we choose and actions we take. The more time we spend with our children the more exposed they become to our

Values, and the easier it will be for them to adopt them.

Summary of Family and Personal Values

What it is:

Our **Values** are what we find important and where we place special significance. Our **Values** reflect our priorities and are at the base of all the meaning we find and derive from life. **Family Values** are often the basis of our dreams and goals for our children and how we wish them to conduct their lives.

Why use it:

The **Values** our child adopts often have a dramatic impact on the career they choose, how they live their lives, the **Relationships** they form, and the happiness and sense of self-satisfaction they achieve. The **Values** we instill in our child in their formative years form the general trajectory of their life.

Family Values and a parent's **Personal Values** fill in the gap until a child is old enough to begin to create their own **Personal Values**. As a child matures and individuates a parent needs to balance their wishes with the wishes of the child, balancing the pride of their **Values** being continued with the respect and support of the new **Values** being established.

Reframe, Replace, and Rewire:

In general, people bond more over their similarities and commonalities than their differences. When we identify (**Frame**) life affirming **Values** family members share, it increases the sense of unity and solidarity of the family. Feelings of pride and belonging fostered thought shared **Family Values** can help minimize or **Replace** feeling of isolation, defiance, and conflict. When the underlying kinship is frequently recognized and celebrated temporary conflicts are able to be quickly neutralized by the over riding sense of **Family Harmony**. Soon, the family becomes accustomed **(Rewired)** to approach most family situations and events with a sense of loyalty and pride.

Family and Personal Values Home Improvement Projects

1. Look over the above list to help you identify your **Values** or use your search engine to find another list of **Values**. Make a list which mean the most to you.

2. Are there any **Values** you have with which you are uncomfortable with or wish you exercised in a different manner?

3. Are there any **Values** which you wish you exhibited more often? List them. What are practical ways you could intentionally start to live according to these **Values**?

4. Now, do the same exercise to list the **Values** of your family members. First take each individual child and adult living in your home and begin to list their **Personal Values**. If they are willing to do the exercise it is good to list the **Values** they see themselves as having.

5. Construct a list of what you feel are your **Family Values**. Take a moment to crosscheck the lists and see what percentage of the **Family Value** list shows up on each **Personal Values** list. This will give you a good indication of your family's common **Value System**.

6. List the activities your family engages in together.

7. What are some other **Family Rituals and Traditions** you would like for your family?

Chapter Fourteen

Negotiating Parental Relationships

In this chapter we will be discussing the relationship you have with the other adults who share a parenting role with your child. Even if you are a single parent you may have family members, relatives, or friends who take on a parenting role with your child for significant spans of time. For clarity purposes we will refer to co-parents as parenting adults who live in the same household and shared parents as adults who live in separate households.

Co-parent Households

While equal sharing of parenting responsibilities such as discipline and time spent with children is often the ideal, it seldom is the reality. This is not only due to factors such as emotional investment, but is often structured in people's personality types, areas of expertise, and knowledge and experience base of children.

It is not unusual for one parent to take on a leadership role for a majority of parenting decisions and the general functioning of the family. Besides personality type, such factors as being the legal guardian or biological parent of the child often dictate who is the household leader. Yet, there is no inherent benefit or harm in one adult being the dominant parental personality. As long as the parental roles are understood, do not undermine each other, and meet the basic needs of both parents and children it matters little if parents are truly equal or not.

In many co-parent households, even if there is a dominant parent, there is a division of roles and responsibilities based on interests and skills. In some cases one parent may rule the organization and functioning of the house itself while another parent specializes in education and extracurricular activities such as band, music, and sports activities. In other cases, one parent is more of a nurturer and likes to provide for the kids and the other parent is more of a teacher and enjoys encouraging the children to do things on their own.

While there are no set good roles and bad roles, there are some foreseeable problems and conflicts which can be resolved with a little observation, planning, and adaptability. Let's explore some of the potential areas of conflict amongst co-parents and some of the things they could do to resolve the issues or act in the best interests of the child.

An area of conflict for many co-parents is in the establishment and implementation of **House Rules** along with the monitoring of the children's adherence to these rules. Often, one parent feels that they are made out to be the bad guy due to usually being the one to discipline and administer consequences to the children. In many cases the other parent perceives the disciplinary parent as being harsh or unrealistic regarding the behavior of the children.

In the above situation the disciplinary parent feels unsupported and undermined, while the nurturing or sympathetic parent feels that they need to balance the situation by protecting and **Advocating** for the children. One parent experiences the other as weak, passive, naive, or uninvested and detached. The other parent's perspective is that the disciplinarian is overreacting, taking things too personally, has unrealistic standards, and forgetting what it was like to be a kid.

The longer that each parent sticks to these perceptions of each other the more likely that each will become more entrenched in their role and the more frustrated and angry they will become with each other. Eventually each parent will likely end up living up to the other's negative perceptions, one being rigid and angry with the children and the other being manipulated to be a savior and easy touch.

The solution to this very common dynamic is often not as difficult as it would seem. It usually involves nothing more than a bit of compromise, support, and a commitment to not undermine each other. This is best accomplished when both adults stop making it a contest of who is right or which way is best, and make an effort to not make their differing perceptions and parenting styles into a ever widening emotional gulf.

Developing House Rules

The following is a list of considerations, recommendations, and communication skills which may prove helpful at reducing tensions between co-parents while establishing concrete methods of being able to be supportive and present a united front:

1. **Schedule a time** to make a comprehensive list of House Rules and Social Expectations you have for your children. The time chosen should be when you will not be disturbed and the children are not present. The meeting should only begin when both parents are relatively calm and composed, and there is no immediate crisis or pressing urgent emergency.
2. **Schedule an appointment** with a professional or mediator to help facilitate the discussion if you have a particular difficulty setting aside a calm and relaxed time or if you or your coparent feel incapable of keeping emotions under control. Please make it **Clear** to the facilitator the solitary **Goal** and **Purpose** of the meeting.
3. **Focus on what each person needs and feels**. This will allow the suggestions and proposed rules to be descriptive and specific, making sure that what is agreed upon is **Clear** and implementable. The use of "**I need/feel**," **Statements** as opposed to comments such as, "*you always*," will help prevent the both of you from feeling attacked, blamed, or devalued.
4. **Take notes during the meeting** and make sure the selected and agreed upon rules and expectations are well documented so that they can be learned and referred to as needed. It is difficult for parents to enforce the same rules and expectations if they have never been explicitly identified and both people have not agreed.

5. **Verbally recognize each other's strengths, parenting talents, and beneficial personality traits.** This will increase or restore a level of mutual respect and trust allowing compromise and agreement to take place. Before getting into the selection process it is good to highlight and compliment each other on what the other brings to the table.

6. **Listen and Attune to each others fears, concerns, objections, and frustrations.** The goal of the meeting is not only to develop and identify a functional set of rules, but also for both adults to feel heard and understood. A person who feels recognized and validated is much better prepared to try out and support new ideas or alternate ways of doing things. Do not contest, debate, or interrupt each other when coming up with the initial ideas on **House Rules** and expectations.

> *Along with the improved functioning of the home and increased behavioral compliance of the children, the goal of the* House Rules *meeting is the increased comfort level of the parenting adults.*

Sometimes it is easier for the parent not bothered by a specific behavior to enforce its prohibition than the parent who is bothered by the social infraction to accept its performance. Issues regarding cleanliness, hygiene, and social etiquette often fall into this category where one parent is extremely annoyed by feet on furniture, not washing hands, or talking while eating and the other parent is not. As a show of support the more tolerant parent can implement those rules to help insure the comfort and emotional well being of their coparent.

A home needs rules and expectations to improve its functioning as well as insure the safety and security of all family members. Yet, a house full of too many rules can end up feeling more like a prison than a home. Therefore, a parent with very high expectations and low tolerances should always be asking themselves if the matter at hand is truly important and worth the battle to enforce. Too many rules can degenerate into control and repression.

When either parent is unwilling or incapable of reaching a compromise of implementing rules they are not fully invested in or being flexible in reducing their highest standards, then it is advisable to seek professional assistance to rectify the situation.

7. **Prioritize the expectations** and introduce them in digestible amounts which are realistic and attainable. If the list of **House Rules** becomes too long and extensive it could become overwhelming and somewhat punitive to the children. The initial adopted rules should contain both those which are most emotionally important to each parent and those which stand the best chance of being successfully implemented by family members.

   When prioritizing **House Rules**, assess the behaviors and attitudes of your children which are most troubling and negatively impact the smooth and harmonious functioning of the home. Identify **House Rules** which would challenge and require your child to act in a more respectful and cooperative manner. Identify or create social skills whose components successfully tend to the unwanted behaviors and attitudes (see **Accepting Criticism**, **Following Instructions**, **Accepting No**, and **Respectfully Disagree**). Discuss instances in which the skills could be identified, taught, and **Praised** and the criteria by which mastery will be assessed.

8. **Establish a time table** for those desired and needed rules and expectations not included on the original list to be introduced and implemented. Schedule future meetings to review progress in house rule adherence and when and how to introduce new ones.

9. **Agree on concept areas for Family Rules and expectations.** The following are some suggestions:

   ✦ *Behaviors and attitudes which demonstrate and promote mutual respect and cooperation*

   ✦ *Personal and household chores and*

responsibilities

- *Cultivation of interests and activities which promote health and personal development*
- *Organization and planning*
- *Guidelines regarding media usage, peer interaction, and social activities*

10. **A formal introduction** (see **Family Meeting**) to the rest of the family of what was decided upon in the parent meeting is often helpful in reducing the amount of resistance to meeting the expectations. A formal meeting is also an excellent opportunity for the parents to look and sound like a united front. A separate meeting with each child to talk over which skills you want to focus on and master is also helpful. In this way you can talk of the benefits of their willingness to co-operate, while giving some indication of possible rewards and autonomy which are attainable through their efforts.

11. **Learn and practice new parenting roles**. Parents who excel at one role can be given an opportunity to succeed in the role dominated by the other parent. A parent who is a task master and whose strength is being a rule maker and disciplinarian can be put in the position to identify, **Praise**, and reward positive behavior. Likewise, a parent whose strengths lie in compliments, **Praise**, and engaging in activities with the children can be assisted in finding things to correct, give consequences for, and **Constructively Criticize**. The parent with one skill set can help the other expand their comfort zone by calmly pointing out opportunities to either challenge and teach or **Praise** and reward (see **Three Voices**).

No two parents will ever completely agree on what needs to be done and how to deal with problems. Support does not mean agreement, and co-parent support, though not always necessary, is extremely helpful in creating a mutually respectful and harmonious household.

It is important for co-parents to avoid ever verbally or through body language criticizing each other in front of the kids. If you ever strongly disagree with an action or statement made by another adult to a child, ask to talk to the adult in private and then express your concerns. If they see your point, ask them to go back and rectify the situation, or you might better understand their viewpoint and find it acceptable.

Yet, if at the end of the discussion you cannot find a comfortable resolution then you should find a way to present both viewpoints to the children in an amicable way to demonstrate that people can **Respectfully Disagree** with each other. When calmly and tactfully articulated, such joint presentations can be very instructive to your children in that teachers, bosses, and employers may have different rules and expectations for which your children need to adapt.

It is critical that co-parenting adults do not cut private deals with a child or keep secrets from each other. We strongly recommend that honesty and open communication become one of your **Family Values**. If your child refuses to comply with this value by becoming increasingly secretive or self-destructive then you need to consult professional help.

Shared Parenting

Much of what we said and recommended in the **Co-Parenting** section applies to **Shared Parenting**. The biggest difference is that each household has the right and responsibility to devise its own rules. No matter how effective and beneficial you find your rules and house schedules to be for your child, you cannot, nor should you try to, dictate these to your shared parenting households.

In our many years providing support to families we have had to monitor ourselves from being excessively protective of the children under our care. So often after a child has made significant improvements under our guidance we become emotionally distraught by the actions of other adults. We think thoughts such as, "*If only they would have said,*" or "*He doesn't respond well to threats.*"

Yet, soon we realized that it wasn't the world's job to adapt to the needs of the kids in our care, but the kid's job to master the skills needed to survive and hopefully succeed in all situations. This is why we are so big on teaching skills to children. Their biggest resource is not us, but the skills they bring to every decision and situation.

Teaching House Rules to Your Children

The following suggestions and recommendations may help you present your wishes and concerns in an appropriate and respectful manner. Always keep in mind that your child needs to learn how to adapt and succeed in various environments and situations (school, job, clubs, teams, etc) with their own rules and expectations. In the end it is the responsibility of your child to adapt and be successful no matter how strict or lax the supervision and structure.

1. **Develop House Rules and Social Expectations** for your own household and put them in writing.
2. **Schedule a meeting with the shared parenting household**. You may want to have this meeting in a neutral setting which is comfortable for the adults from both sets of households.
3. **Present your House Rules** to the parents of the other household. Let them know your reasons for the rules and the benefits of those rules.
4. **Ask to see their House Rules** and if they can share anything that they are doing which might be beneficial in your home.
5. **Thank them for listening and sharing**. Let them know how helpful you find this exchange of ideas. Offer to incorporate any strategies or functional habits they are using which you could see benefitting your child.

No matter how contentious your overall relationship with your ex or with a step-parent, you owe it to your child to have as strong an alliance as you can forge. If you are a step-parent and are dealing with a bio-parent, your efforts to bond and gain their trust are because of your common interest in the welfare of your child. Complimenting or praising a shared positive or endearing personality trait between bio-parent and child is often a good way to show your appreciation and respect of their valuable role in their child's life.

If your relationship with the shared parent household is extremely contentious and either you or they find it difficult to speak in a respectful manner, then we strongly recommend that you find a third party such as a mediator or family **Advocate** to help facilitate the meeting and all other communications. No matter how deep the division, personality conflicts, or emotional bitterness, you owe it to your child to model mutual respect and cooperation.

Just as in the case of co-parents, it is best not to hoard sensitive information or keep secrets away from shared parents. A child's need to keep secrets is often motivated by a need to manipulate, undermine, and pit one household against the other for personal gain. If you feel you need to keep information from other adults with whom you share parenting, we strongly urge you to process this plan with a clinician or helping professional to help you in sorting out whether this is in the best interest of your child.

While sharing your negative perceptions and feelings towards a co-parent is to be avoided, so is speaking ill of shared parents. Likewise, never ask your child probing questions regarding the functioning or parenting decisions of the other household as this puts your child in the middle, needing to choose sides. Although this is tempting at times, it is not in the best interest of your child who is the recipient of "**Shared Parenting**."

Since your child is spending time in two homes, voicing negative feelings or showing distrust in the other parent's decisions is counterproductive and can lead your child to feeling confused, angry, or uncooperative in one or both homes. As mentioned earlier, it is not a moral victory to have your child only behave and be successful in your home.

> *Your child's success isn't a parenting contest between two households, but a statement of their ability, where ever they are, to be respectful and happy.*

A child from a divorced family is often very resistive to being disciplined by a step-parent. A step-parent can only try their best to enforce rules in a manner consistent with the biological parent in the home. It helps to have the bio-parent state to the child their agreement with the step-parent and desire for the rules and expectations to be so enforced. This is another area in which the co-parent **Family Meeting** is so beneficial in reducing a child's resistance and anger towards a step-parent.

Step-parents, foster parents, and all other care giving adults need to avoid making any potentially insulting or negative remarks regarding the bio-parent. Even if a child is angry or conflicted about their bio-parent, insulting remarks regarding a bio-parent's personality or character can be internalized by the child as a genetic insult toward them. If their parent is untrustworthy, bad, selfish, or incompetent then the child may see themselves as damaged goods or "born to be bad."

The authors of this book were once houseparents for a group home for a few years. While the children stayed with us full time, the goal was usually for them to return home. The majority of the kids in our care went on an occasional home visit to practice their skills, and then more frequently to begin the transition to living at home. We tried to establish strong **Relationships** with their biological or adoptive parents, meeting with them before and after these visits.

Using many of the strategies and perspectives outlined in this chapter we did our best to stay sensitive to the needs of both the parents and the kids. We included the parents in discussions regarding how to practice skills with their child, what skills to focus on, and how to transfer what was working at the group home back into the family home. Though we formed strong **Relationships** with the kids we made sure we did not **Replace** or undermine the parents' roles with their child.

An area of special concern for us was to not do things which could not be duplicated by the parents. We celebrated all important events such as birthdays, holidays, and accomplishments. If possible we had the child celebrate such occasions both with us and with the family and offered for the family to be present at our celebration with the child. We coordinated all gifts through the parents making sure they were comfortable with the expense and 'message' of the gift. We also kept the parents apprised of the current interests of the child to help them in their choice of gifts.

We recommend that all non-biological parents or caregivers, when possible, include bio- parents or get their input regarding gifts for their children. We also caution all non-biological parents to not upstage or buy gifts beyond the fiscal capabilities of the bio-parent.

Summary of Negotiating Parental Relationships

What it Is:

Shared Parenting is when more than one person lives with and shares in making parenting decisions. Even single parents often find themselves sharing parenting responsibilities with a family member, relative, or friend. In this chapter we suggested ways of setting up and implementing **House Rules** and **Social Expectations** when either your child is with you full time or is spending a portion of time living in multiple residences.

Why use it:

Parenting is most effective when **House Rules** and **Social Expectations** are well identified, consistent, and tied into specific behavioral and social goals of family members. The autonomy of each separate household needs to be respected. Undermining the authority of or keeping secrets from any parent is to be avoided and often aids in a child's poor performance in the home. The sharing of ideas, strategies, and goals amongst parenting adults and households is extremely helpful in your child's ability to be cooperative and respectful and not pit one adult against the other for personal gain.

Reframe, Replace, and Rewire:

The goal of parents having the exact same expectations and being consistent on how they enforce those expectations while noble is not very realistic. The goal of parental consistency becomes attainable when one **Frames** the goal in terms of everyone following mutually agreed upon **House Rules**. **House Rules** and **Social Expectations** implemented through the use of the basic social skills allow parents of different temperaments and personality types to get on the same page. The tie between **House Rules** and skills promoting mutual respect allow parents to **Replace** tensions and arguments over parenting style with **Clear** and **Specific** skills to be fostered, without a need for power struggles and debate with the children. The longer the agreed upon **House Rules** and interaction styes with the kids are enforced, the easier it is for them to become habit. The habit of focusing on House Rules being followed in a respectful manner will help **Rewire** family members into approaching each social interaction in a calmer and more harmonious manner.

Negotiating Parental Relationships Home Improvement Projects

1. What are the **House Rules** you want to have? Think of this as a brain storming activity and include all your ideas.
2. What are the **Social Expectations** you want to teach your children?
3. Look over the suggested format of **Developing House Rules** in this chapter. What seems daunting to you? Are there suggestions which seem unrealistic to you? Explain.
4. If you were able to follow the format in **Developing House Rules** what would be the benefit for you and your children?
5. What are your fears for your children if others who share parenting responsibilities do not enforce the same rules or social expectations?
6. If professionals have recommended some **House Rules** for your family which do not seem realistic, explain your concerns. Thinking back to your **Personal Values**, do any of their recommended **House Rules** which seem unrealistic actually honor your **Value System**?
7. Develop your **House Rules** and make a plan to implement them.
8. How can you use the **Three Voices** to learn and practice a new parenting role?

Chapter Fifteen

Sibling and Family Harmony

Almost every child is dependent on adults to teach them how to share and be sensitive to the feelings of other children. Some children learn compassion and empathy pretty quickly and at an early age, others can struggle with being sensitive and supportive of peers and siblings for the bulk of their childhood. Even children who are caring and sensitive by nature have a difficult time keeping arguments and conflicts from occasionally occurring when interacting with their brothers and sisters.

Whether you decide to have a formal structure for family communication (see **Family Meeting**) or not, it is beneficial to foster opportunities for your children to express appreciation of and gratitude for each other. Such expressions of care and appreciation create a culture of support, family pride, and respect. These deep sentiments help your children weather the inevitable conflicts and squabbles that come with the day-to-day interactions of living in the same home.

Teaching and mastering of skills such as **Maturely Registering a Complaint**, **Entering a Conversation** or **Conversation Skills** can go a long way in keeping sibling conflicts from becoming a parental nightmare where you're put in the position of being referee and judge. A child who is allowed to shout out complaints with shrill screams of, "*Mom!*" or "*Dad!*" from rooms away followed by, "*Tommy's being mean!*" or "*He won't let me have a turn!*" is bound to become bothersome to the entire household. As we have mentioned on numerous occasions in this book it is often not *what* your child is saying that is inappropriate, but *how* they are saying it.

When a child is expressing a concern they should do so maturely and respectfully. Here is a skill that will help increase the harmony and respect level of your home. If your child has something they want to say to you, they should not just shout it out from where they are, but instead be taught the formal skill of **Maturely Registering a Complaint** (figure 15.1). You can change the name of this skill to words appropriate for the age and maturity level of your child; the skill components will remain the same.

Maturely Registering a Complaint

1. Find the person to whom you want to speak
2. Wait for a pause in their conversation
3. Say, "Excuse me"
4. Present concern in a soft and respectful voice tone
5. Listen to instruction or guidance given
6. Repeat back instruction or guidance
7. Accept Situation or ask to **Respectfully Disagree**

**figure 15.1*

With the introduction of this format, the expectation that a child is not to yell out complaints from a distance is **Clearly** stated. All the parent needs to do is remind the complaining child of the skill or sit quietly until the child remembers and comes over to them. You may want to have a one word signal to say such as, "skill," or "concern," or some other sound that signals or "**Cues**" your child that they are to use the skill in question (see **Cues and Prompts**). Please note that the second step of this skill can obviously be omitted if you are not in a conversation when they find you.

If you are unable or feel it is best not to go to the room where the conflict is occurring, you could use a sound such as a clicker or some appointed noise to be made by your cell phone or hand held device which your child will recognize as their **Cue** to come and find you and to then use the skill. The more often you delay responding or dealing with your child's complaint until they formally use the skill of **Maturely Registering a Complaint**, the quicker they will stop relying on lung power to have you intercede in the sibling conflict.

Many immature children will want to use the skill in a very loud voice in order to insure that their sibling hears and reacts to what they are saying. This should not be tolerated and the process not move forward until your child is able to speak to you in a normal voice tone. You may want to consider instructing your child to sit quietly for a minute, and then in a voice barely above a whisper invite them to maturely register their complaint.

If both participants in the conflict want to give "their side of the story" choose who you want to listen to first and instruct the other child to go to another area. Let them know that they need to stay quiet and wait till they are called, or they will lose the opportunity to **Maturely Register a Complaint** at this time.

Just as in the case of **Respectfully Disagreeing** you don't want a child to overuse the skill of **Maturely Registering a Complaint**. If your child overuses the skill tell them that they need to use the solutions you've already given them and that they now need to **Accept No** regarding their request to register a complaint.

It is often a tough call determining if the bigger, older, or more sophisticated child is guilty of bullying or tormenting their sibling or if the little, younger, or less sophisticated one is just trying to get the older sibling in trouble. In many cases both are responsible. Yet, as we've mentioned numerous times in this book the use of skills is far more important than the topic or assessing who is right and who is wrong. *Increased cooperation, respect, and harmony is the objective and not deciding case by case who "caused" the conflict.*

When children are having difficulty getting along or playing together in a harmonious fashion it is often beneficial to isolate them from each other, or give them separate tasks to do. While this is usually an excellent temporary solution, it does not have your kids learn ways of interacting together in a cooperative and enjoyable manner.

Our duty is to find ways of **Replacing** old habits that fostered arguing and fighting with activities that promote working together, teamwork, and having fun. While we and they strive to identify and engage in these conflict free activities, we want to be working on having our children practice and master skills involving sibling cooperation such as *Giving and Receiving Compliments, Teamwork, Asking for Assistance, Helping Others*, or any other social skill you can design which **Replaces** conflict with cooperation. In this manner we are filling the void often created when we just demand that our children "stop fighting" and get along with tangible and enjoyable substitutions and **Replacements** (**Replacing Over Extinguishing** in **Maximizing Therapeutic Growth**).

Probably the most powerful way to have your children learn how to enjoy playing together is for you to hand pick the activity and alternate between doing the activity with them and observing/ monitoring them playing together (see **Exercise**, **Laughter**, **and Play** section in **Liking Your Own Skin**). The activity can be anything from basketball or throwing a frisbee to charades or a video game; the important thing is that you teach and role model giving compliments, working together, and being supportive. These times of observation and participation are great opportunities to have your children compliment and cheer each other on, pat each other on the back, note improvements, give high fives, and generally rally around and support one another.

We Are Family

The Parental Tool Box you are assembling is ideal for creating a culture of mutual respect and harmony in your household. It is not by accident that up to this point we have never once talked about "gaining control" over your kids through "behavioral management." ***The Parental Tool Box*** *is designed to promote personal growth and familial support through* **Strength Based** *skill development and not through gaining control over others.*

Since the skills are **Strength Based** and positive, it not only allows but encourages sibling involvement in supporting each other to master their skills and share in their successes. Earlier in this section we talked of the benefits of having antagonistic and conflictual sibling **Relationships** being **Replaced** with fun and supportive ones in which siblings are assisted and encouraged to compliment each other and work/play together.

Family unity is heightened when the successes of individual members are recognized and celebrated. Many families find it beneficial to make skill mastery of an individual child a family goal where everyone gets rewarded and celebrates the occasion. The reward could be anything from a meal at a favorite restaurant to a fun family trip. In this fashion siblings can be highly motivated to give full support and assistance to their brother's or sister's skill mastery.

While families often find that one child in particular is in need of social skill development it is often beneficial to assign all family members, even parents, skills to master. This can help normalize the process as well as emphasize that everyone needs to grow and develop. In this fashion skill development can quickly become a fun activity embraced by the entire family, rather than a therapeutic intervention aimed at one "problem child" in the family.

Almost every person can use support to help insure they find the time and initiative to engage in all their interests, hobbies, and productive activities. Combining skill goals into an individual **Activity Chart** is a great way to get the entire family to grow and be happier people. **Personal Activity Charts** are a great way of helping you find the discipline and support to do the things you want and enjoy. They are also a way for you to guide your less motivated or bored children to expand their world and find interests and activities which enhance their self-esteem and love of life. Our fondness for **Activity Charts** is demonstrated by the fact that they are mentioned often in The Parental Tool Box (see **Parenting in the 21st Century and Visual Guides, Aids, and Documentation**).

Many of you are reading this book because you have a child whose frequent acting out and argumentation is causing your house to be in a fairly constant state of turmoil. While we are confident that the use of many of the skills in ***The Parental Tool Box*** will greatly improve the home environment, we also realize how disruptive an acting out child can be on the functioning of the family.

Disrespectful acting out children demand a lot of our attention, time, and energy often at the expense of time available to our more complaint children. We should try our very best to spend more fun time with our respectful children than with our non-compliant kids. This often takes planning and the use of support systems and friends who will baby sit while we go out and have fun with the children whose relationship with us is pleasant and rewarding.

In a two adult household it is often beneficial for one parent to stay at home with the troubled child while the rest of the family goes out to enjoy each other and recharge their batteries. Everything we said regarding self-care in the chapter entitled **Give What You've Got** applies to every family member and not just the adults. The sad reality is that any parent who spends the bulk of their time and uses almost all their energy combatting an acting out child is robbing their other children of care and unintentionally making acting out to get attention more likely. Our years of working in residential care with very reactive aggressive children has taught us the realities of the needs of these children, yet it also taught us the importance of somehow finding the time for the other children in our care.

Summary of Sibling and Family Harmony

What it Is:

Sibling and Family Harmony is a the result of developing a family culture of mutual respect and support. Empathy and the ability to share statements of appreciation between siblings is usually dependent on parental instruction and guidance. A family that engages in fun activities and encourages its members to find and develop personal interests and hobbies is often one that succeeds at creating **Familial Harmony**.

Why use it:

Households that have a high level of **Sibling and Family Harmony** become havens from the stresses of the outside world.

Children in a harmonious home are more likely to develop strong and life lasting ties to each other and be generally happier individuals.

Reframe, Replace, and Rewire:

The **Clearer** and more **Specific** a parent is in describing house expectations regarding all communication patterns in the home, the more harmonious the home can become. **Reframing** the goal of all family communication in terms of harmony and mutual respect will go a long way towards reducing the frequency of verbal complaints and conflicts. Consistent monitoring and keeping high standards regarding respectful communication patterns will help **Replace Family** tension and chaos with **Harmony** and comfort. A harmonious living environment **Rewires** all family members to feel more comfortable within themselves. This, in turn, will have them be more patient and understanding, and less demanding of others.

Sibling and Family Harmony Home Improvement Projects

1. Think of an activity to engage with your children which can incorporate giving compliments and **Praise** to one another. One example is to take turns kicking a soccer ball to one another. Each person must compliment the person to whom they are kicking the ball. Now schedule this in your family calendar within the next five days.
2. Practice teaching the skills of **Maturely Registering a Complaint** to someone you trust.
3. Teach the skill of **Maturely Registering a Complaint** by making your own rap song. Perform this rap song for your children as you teach the skill.
4. With what skill could everyone in your family use some practice? In a **Family Meeting** agree on how each person can practice this skill over the next week. Come up with an incentive for the entire family if you all successfully practice during the week.
5. Has anyone in your family been overlooked recently? Make a specific plan to spend time with that person in a manner they would like.

Chapter Sixteen

An Ounce of Prevention

Converting Problem Areas Into Skills

Children who have mastered the skills which teach mutual respect are less likely to get into frequent arguments and conflicts with others. This is one reason that we have so strongly recommended and discussed the benefits of having your children learn how to **Accept No**, **Accept Criticism**, **Follow Instructions**, and **Respectfully Disagree**. For if even conflicts due arise, your child's ability to use these skills will keep the problem from escalating as your child quickly responds to your intercessions.

In this book we have and will continue to identify and suggest many other social skills for your child to learn and master. The list of potential skill titles is almost endless and most children only need to master a handful of skills to become happy and delightful people.

There is no magic formula for coming up with a skill for your child to learn; all you have to do is identify a problem area and come up with a skill title which addresses that need. In the spirit of being **Strength Based**, solution oriented, and supportive we recommend **Replacing** the old habit with a new desired one. The name of the skill should be goal oriented, not focusing on the problem behavior.

Some examples of how to do this would include a child who lies or steals could be given a skill of *Honesty*, *Trust*, or *Respect for Others*. A child who self-harms, has substance abuse issues, or is always bored could have *Self Care*, *Productive Use of Time*, or *Healthy Living*. A child who swears a lot could have *Express Feelings* or *Vocabulary* to help them find alternative means of expression. A child having trouble making their way in life could be assigned *Self-Responsibility*, *Self-Reliance*, or

Autonomy.

Similarly the steps or components of the skill would vary according to your expectations and the needs of your child. Oftentimes, skills will not involve steps but rather a short hit list of objectives or things to keep in mind.

The steps to **Maturely Registering a Complaint** could be modified a little to teach the skills of *Entering a Conversation* or *Conversation Skills.* In *Entering a Conversation* (*Not Interrupting*) you could reduce it to the first three steps. If you chose the title *Conversation Skills*, you could keep steps one and three and then add areas to stay mindful of such as staying on topic, listen to what others are saying, don't dominate, and speak at the same volume as the other person.

A skill such as *Self-Responsibility* could involve a whole slew of various activities and areas needing attention. An abbreviated list could include things like: getting and maintaining a job; scheduling/planning; seeking training and education; return calls/emails; doing chores; being on time for appointments/school/work; volunteering; daily practice of discipline; practicing an instrument or doing art; doing research; and networking.

While your personal list of areas for your child to show responsibility may be quite lengthy and extensive, it is best to focus on just three tasks at a time. Once those are mastered you can move on to the next batch. Changing the target name to *Self-Reliance* and then to *Autonomy* as you introduce each new batch of objectives allows you to fully recognize and celebrate their mastery over the previous set of tasks.

We've mentioned before that while mastery of a skill takes somewhere between four to eight weeks, it is usually self-defeating if your child takes longer than three months to master a skill. If your child is having trouble mastering all the elements or steps of a target skill in a reasonable amount of time, it is best to emphasize the aspects or the skill they have mastered and find another related skill to assign them which effectively deals with the problem areas that linger.

As an example let's say that you assigned your child the skill of **Following Instructions** because often when you assigned a task or gave a directive your child responded with some combination of arguing, yelling, whining, complaining, or procrastinating. While a great percentage of the time your child no longer reacts and resists doing tasks, they still frequently perform the task in a substandard fashion. In this situation you could reward their compliance by celebrating their mastery of **Following Instructions** while **Replacing** it with a new target skill such as *Organization, Focus, Mindfulness*, or *Planning* to help them improve the quality of their work.

Our success in teaching our kids important social skills is often impaired by expecting perfection or having unrealistic expectations.

> *Mastery does not mean perfection; it means your child has* **Replaced** *an undesired habit they did a majority of the time with a desired new habit they engage in often. We want to recognize, reward, and celebrate our children's efforts, progress and development.*

A young, emotionally immature child or a child who struggles with attention issues may still be dependent on **Prompts**, reminders, and **Visual** or **Auditory Cues** to execute their target skills at a high level. While there is no universal standard by which to evaluate whether your child has mastered a skill or not, one can always look for effort, good intentions and mutual respect as general guidelines.

Just as there is no perfection in human nature, growth and development is not always a straight march forward but often involves plateaus, slips, or a temporary step backwards. It is not unusual for your child's performance of a skill previously mastered to deteriorate or for old undesired habits to re-emerge.

The need for a "refresher course" or "booster shot" is expected and not a failure. Most new habits and skills go to the wayside after a vacation and need to be reestablished when returning to normal routines. Posing this need to tighten up or revisit a skill will usually be successful if the child is not made to feel that they have "regressed" or that "they are back to square one."

Your child's overall acceptance or resistance to the introduction of a new skill or a revisiting of an old one will be highly influenced by the reasons and benefits you pose and your voice tone (see **Attunement**).

The more you adhere to implementing the **Strength Based Approach** *to creating a mutually respectful household outlined in this book, the more you and your children will be able to view criticism as an opportunity for growth and not an attack on one's character.*

Presenting New Skills to Your Child

In this book we have suggested steps/components for teaching skills. As an example in the skill of **Following Instructions**, we recommended that a thorough but concise format would be the following (figure 16.1):

Following Instructions

1. Listen Attentively;
2. Say OK;
3. Repeat Back Instructions;
4. Do Task;
5. Check Back.

**figure 16.1*

When creating a new skill for your child think of the steps or components which will both successfully meet your expectations and **Be** very **Clear** to your child. A skill with too few steps will often have many cracks for your child to slip through while one with too many steps will be overwhelming and unlearnable for many kids.

We have found that a fairly natural way to introduce the components is to follow this basic **Script**:

> *"So, Tommy I'd like us to work on you being more successful when your Dad or I give you a task or chore to do. We will call this* **Following Instructions***. When I say follow*

instructions I mean that first you listen to me attentively and say OK so that I can tell that you are listening. Then to make sure that we are both clear on what you are supposed to do, I want you to repeat back what I said. This way I can make sure I haven't given you too much to do at one time. Understand? After you've repeated it back and we are on the same page, then I'd like you to do the task and check back and let me know when you are done."

A key phrase in the above **Script** is to introduce the steps by saying, "*What I mean by (insert skill) is...*" and introduce the steps or components which fully and concisely meet your expectations. Be sure to say all this at a relaxed and relatively calm time in the home or in the car. Have your child repeat back the components or steps a few times until you are assured they are **Clear** on how to do the skill, its goal, and mutual benefit.

Cues and Prompts

While **Cues** and **Prompts** are often used as interchangeable terms, for the purpose of assembling your ***Parental Tool Box*** we will make a subtle but important distinction between the two terms. A **Prompt** is when you make a specific request for your child to use a specific skill. This could be done indirectly by asking your child to review the steps of **Accepting Criticism** or **Accepting No** before saying no to a request or before you begin giving them corrective feedback. For example, before telling them to go clean their room you could say, "*Could you tell me the steps of* **Following Instructions**?" or immediately following some corrective feedback you could say something like, "*This would be a great opportunity for you to use the skill of* **Accepting Criticism**."

A **Cue**, on the other hand, is the use of a predetermined verbal or visual signal to remind your child to use a specific skill or respond in a specific manner. Your child is supported and guided to succeed and respond using the desired format. Touching your ear, or saying, "*Pizza*," may be a **Cue** letting your child know they are supposed to say, "*OK*," or to use the skill of **Maturely Disagreeing**.

Cues and **Prompts** are teaching tools and are to be presented in a positive, **Strength Based** fashion. Many kids prefer subtle **Cues** that others don't know which allow them to get guidance without feeling embarrassed or being put in the spotlight. Other children like humorous **Cues** which help break the tension of the situation. We had one child who overcame his tendency to get angry when criticized by our using the verbal **Cue** of, "alfalfa". In even the tensest of situations he could not resist smiling whenever we said, "alfalfa" and this greatly assisted overcoming his anger and master the skills promoting mutual respect.

Many parents often mistake warnings and threats for **Prompts**. While **Cues** and **Prompts** encourage teaching and the practicing of desired skills, warnings and threats often attempt to reduce teaching or emphasize the "badness" of the behavior in question. Telling a child to, "*Stop arguing!*" or warning them, "*If you do that one more time!*" is neither supportive nor encouraging and more often than not a trigger for the child to act out or engage in a power struggle.

The parent who warns their child to stop what they are doing or they will receive a consequence, is unintentionally making skill practice into a form of punishment that the child can only avoid by immediately "behaving." This threat makes it more about crossing a threshold and getting you angry and not so much about their using a skill. Even if you aren't getting frustrated or angry, it allows your child to deflect the issue away from their behavior and make it about your mood or the fact that it is bothering you. Any form of warning has a tendency to personalize the teaching and make it about feelings and attitudes and less about skill usage and an opportunity to show growth and increased respect.

Prompts and **Cues** are teaching tools and their goal is not to prevent teaching or skill practice from occurring, but to maximize its frequency and supportiveness. Warnings and threats often cast teaching in a negative light, making it a chore and a punishment. It is vital to always keep in mind that teaching skills frequently and early on before non-compliance escalates helps keep the edge and urgency which so often precedes tantrums and power struggles from emerging.

Teaching and learning are most effective when both teacher and student are having fun and being successful. The goal of almost everything in this book is to increase the success and happiness of parent, child, and household.

Verbal Contracts and Safety Plans

Throughout our many years of working with children and families we have found a well prepared, short term verbal contract to be a very effective tool for getting a child, especially one older and more mature, to be successful in a chronically difficult area. Kids with long term issues regarding anger, honesty, bullying, swearing, and any number of oppositional or harmful behaviors often make progress by giving their word to try their best.

Verbal Contracts work best when they are the result of calm and serious conversation in which the adult shows both confidence and belief in the child's ability to succeed. The goal should **Be Specific**, such as to talk in a quiet voice or even to work on saying OK over the next several minutes or hours. When a child commits to giving their best effort, they are more likely to successfully respond to **Prompts** and **Cues** and appreciate your support and guidance to have them succeed. **Verbal Contracts** made with one child are often good to share with the rest of the family allowing them to support their sibling and help them reach their goal.

Many children, especially young or immature ones, will try to commit to accomplish things well beyond their capabilities. It is important that you help them construct a **Verbal Contract** that they can meet. If they want to say they will never swear again, or go two days without swearing, you may want to amend the contract to going two hours with two or less errors and immediately responding to any **Prompts** or criticism regarding any errors.

Safety Plans are agreements made with highly volatile children and young adults who engage in risky or destructive behaviors that sometimes result in harm to self or others or significant damage to property. The goal of the contract is for the child to know what to do when they begin to feel the intense feelings that immediately precede their dangerous and harmful behaviors. It is called a **Safety Plan** because the child commits to and tries to practice safe and calming alternatives to **Replace** their old destructive habits. A **Safety Plan** usually articulates one to three plans of action they can implement when they feel unsafe, or if you as a parent ask them to do so when you see they are becoming an immanent danger to themselves or others.

Safety Plans could involve anything from going to a specific safe area to listening to music to hitting a weight bag. It is for you and your child to discern what would work to help them calm down and regain control over their feelings and actions. We strongly recommend that you consult with a professional if for any reason you have concerns that you and your child are unable to design a reliable and effective **Safety Plan** or find yourself creating multiple plans.

In most cases it is vital for the entire family to be aware of the **Safety Plan** to help make sure that it is able to be implemented without any interference or delay. In this way, everyone can be assured that they are truly acting in a supportive and helpful fashion and not unintentionally doing something which intensifies or enables destructive actions to take place. Everyone in the family should have a **Script** to follow. Usually this involves siblings going quickly to a separate area allowing the parent to de-escalate the situation and help the troubled child enact their plan.

Just as is the case in a fire drill, the family needs to rehearse what to do in a family emergency. Every family member should know what they are to do if their parent uses a **Verbal Cue** such as, "*I think Terry could use some privacy right now,*" which signals that the enactment of a **Safety Plan** might be necessary.

When Tantrums Happen

Having your children master skills which foster and demonstrate mutual respect and applying many of the verbal and behavioral strategies contained in this book will greatly reduce the likelihood that your child will act out or have a tantrum. Yet, even when a tantrum happens there are recommended tools and strategies to help foster and insure future success.

How to Respond to Tantrums:

1. *Get on the same level as your child.*

2. *If they are in movement, stay in vicinity without crowding or confronting them.*

3. *Assure them they are safe and will be OK.*

4. *Be patient and calm.*

5. *Do not attempt to speak louder than your child. When possible wait for pauses or breaks to offer encouragement,* Give Instructions, *and identify improvements.*

6. *Use* "When/Then," Statements *to guide them while gently maintaining expectations.*

7. *If they calm down but refuse to move forward, give them space while still ensuring safety.*

8. *Engage in some form of* Relaxation Techniques *and review skill usage to help assess when they are ready to move forward.*

9. *When they are ready, have them process what happened (verbally or written), and have them verbally reassure you that they are OK and ready to calmly move on.*

10. *Offer them some alone time if they feel they need it.*

The goal of how you respond to a temper tantrum or any acting out behavior is not in winning a battle of the wills, but responding in a way which restores respect, safety, and teaches skills which make further occurrences of such behavior unlikely. The components listed above deal with three general concepts.

1. **Create safety and personal comfort**. Safety and comfort are increased when you get on the same level as your child and "track" their movements from a mutually comfortable distance. Getting on the same level as your child even includes when your child goes into the fetal position (see **Parenting the Non-Responsive or Implosive Child**).
2. **Be Patient**, supportive but firm in your expectations. A parent should be empathetic of their child's distress, supportive of any signs of improvement ("*Thank you for bringing your voice down and not swearing*,"), and firmly maintaining the requirement to show respect (see "**When/Then**," **Statements**).
3. **Be thorough and instructive**. Letting your child move on before they are composed and respectful will usually result in additional acting out behavior and tantrums or a lingering disrespectful and punishing attitude.

Summary of An Ounce of Prevention

What it Is:

An Ounce of Prevention is the ability to create skills for your child which will quickly improve and through time **Replace** old unwanted habits with new desirable ones. **Cues** and **Prompts** are ways for us to remind our child they now have an opportunity to use a skill on which they are working. **Verbal Contracts** made during calm times allow our child to make a commitment to using new skills while seeing the skills as a means of support. **An Ounce of Prevention** allows us to tend to important issues when our child is in a good emotional state. It allows both us and our child to discuss and problem solve potentially tense and emotionally charged topics in a calm and respectful manner.

Why use it:

When we use the skills of prevention and proactive teaching we are able to avoid, avert, and lessen the intensity and duration of emotionally charged habits and events.

Reframe, Replace, and Rewire:

Through the use of **An Ounce of Prevention** we **Reframe** conflicts and battlegrounds into tangible and proactive ways of creating mutual support and understanding. Through strategies such as skills, **Prompts**, and **Cues** we **Replace** old habits of conflict and defiance with ones of mutual respect and comfort. Through frequent use of the skills and strategies new habits are formed and the family is **Rewired** to interact in a new and rewarding way.

An Ounce of Prevention Home Improvement Projects

1. Name a parenting skill which you have stopped practicing and is in need of a "booster shot." Make a plan on how to start using this skill again.

2. In a **Family Meeting** have each family member name a habit or behavior they would like to change/add. Come up with a playful **Cue** family members can give to remind each other to stay on track.

3. Think of a time your child engaged in a temper tantrum. Write a **Script** using "**When/Then**," **Statements** and a **Relaxation Technique** to help guide you in how you could respond in the future.

4. Share the **Script** from #3 with someone you trust and ask them to role play it with you (you play the role of your child). After the role play, discuss whether you both think this would have helpful during your child's temper tantrum. Is there something you want to add or change in your **Script**?

Chapter Seventeen

Guilt, Regret, and Parental Satisfaction

We imagine the majority of parents reading this book have had many difficult times with at least one of their children. In most cases, the bad times have outweighed the good, and it has been difficult to stay hopeful and optimistic about your chances and abilities to successfully parent your child.

The emotional toll the battles, power struggles or emotional implosions, and self-harming behavior of your child most likely has been quite devastating to your self-esteem. Your anger, frustration, and bewilderment may have made you do and say things which you are not proud of and wish you could take back.

Given these experiences, very common among parents of troubled children and teens, it is understandable that you may have developed many regrets and are filled with guilt and shame (Kaufman, 1992). Many of you probably feel judged and blamed by friends, peers, family, and professionals who know your child or parenting history.

We've mentioned a few times that this book is not about blame but rather just expanding your ***Parental Tool Box*** to use in future situations and teaching with your child. While there is no magic wand, we believe that most parents will be able to use this book to assemble an expanded toolbox which can help your child become more cooperative and respectful as well as more appreciative of your efforts.

Even if you have previously tried a variation of some or many of the behavioral, relational, and social tools contained within this book, your persistence in refining and honing your skills will eventually be rewarded. The rewards might be mainly due to the heartfelt knowledge that you are doing your best to be a caring and effective parent.

On a number of occasions, we have mentioned that how one says something is as important, and often more important, than what one says. Oftentimes, potentially effective parenting gets lost when our anger and frustration override or destroy the best of our intentions.

Likewise, we cannot stress the importance of when you decide to say something to your child. When your child is angry and defiant, it is not time to logic with then or give them ultimatums, but rather, time to help them get back under control by using the skills of *Cooperation* and *Respect*.

Each error you've made in the past has been a missed opportunity and can help guide you in the selection of the tools you use and master from ***The Parental Tool Box***. While we are not here to judge or blame you, neither are we here to absolve you. Feelings such as regret and guilt live in your heart and can haunt your thoughts and self-esteem. If they exist for you, it is for you to resolve, maybe with the assistance of a therapist. Yet, we can offer some perspective and recommendations to help you work through, resolve, or use these feelings in a positive manner for you and your child.

Our first suggestion is for you to be very honest with yourself. Maybe your feelings of regret and guilt are mainly unwarranted or maybe they are a cry from within yourself for a need to change how you emotionally and cognitively respond to your child. Only you have the power and control to resolve or positively use these negative feelings and thoughts about yourself.

One of the dangers of entertaining these negative feelings is that it may prove to be overwhelming, cause you to emotionally shut down, or give up trying to improve your relationship with your child. *The very fact that you're reading this now shows that while you may be skeptical or even doubtful that this book can prove useful, you haven't totally given up all hope.*

Another danger is that you may begin to use your feelings of guilt and regret to explain, justify, and excuse your growing anger and frustration with your child. This could lead you to either convince yourself into accepting things as they are, or justify your aggressive verbal and emotional attacks on your child as necessary acts of self defense.

You could also use these feelings as an exercise in excuse making as to why you parent the way you do and consider yourself disabled or a victim. This style of thought can be fortified by a diagnosis you may have, your own family upbringing, a period of depression you previously suffered, or interpretations you've made of statements and observations by a therapist.

You do have the option of looking into your heart of hearts and reviewing the history of the intentions and motivations underlying your actions and parenting decisions. In this way you can use your guilt and regret to help you assess the purity of your efforts. We have said on many occasions there is no perfect parenting or even one definitive right action in a given situation.

The times which you have given in to anger and frustration and strayed from care and concern are surely worthy of remorse. We can learn from those times and moments and use that knowledge to guide us in the selection of skills, strategies, and perspectives we want to cultivate.

Guilt and remorse can be beneficial emotions when they motivate you to do and see things differently through the development of additional parenting skills. *Trial and error is an important and often necessary step in learning, and guilt and regret can inspire us to make the most of past mistakes by mastering new techniques.*

It can be particularly difficult as a parent to see others succeeding with your child or see your child showing respect or having fun with others. Yet, there are many reasons why your child might perform for others or be more willing to start new rituals with others.

One is that it is often hardest to parent your own child. Many human service providers wish that their own child listened to them as well as the children with whom they work. Another factor is that facilities, programs, and therapeutic groups and milieus have a lot more controls which help avoid the teaching being contaminated or undermined by outside influences. The lack of history also allows clinicians to begin a fresh therapeutic relationship without having to deal with much of the emotional baggage and reflexive negative responses.

We hope naming these factors can help you overcome any feelings of hurt and envy which could further distance you from your child. Feeling defeated, emotionally abandoned by your child, or in competition with those who have been helping will likely make it difficult for your relationship to improve.

It is important to find ways to see and feel how everyone is coming from a caring perspective.

> *The more your child sees everyone as being on their side and on the same team, the easier it will be for them to master skills of respect and cooperation and use these skills in every environment.*

There appear to be two roads that lead out of the emotional pit of guilt and regret. The first road that we alluded to earlier is to use these feelings as motivation to make changes and develop skills to create a better future. This road is premised on your ability to learn from the past and to use the past to come up with a new route. In this way your new habits and refurbished relationship with your child are born out of the knowledge gained though experience. The past is no longer just a source of pain, guilt, and regret, but becomes the very soil out of which a bright future is reaped.

Feelings of guilt and regret arise out of the frustration, pain, and hurt of the past. The fact that one can't change the past makes it particularly difficult for many to overcome their negative feelings regarding prior events and times. While acceptance is often recommended, it does little to end old patterns or motivate one to develop and implement new skills.

A person who feels good about their current situation is best suited to be able to get over feelings of guilt and regret. Guilt and regret can haunt you when your past is viewed as causing a current existence of pain, failure, or discontentedness. That past becomes transformed into a positive one when your current life is perceived as being successful and rewarding. Many of the old "mistakes" become necessary "steps" to your current satisfaction.

We have never met a successful artist or businessperson who regrets their early years of struggle and frustration. If anything, they often state that the hard times only make their current success all the more sweeter, richer, and satisfying. Similarly, we have yet to meet a parent whose relationship with their child became close and rewarding while remaining mired in guilt and regret. Their feelings of gratitude and being fortunate easily outdistance regrets over past actions. While still wishing that individual things might have gone differently, many parents wouldn't change a thing if they felt it would tarnish the current relationship with their child.

In essence, guilt and regret are not inherently bad emotions or a death sentence for your self-esteem or your relationship with your child. These emotions can be used in a positive manner and help inspire you to cultivate a rewarding relationship with your child. We see the past through the eyes of the present, so while you can't change the past you can definitely transform its meaning and the role it plays in your view of yourself.

We cannot promise that your feelings of regret and guilt will be dissolved by using the skills in this book to develop a rewarding relationship with your child based on mutual respect and appreciation. We can say that it has been our experience that parents who feel increasing successful with their child and take pride in their relationship are often able to view the past in a positive light.

No Perfect Tools

Along with the fact that there is no perfect parent, there is also no perfect tool. The skills, strategies, and perspectives presented and described in this book have been proven to be effective in helping parents, children, and families become more harmonious, happy, and autonomous. While a majority of children will be able to master the vital social skills necessary to avoid the need for continued placement or interventions, some will have mental, biochemical, and neurological needs and issues requiring prolonged interventions or placement.

While the efforts of improving and expanding a ***Parental Tool Box*** will benefit most every child and family, it will not keep every child from needing additional services. Such need for services are often alleviated by skill improvement, although in many cases a child's issues are such that improved social skills alone are insufficient in having the child become safe, functional, or autonomous. Problematic issues often necessitating additional interventions include acute mental illness, neurological processing, biochemical imbalances, addictions, and severe trauma, just to name a few.

Please do not let your feelings of guilt and regret regarding your child's difficulties in social and interpersonal functioning prevent you from consulting with and seeking the assistance of professionals. The world of therapeutic care is very broad and vast. So many times vital help is only a phone call or an assessment away. Whenever you have a question or concern regarding your child, it is valuable to access professionals to answer your questions or direct you to someone who can provide you with information and/or answers.

Summary of Guilt, Regret, and Parental Satisfaction

What it is:

It is not unusual for parents who have had intense or extended periods of conflict with their child to regret and feel guilty about past actions and mean words born out of their anger and frustration. Feelings of failure and incompetency can grow and defeat a parent making their regret, guilt, and remorse dominant and reoccurring emotions affecting their health and self-esteem.

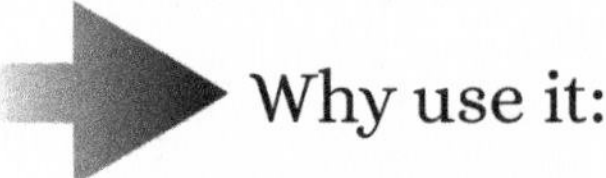

Why use it:

We cannot change the past, but a parent who uses their past to guide and inform the present is able to restore their pride and self-worth. By assembling a versatile and practical tool box a parent can insure that their actions and words are able to express their best intentions. The knowledge that you are acting and responding to your child in healthy and respectful ways will go a long way towards **Replacing** your feelings of guilt and regret with those of the self-satisfaction that you are doing all that you can do as a parent. Success in the present is the best way to alleviate regrets of the past.

Reframe, Replace, and Rewire:

Feelings of guilt and regret can sometimes be justified. Whether justified or not, what is important is that these feelings inspire you to do better in the future and not to give up or become paralyzed in the present. Oftentimes parents have unrealistic expectations of themselves and or their children. Much is gained when parents **Reframe** their goals as opportunities and not as urgent and crucial duties and obligations. One can **Frame** poor skill usage as missed opportunities rather than unforgivable disasters or failures.

By being patient with yourself and your children and practicing the skills of mutual respect whenever you are able, you can begin to **Replace** guilt and regret with self-appreciation and feelings of success. Slowly through the repetition of celebrating the improved skills and communication patterns demonstrating mutual respect and **Familial Harmony**, you will be able to forgive both yourself and your child for the occasional missed opportunity, and see it as just a part of the learning and change process. By focusing on the successes and viewing mistakes as fixable missed opportunities, you will **Rewire** yourself to approach all conflicts and social errors with calm and confidence.

Guilt, Regret, and Parental Satisfaction Home Improvement Projects

1. Remember back to when you first knew you were going to be a parent? What did you hope being a parent would be like?
2. How would you like your relationship to be with your child in one year?
3. How would you like your relationship to be with your child in five years?
4. Describe how you want your relationship to be with your child when they are 30.
5. What can you do now to work towards the relationship you want to have in the future with your child?
6. List your positive qualities as a parent.
7. In what areas of parenting do you wish you could be different?
8. Try the following mindfulness exercise. Find a place to be alone without any interruptions. Get in a comfortable position and relax your body. You might want to refer to the body scan exercise to help you fully relax. Set a timer for 10 minutes and repeat the following statement: "*I forgive myself as best I am able for any harm I may caused myself or others, both knowingly or unknowingly through my thoughts, words, and actions.*"

Chapter Eighteen

Being Your Child's Advocate

At the beginning we mentioned that though this book could benefit any parent, it was mainly written for parents of children with significant behavioral, social, and emotional problems. It is designed to negate out-of-home placements; fill in the gaps left by the reduction and/or removal of aftercare services; and to help in the transitions from program to program and from program to home.

The emphasis on short term specific interventions and least restrictive settings has resulted in children often going from one treatment to another even when they have graduated positively from a previous program. Parents, too, are in constant transition as they adapt to the new treatment teams and clinicians who become significant figures in their children's lives.

It is very understandable that many parents become bewildered, lost, and frustrated as they try to successfully "navigate the system." Parents are expected to adapt and support each program and intervention service their child receives despite significant changes in approach, vernacular, and assigned parental role.

We will now offer some suggestions of how you as a parent can find the sweet spot whereby you **Advocate** for your child while showing due respect for all the professionals with whom you come into contact. We will discuss how to hold professionals accountable while remaining a vital and team oriented **Advocate**.

Any tool is able to be misused or used as a weapon causing further damage or injury. In our presentation of basic tools of **Being Your Child's Advocate** we will attempt to guide you towards proper use of the tool, as well as warn of some of their possible misuses.

Advocacy Tools

1. Be a Good Historian

One of your important roles is to help reconstruct your child's history so that the professionals are made aware of the chronology of significant events in the life of your child. While your child's story is usually part of their file information, you will often be interviewed by professionals as they build on the information already documented.

The telling of your story can never be fully represented by written social histories, and each time you are interviewed is an opportunity for the interviewer to get a **Clearer** and more powerful picture of your child's gifts and struggles. Any insight into your child's inner world and recognition of their patterns are very useful and can prevent therapists and programs from starting over from the beginning or repeating previous mistakes.

It is important not to just tell your "side of the story" or paint a picture with a specific goal or agenda. Therapists and clinicians are trained to recognize such strategies with the result that your interpretation might be discounted or received with skepticism. The recounting of your child's emotional and psychological reactions to the events in their life is valuable, as are your reactions and the rest of your family's. Yet, doing so with an agenda or finding someone to blame will render you a less credible and reliable **Advocate** and family historian.

2. Seek Treatment Appropriate for Your Child

If your child is struggling at home, at school, or socially you want to find out what treatment is available. Make calls and conduct research to find resources and contact professionals who can conduct an assessment of your child and the services for which you qualify. Local agencies and therapists who specialize in adolescents will either be able to assist or direct you to someone who can help identify what is available and potentially beneficial.

If your child currently is in placement or receiving interventions that are scheduled to end in the next month or so, you want to be investigating with the organization what the discharge plan is and begin to identify what future services are required or recommended.

3. Shop Around

Any time you identify or are told what treatment your child needs (individual therapy, out-of-home placement, alternative school, or after school program), shop around to find the program which best fits your child's needs (Pozatek, 2011). Meet with therapists and visit facilities to ascertain if the program style and content seem appropriate and a good match. Ask questions to insure you understand what will be involved. When it comes to interviewing individuals such as therapists, administrators, social workers, and mentors, take your time to find a good match. Look for compatibility of personality type, communication style, and teaching style.

4. Hold Professionals Accountable

Know the job description of those who are providing services for your children and make sure that they are providing the services for which they were contracted. Set up meeting times to review how things are going and ways you can be of most assistance. Obviously you are not to expect any professional to violate confidentially, but they should be able to keep you informed of progress being made and any areas of concern.

When information is provided, or a diagnosis, medication, or specific intervention is suggested, it might be prudent to get a second opinion. Often times it is very reassuring when multiple professionals make the same assessment and recommendation.

If your child is in placement, set up regular times to speak with a representative of the facility to give you updates and to answer any questions you might have. You should always make sure that you verify anything your child is saying regarding his interactions with peers or staff. Such a contact person is vital to insure that you are not being deceived or put in the middle by your child. You will want to know who to contact to allow for the free flow of information and to minimize misunderstandings.

5. Abide By the Rules

Many programs have rules and guidelines which may be emotionally difficult for you to accept and support. This may include when and how you have contact with your child; what you can and can't do on visits; food and gifts you can bring your child; or the access to and use of media and personal belongings.

Once you've made a commitment to the program, it is vital that you follow and support the policies and rules. Cutting corners or supporting your child to subvert the structure and guidelines is poor modeling and counterproductive.

As your child's **Advocate** it is important that you ask questions and air concerns, but as long as your child is engaged in the services you must accept and support the rules and guidelines as they exist. If you feel discounted, left out, or marginalized it is important to address these issues in a direct and open fashion by talking to the appropriate representatives of the program.

In many cases cooperation and patience usually prove to be most beneficial. If problems and emotional concerns persist, it is important to access a third party to serve as your **Advocate** (social worker, therapist, mediator, educational consultant, etc.).

Before ever deciding to terminate treatment be sure to get an objective second opinion to see if your concerns merit such a move. As your child's advocate you want your child to receive quality treatment, but numerous terminations and changes can be unsettling for your child and make him more resistive and uncooperative to future interventions. In such cases, children will often register persistent complaints to prod their parents into "saving them" by pulling the plug on treatment.

The changes our kids need to make are seldom comfortable or easy for them. If they can depend on us to bail them out, they will likely not emotionally invest or give their best effort to learn skills and grow. So, while it is important for parents to stay involved, it is equally as imperative that you allow the professionals and treatment providers to do their job. *A good parental* **Advocate** *is one who protects the best interest of the child.* Often the best interest of the child is served by patience and a commitment to the services chosen.

6. Therapeutic Consistency

One of the major things to **Advocate** is for therapeutic consistency. *While treatment may change over time, it is important that the therapeutic thread neither gets dropped nor broken.* The thread can be continued if some caring individual maintains a long term relationship with your child. Often this can be a therapist, counselor, educational consultant, or mentor who remains involved with your child through all the changes and interventions.

Such individuals remain a resource, attend treatment teams, and consult with you regarding your child's needs throughout the years. They are there for you and your child in good times as well as the bad, and can help you understand and integrate all that you and your child are exposed to from a service and intervention perspective.

Therapeutic consistency also involves a way for treatment to be practically and functionally integrated. Therapeutic consistency helps your child understand the path they are on and helps reduce the perception that nothing is working or that it is unrelated to previous interventions. Many parents may need assistance in recognizing the therapeutic thread that spans and runs through all treatment. Yet, your role as **Advocate** is strengthened by acquiring and maintaining a vision and grasp of the therapeutic thread. If for any reason the thread is dropped or lost track of, the **Advocating** parent can seek out the assistance needed to regain consistency.

7. Giving and Receiving Feedback

The skills of cooperation such as **Accepting Criticism** and **Respectfully Disagreeing** apply to us as well as our kids. Mastery of the skills will greatly assist your effectiveness as an **Advocate** for your child. The more respect you show workers, clinicians, and agency administrators the more likely it will be for them to listen to you and consider your input. Be careful not to have the content of what you are saying get lost in the defensive or offensive manner of how you are saying it.

Voice tone, body language, and not interrupting others are often key in your ability to be heard during a meeting. Remembering to be descriptive will help you avoid blaming or labeling those who are providing services for your child. Working together does not mean completely agreeing with everything being said. Staying open to the suggestions and viewpoints of others often allows them to remain open to your observations and concerns. Expressing your concerns is very different than making judgments and accusations.

It is easy to feel overwhelmed and insecure in a room full of professionals. Using skills of preparation (see **Scripts** and **Dress Rehearsals** and **Visualization**) may ease your anxiety and improve your presentation during formal meetings. Bringing along an **Advocate** for yourself will also increase your comfort level as that person can assist you in **Advocating** for your child.

When receiving criticism remember to say, "*OK*." When **Respectfully Disagreeing** remember to lead with statements of understanding and appreciation before voicing your concerns, making an observation, or expressing discomfort with what is being said. A good **Advocate** seeks cooperation not conflict; it should never be an 'us-versus-them' situation. Rather it should involve a vigilance to get everyone working together towards a common goal of the long term success and happiness of your child.

8. Planning, Transitions, and Being Proactive

Whether the next step is coming home or entering a step down or step up program, it is important that the transition be done in a therapeutically thoughtful way. Your child should be prepared for the transition, reach closure with their current placement, and understand the goals and the reasons behind the next step.

Even if your child's discharge or graduation is known well in advance, agencies and treatment facilities often need gentle reminders to make sure that a reasonable transition plan and schedule is in place. The transition plan should include the transferring of skills and successes to the next placement along with treatment goals and team recommendations.

If home visits are available and your child is returning home soon, work with the agency/program to schedule visits to make the transition as smooth as possible. Visits are used to evaluate how well your child is able to transfer skill growth to the home environment. Problem areas should be identified after each home visit and worked on at the facility before the next visit. If possible, increase contact and information flow to maximize both the facilities knowledge of home behavior and assistance in having the treatment goals of the program coincide with your home transition goals.

Request that questions your child has which are producing anxieties regarding their next placement get answered. Ask if the facility has a format for your child to reach closure with staff and clinicians and request that the treatment team design a closure plan if the facility does not have a standard procedure.

Most children have an adjustment period before leaving one facility and then another adjustment period upon arrival at home or a new placement. Studies show that problems and behavioral regressions resulting from these transitions can be greatly reduced and avoided if a child is supported and taught how to deal with the transition (Reedy, 2015).

9. Be Descriptive and Respectful

Before closing we want to emphasize the importance of an **Advocate** being descriptive and respectful. A parent who truly understands that 'how you say something is often more important that what you say' will find the entire system more friendly and manageable.

Often when strategies or skills are introduced to a parent by a clinician, therapist, or staff member the parent will curtly respond and close the door with, "*I've already tried that,*" or "*That never works.*" While a parent's frustration regarding being told to use previously tried strategies is understandable, the finality expressed in these statements bars any discussion of how to make things work better from being explored. It is also important to remember sometimes strategies may have had limited success because of needing more practice and repetition.

As we stated on numerous occasions there is no magic wand and there are a limited number of tools to explore and use. Therefore, there is a great probability that you will be asked to incorporate strategies, teach skills, and address areas that you have tried before with varying amounts of success. In such a situation describe in detail what you tried and what happened. Ask the therapist what will be different this time.

Try to avoid saying, "*I told you so,*" when a treatment strategy does not go as planned by the professional. If a previous observation or a prediction of yours proves to be true it will do little to rub people's face in it. As your child's **Advocate** it would be more beneficial to focus on the future and to offer suggestions of what could be done now. As a parent of a child in need of treatment there are many benefits to having good **Advocacy** tools.

- ✓ *You will feel better about yourself and feel less overwhelmed or intimidated by professionals working with your child.*
- ✓ *You will be an integral part of your child's treatment design and implementation.*
- ✓ *You will be able to better access treatment for your child and monitor their success.*
- ✓ *You will be better able to join with all providers and avoid any tendency to fall into detrimental and counterproductive 'us-versus-them' scenarios.*

We could write an entire book on recommended strategies on how to be an effective **Advocate** for your child, and maybe one day we will. Hopefully this short section convinced you of its importance and gave you a glimpse of how it might be accomplished. We hope that many of you will also try to find an **Advocate** for yourself who can help you **Advocate** for your child.

Summary of Being Your Child's Advocate

What it is:

As a parent you have a privileged position and perspective on your child. Your emotional investment and knowledge are assets that make you a prime candidate to **Advocate** for your child. **Being Your Child's Advocate** means that you try your best to insure they are receiving quality treatment in an effective manner. Often times being a good advocate means surrounding yourself with caring people who are supporting you as well as your child. In the end, a good **Advocate** is a good team member who is dedicated to their child succeeding the right way, in a way that will have lasting benefits.

Why do it:

A child who sees you as being on their side and as their **Advocate** is more apt to try to succeed and work their way back home. It is difficult to overstate the sense of self worth a parent can achieve when they successfully **Advocate** for their child and are seen as a valued asset by the professionals working with your child. When everyone functions on the same team on behalf of the child, transitions are made much easier and gains and improvements in your child's behavior and emotional well-being last.

Reframe, Replace, and Rewire:

It is not unusual for parents to develop an adversarial stance towards professionals and "the system." This often occurs when parents feel insulted or blamed by criticism they receive and guidance offered. Such ill feelings are often exaggerated when a parent feels that professionals are making assessment errors based on their limited exposure to their child. A parent's ability to **Reframe** their role with professionals from adversarial to their child's **Advocate** can often remove the tension and get things moving in a positive direction. When a parent **Replaces** anger, hurt, and defensiveness with the **Advocacy Tools** outlined above, productive and mutually respectful relationships with professionals become very likely. **Mastery of Advocacy Tools** will **Rewire** a parent's biochemistry resulting in approaching meetings and discussions regarding their child with increased ease, comfort and confidence.

Being Your Child's Advocate Home Improvement Projects

1. What are some ways in which you could improve upon **Being Your Child's Advocate**?
2. Think of a time in the past when your intention was to **Advocate** for your child and it did turn out the way you wanted. Describe what you wanted to happen.
3. Describe what did happen?
4. If you were to go back in time, what would you do differently to better **Advocate** for your child?
5. Look over the **Advocacy Tools** listed in this chapter, Which of these tools are you very successful using? Which of these tools are you willing to put more emphasis on to better **Advocate** for your child?

Chapter Nineteen

Listening and Problem Solving

On numerous occasions we've recommended that you have an array of formats to help govern how you and your child dialogue. These styles of verbal interaction provide recognized structures to follow, each having slightly different goals and rules. The identification of each format makes it easier for your child to see why one form of expression may be considered inappropriate or getting off track in a given interaction. Getting back on track is as simple as reminding them of the components of the specific form of interaction or reviewing the apparent **Goal** and **Purpose** of the current discussion.

In the end it is your decision whether you need to shift formats in mid conversation. Shifting from one format to another is acceptable if both you and your child identify the new format and can make the switch to the goals and procedures of the new format.

We will now give a short description of various formats that span the spectrum from listening to active problem solving. *We listen when our child's major need is to express and process their feelings, and we problem solve when our child needs a plan of action or has an ethical decision to make.*

1. Venting

Venting is a format on the far end of the listening continuum. In a proper **Venting** session your child does all the talking and you are there to show deep interest in what they are saying. When your child **Vents**, your job is to show care and concern and validate their feelings by nods, smiles when appropriate, and an occasional word of **Praise** or sympathy. We know **Venting** works when our child feels some relief from talking the situation out with you and when they are able to refocus back to the activity at hand. **Venting** is not useful if your child continues on and on, repeating the same information over and over, and is not able to refocus their energy into another activity. You'll also know it is not useful if you redirect your child to another activity and they immediately find someone else to whom to **Vent**.

Venting is not appropriate, and we need to verbally intervene if our child is becoming a danger to self, others, or shows signs of being ready to begin damaging property. If your child is blaming or verbally attacking you personally, then you need to intervene by using calming techniques and remind them to use "**I Feel**," **Statements** to help avoid blaming. If they are unable to hear or do this, then it is time to stop and deal with their behavior through skill identification and encouragement.

2. Active Listening

In **Active Listening** our verbal role is mainly to repeat back to our child what we hear them saying. Sometimes you can parrot back almost word for word what you heard, such as, "*What I hear you saying is that you think Tina is avoiding you and talking behind your back.*" At other times you can **Frame** what they are saying such as, "*You've been talking about things you could do during football practice which can catch the coach's eye.*"

In **Active Listening** you are able to make many more statements of support, concern, and empathy than during **Venting**. A parent engaged in **Active Listening** is often heard to say things like, "*That must be so hard to hear!*" or "*How do you feel when he doesn't return your call?*" or even, "*You're doing a great job not getting into arguments with Phil!*"

Many children, especially younger ones, find having their words said back to them to be comforting and validating. Children with the maturity of a teenager prefer more **Framing** and summaries of what they have said with the occasional repeating back as a point of emphasis.

You can use the skill of **Active Listening** to **Attune** to your child and/or have them feel that you are attuning to them. This can be accomplished by asking them to expand on or clarify what they are feeling. In this manner you are having them reflect on and share their feelings which often helps deflect or **Redirect** their anger, while at the same time validating their emotions by having you attentively listen.

Using **Active Listening** in this manner accomplishes several goals all at the same time. One, it can help your child focus on the underlying feelings of hurt, frustration, embarrassment, etc. and dissipate the desire to angrily complain or argue the topic. Two, it can provide you an opportunity to **Attune** to their feelings and not react to their aggressiveness or get into a power struggle over the topic. And three, it can help your child feel validated and **Attuned** to by the mere fact that you are showing care by wanting to hear more about their feelings.

There are some children such as those on the autism spectrum, with high anxiety, or ADHD who react very negatively to having their words parroted back to them. It is wise with these children to mainly summarize and frame and to get their permission to say what you heard them saying. Many of the children with the issues listed above are fine with you repeating back what they say, if you ask first if it's OK. Obviously, we should honor their wishes if they decide they do not want us to repeat back verbatim what we heard.

If during this session your child begins to pose a specific problem which is bothering them or they want help on a situation, then move on to a **Problem Solving** format. We will now present an example in which you would encourage your child to select a solution from a few options.

3. Problem Solving

We mentioned above that the need for **Problem Solving** could arise during an **Active Listening** session. Often we perceive our child is struggling with something that needs to be solved. Generally, a **Venting** and **Active Listening** session is initiated by your child wanting to process their emotions or talk about something bothering them. In applying the rest of the skills addressed in this chapter, you will take a more directive role in the flow and goal of the conversation.

Problem Solving

Here are some steps for dissecting a problem (figure 19.1):

Problem Solving Steps

1. Identify the problem/issue needing a solution or action.
2. Help come up with three options.
3. Explore the potential advantages and drawbacks to each option.
4. Have them pick the solution that promises the most success and with which they are most comfortable.
5. Schedule a time to review how things went.

**figure 19.1*

We often can see that 'something' seems to be bothering our child, and when they show no signs of "coming down with something" we suspect that they have 'something' weighing on their mind. At these times it is beneficial to approach our children with a calm concern to gently inquire what is bothering them. Most children are usually reluctant to "talk about it" but calm persistence usually pays off. After a while our game of 20 questions will generally point us in the right direction.

At the root of their distraction is usually a problem with a peer, boss, teacher, or social situation that they are undecided or lost as to how to respond or what to do. Once the problem has been identified we suggest you help them identify a solution they are comfortable with by using the following format.

With more mature children our goal is that they become more autonomous and learn how to solve their problems by encouraging them to come up with their own options. With less mature children we may have to help them identify an option or two.

We recommend that you continue seeking options until three are identified. Having only two options seems too much like choosing between opposites and isn't much of a choice. Most kids find considering more than three options a bit overwhelming and tough to keep straight.

Let's imagine that your child is unusually quiet and is just hanging around his room. You approach him and ask what's up and he says, "*Nothing.*" Through additional questions you discover that he's interested in a girl and he's unsure of what to do. You have him identify three things he could do: ask her out; invite her to a group outing; text her.

You have him explore the benefits and drawbacks of each option. Examples of some possible things your son might identify are: 1) I could get a date with her; 2) she says no; 3) we get along on the group outing; 4) she brings a date to the outing.

The range of topics you could use this format is almost endless. Generally, the goal of **Problem Solving** is to have your child choose the option that most appeals to them. This will sometimes not be your first choice, but, unless it involves breaking the law or potentially physically harming themselves or others, it is fine to let them learn by trial and error. You could let them know that you would have chosen another option, but such input might make them redoubt themselves and they may give up or feel a need to start the process over from the beginning.

Scheduling a time to review how things went is one more way for you to show that you care about what is happening in their life. The review time also lets you see if they followed through on their decision and if the issue is resolved or needs further attention.

The recommended format for **Problem Solving** can be modified to your tastes and goals. Some parents want a more active role in problem solving and desire a consensus rather than letting the child choose. Other parents, due to their child's track record regarding decisions or a lack of maturity or social awareness, feel that they need to take the lead in identifying the options and explaining to their child the possible benefits and drawbacks. Yet, if your goal is to have your child become an autonomous adult you at some point need to let them have more executive decision power regarding the choices they make in life.

4. Self-Advocacy

This is the label we give when the goal of your discussion is to have your child stand up for themselves, question authority, or make sure their desires and goals are voiced and recognized by others. We often encourage our kids to **Advocate** for themselves anytime we feel that their good intentions, efforts, views, skills, and talents go unnoticed or are under-appreciated. Likewise, we feel they should stand up for themselves if they have been falsely accused or misjudged. At times our children know how to **Self-Advocate** and all they need is our support and permission. However, in many situations our children can use help and assistance in preparing how to best **Advocate** for themselves.

The two biggest concerns we have when our kids **Self-Advocate** is that they do it in a mature respectful manner and they say the right words in the right way. These concerns are best addressed by having our children practice and rehearse their presentations until they are comfortable and confident in their presentation.

These concerns can be fully addressed by incorporating two skills presented earlier in this book, **Respectfully Disagreeing** and **Scripts** and **Dress Rehearsals**. Paying attention to the goals and components of these two skills and techniques will be an effective preparation so your child can present their ideas comfortably and respectfully. Such practices will not insure that your child's efforts at **Self-Advocacy** always achieve their goal, but it will greatly assist them in becoming more articulate and in providing alternatives to becoming combative or out of control.

5. Advice

Giving Advice has been a hallmark of parenting since time immemorial. Parents have used advice giving as a means of trying to have their children benefit from their experience and wisdom. **Advice** *giving is not telling your child what to do, but rather giving them information for them to consider when they make decisions.* A parent giving **Advice** is providing their child with perspective and recommended options of how to continue, what to look out for, or possible repercussions of taking a specific course of action.

Advice given in anger or with an expectation of it being followed isn't really **Advice** but an instruction. Too often parents use advice as a forum to indirectly criticize their child or express their frustration with their current direction. Also many parents spend too much time expressing their opinions. Instead of the child hearing their parents' care and concern the child feels lectured or reprimanded.

The skill of **Advice** giving is in it being concise and illustrative rather than pointed and judgmental. *The goal is for the child to feel their parent's wisdom is based on respect and support.*

Summary of Listening and Problem Solving

What it is:

In this chapter we outlined five potential formats of **Listening** and **Problem Solving** which span the entire realm of relating to your children from passive and attentive listening, to active guidance, to voicing your perspective and recommendations. These formats were offered as general tools that you can adapt and modify according to your needs and relationship with your child.

Why use it:

The ability to identify and use various methods of having your child process their feelings and make decisions allows you and your child to have specific ways of approaching and resolving many sensitive and important issues. A parent's awareness of which format fits what situation helps in averting arguments, frustrations, and hurt feelings that can occur when child and parent have differing goals and agendas. A child is more likely to approach and share with a parent who can adapt their interaction style to the needs of the moment. Open and supportive communication between parent and child often results in increased mutual trust and respect.

Reframe, Replace, and Rewire:

In this section we outlined five specific **Listening** and **Problem Solving** formats to use with your child. Identifying which format you are using in a given situation helps you limit and avoid many unnecessary conflicts, arguments, and power struggles. Identifying which format you plan on using both **Reframes** the style and content of the discussion while allowing you to quickly redirect your child when they stray or become emotionally inappropriate. Guiding the discussion along the chosen format **Replaces** meandering and potentially volatile discussions with productive ones with a stated structure and goal. Frequent use of the various formats will **Rewire** your child into only providing the relevant material and emotional tenor consistent with the given topic.

Listening and Problem Solving Home Improvement Projects

1. Are there times in the past when you think that **Venting** was helpful for your child? Describe the situation and how you were able to support them in **Venting**.

2. Can you think of times when **Venting** was not a good idea for your child? Describe the situation and explain at what point it might have been good to try a different approach.

3. **Active Listening** requires **Attunement** with your child, giving them your complete attention by letting them know you have heard what they are saying. Think back on the last 24 hours you spent with your child. Take a piece of paper and draw a line down the middle. On one side of the paper write down the times in the last 24 hours you were engaged in **Active Listening**. On the other side of the paper, honestly write down the times in the last 24 hours when you were really not fully engaged in listening to your child and can hardly recall what they said.

4. Look back over your **Family and Personal Values**. If you are intentionally living by your Values, what changes could you make to engage more frequently in **Active Listening**?

5. Think of a problem you are currently having in your life. Using the **Problem Solving** model above, either write out the steps or talk through the steps with someone you trust.

6. Describe how you will use this **Problem Solving** model with your child.

7. What are some ways in which you wish your child would practice the skill of **Self-Advocacy**? How can you help them in using this skill?

8. Think back to your childhood. What are some memories you

have of adults giving you **Advice**? If there are times when you did not follow their **Advice**, or listen to it, what do you wish they would have done or said instead?

9. Ask your child to rate you on a scale of 1 to 10 on how helpful your **Advice** is for them (this will take courage).

Chapter Twenty

Family Meetings and Discussions

Even in a small or moderately sized family it can be hard to make sure everyone is kept informed and up to date on household news. As a parent it can become a little unnerving to have to repeat oneself numerous times to each family member or be left out of the loop on some basic information about one of your children.

Most parents value family activities and feel that time spent all together is important. While one-on-one time with individual members is also rewarding, many parents feel that family time is both important and often rare in our ever increasing busy individual lives. The various forms of electronic media and communication devices can often keep us in contact somewhat frequently, yet it seldom lends itself to interactive family time.

Family cohesiveness, support, and understanding can be greatly enhanced by some form of organized and scheduled time to meet and talk. This could be done weekly at the dining room table or even in your vehicle as you drive somewhere together as a family.

While some families need and thrive on formal meetings, others find more informal discussions to be more comfortable and enjoyable. The more informal the meeting, the harder it is for it to be productive, consistent, and well monitored. Yet, any format is acceptable as long as everyone feels recognized, heard, appreciated, and the meetings happen often enough to meet your family needs.

It is rare that every family or family member gets excited and motivated by the prospect of a **Family Meeting**. Many families, therefore, have found it beneficial to schedule them right before a fun activity such as watching a movie together, going out to a favorite restaurant, or playing video or board games together.

Here is a partial list of some of the potential benefits and purposes of planned family discussions and meetings.

Benefits of Family Meetings

1. *Information can be shared quickly and efficiently. Every family member can receive news and changes in plans at the same time which avoids someone accidentally being left out or hurt that they were the 'last to know.'*

2. *Meetings can be held to inform everyone of schedules, routines,* **House Rules**, *or any temporary changes in any such topic due to previously unforeseen circumstances.*

3. *New rules, household routines, responsibilities, or chores can be discussed and chosen.*

4. *Families can make and decide on plans for the coming week involving anything from dinner menus and cooks to which child's activities or sporting events they will be attending.*

5. *Meetings can be to recognize a family member's efforts and accomplishments in a specific area such as school, job, art, or social activity.*

6. *The meeting can be to set individual or family goals and to decide what treat or reward will accompany accomplished goals.*

7. *The meeting objectives can be to resolve problems, conflicts, or hurt feelings between family members and to identify ways for each family member to be supportive or helpful in resolving these conflicts.*

8. *The meeting can involve the review of previous decisions and discussions of how well things have gone since then.*

9. *The meeting can be a vehicle for individual family members to tell stories, give updates on their activities and interests, or do a performance of their choosing.*

Many families let their kids lead **Family Meetings** as a reward for maturity and an incentive for increased responsibility thus encouraging them to take a more vested interest and pride in how the home functions. Family discussions and formal meetings can help foster even stronger familial **Relationships** and family pride. All in all, **Family Meetings** can be structured and run in any manner which fits your families needs and interests.

Summary of Family Meetings and Discussions

What it is:

When a family routinely gets together and follows a basic format to talk over a predetermined topic, then they are engaging in a **Family Meeting** or discussion. What makes a "family meeting" a **Family Meeting** is not so much its specific format or level of formality but that it happens frequently and has a consistent structure and flow.

Why do it:

Family Meetings and **Discussions** demonstrate to each family member the importance and significance of the family as a whole and of their relationship bonds with each other. **Family Meetings** are an excellent vehicle for being able to guide and monitor how family members speak to each other. It also is an opportunity to have the youngest as well as the oldest members of the family lead discussions and get more comfortable speaking in front of groups.

Reframe, Replace, and Rewire:

Family Meetings do not have to be a formal meeting at a designated spot or even inside the house but can occur anywhere and anytime the family is together. What is vital is that everyone understands the value and importance of the meeting and gives their attention and input during the course of the meeting. Therefore, it is important that one **Clearly Frames** the beginning, purpose, and results of the meeting. **Family Meetings** can greatly improve family communication patterns **Replacing** rumor and misrepresented parental sentiment and **House Rules** with **Clear** and **Specific** recommendations and house policies. Frequent use of **Family Meetings** will help **Rewire** the family into acting in a consistent manner and emotionally investing in the general functioning of the home.

Family Meetings and Discussions Home Improvement Projects

1. What are topics you would like to discuss in a **Family Meeting**?
2. What are some ways you can reward everyone in the family for their positive participation in **Family Meetings**?
3. **Activity Bags/Boxes** are a useful tool for all families to use. This is an exercise to do with your children so take your time to make it a pleasant experience. Get 3 pieces of paper which are different colors (such green, purple, and red). Each of the colors will identify activities which you can do with your child for a specific amount of time (such as: green = quick; purple = short time; red = extended time). Now write down different age appropriate activities you can do with your child which can be accomplished in the specific time slots.

   Here are some examples:

   Green *(1 to 5 minutes)*

   - ✓ *Read a poem together.*
   - ✓ *Listen to their favorite song and have them explain why it is important to them.*
   - ✓ *Pick out a dessert to get the next time you go grocery shopping.*
   - ✓ *Write something nice about a family member (or draw them a picture) and hide it where they will be sure to find it.*

   Purple *(10 to 20 minutes)*

   - ✓ *Look at some old family pictures and talk about what was going on in the pictures.*

- ✓ *Take the lyrics to a favorite song of your child's and together create humorous lyrics.*
- ✓ *Plan a special 5 course meal for a family celebration.*
- ✓ *Have your child show you their favorite game.*

Red *(30 minutes or more)*

- ✓ *Go for a walk outside.*
- ✓ *Pack a picnic and find a special place to go eat it. If it's pleasant weather, go outside. If it's cold or rainy, pack the picnic and go to a public place where you can eat or find a different place in your home to eat.*
- ✓ *Make a card to send to someone important to all of you*
- ✓ *Play a game together.*

Cut up the ideas into strips which you can put into a chosen bag or box and decorate it together. This **Activity Box/Bag** can be kept in a convenient place and when you are at a loss for how to motivate or reward your child, reach into the bag and pull out an activity which can be done in the amount of time you have available.

There are several reasons to make this **Activity Bag/Box**. One is to give you ideas when you are at a loss for what to do. Another is to spend some time with your child coming up with ideas which can be fun, rewarding and age appropriate. That is why it's so important to do this with them. The making of the activity slips and the decorating of the box can all be done in a **Family Meeting**.

Use your imagination and have some fun as a family in making your **Activity Bag/Box**. This is an opportunity to spend positive time together and can be adapted for any age of your child from 3 to young adulthood. We've known grandparents to get in the fun as well.

Chapter Twenty One

Parenting in the 21st Century

As far as we know, parenting has never been easy. So while some insist that parenting is natural and instinctual, historical documentation does not seem to support this viewpoint. Each era and individual society has its unique challenges and difficulties regarding the healthy upbringing of children.

The escalating speed and complexity of modern life places an enormous stress on parents and families. The growing number of single parent and shared parent families also presents some daunting challenges. Exponential growth in technologies having to do with instantaneous social and global news as well as mass communication is making it harder and harder for parents to be able to control, regulate, or even shepherd the sensitive information being introduced to their children.

It wasn't so long ago that the majority of families lived in small communities or spacious rural areas where people of like mind and values congregated. While differences in parenting styles and beliefs always existed, children generally had a very limited view of their options with most kids seeing their friends parented in a fashion similar to themselves.

Today, children are aware of an expanding menu of parenting styles and attitudes making their parent's decisions more susceptible to being negatively scrutinized and compared with other parents. Many popular "children's movies" involve story lines focusing on children having to overcome their parents ineptitude or on their being envious of their friend's cool parents.

Sheltering and protecting our children from influences we do not want them to be exposed to is becoming harder and harder and in many situations down right impossible. Whether we like it or not, parenting has become a high profile commodity in modern society. Most of us can no longer parent in isolation or in a restricted community of like minds and hearts. We are now in constant competition for the development of our kids values with a consumer society bent on getting children's attention and winning their allegiance through whatever device necessary.

A critic of democracy once said, "*Imagine how difficult it would be to parent if you were elected by your children every couple of years.*" While parents aren't elected, many feel that they are being forced into a popularity contest with other parents.

How does a **Parent in the 21st Century** teach values, discipline, and say, "*No,*" to their children's requests and still win their love and respect? How does a parent do the right thing when others around them are doing the convenient thing? How does a parent deal with the technologies that they can partially restrict or prohibit in the home but cannot prevent their child from engaging in beyond their eyesight?

While some parents might desire us to go device by device and make suggestions and recommendations about the proper way to intervene or manage these technologies, this type of thinking is fundamentally misunderstanding how technology impacts our lives. We use our modern devices to achieve the same basic activities we've always engaged in: socializing with one another; unwinding and relaxing; or various hobbies, such as arts and crafts, to name a few. Each of these activities has their own value and can be moderated accordingly. It is not terribly important if the child is socializing on the phone, a video game, or some form of virtual reality; and the restrictions need to be based on the underlying activity, not the specific medium being used to engage in it (Grandin, Moore, 2016).

Instead, we focus on how you can maximize positive influence with your child to help shield them from the allure of possible negative aspects of our technology based consumer culture. There are ways in which your child can use emerging technology without diluting or harming the quality of their relationship with you. Focusing on gaining social skills, learning new information, and developing age appropriate **Relationships**, whatever the medium, is the message you want to give your child regarding the use of technology.

In **Give What You've Got** we talked about how play is an essential element to the learning process. Educational games have been a popular part of pop culture and media for centuries. Therefore, it is important to point out that many games are worthy additions to your child's life and activities. With a little research you can identify many worthwhile games for your child to enjoy.

Worlds Apart

In many ways modern inventions, machines, and electronic technologies are making it easier for us to spend more time with our loved ones. Tasks that used to take us hours to do can now be done in minutes, if not seconds. Research and clerical tasks that previously demanded you remove yourself from the family can now be done in their presence with little, if any, shift of your attention.

The many forms of written, audio, or visual instantaneous communication devices make it possible to contact our family members at any conceivable time. One can see and talk to family members even if you or they are thousands of miles from the family home. Likewise, we can document in real time any photo, video, or audio of an event, celebration, or sentiment we want to share.

While all the above is true, the majority of parents are finding it harder and harder to increase the quality and quantity of time they spend with their children. Despite all of our conveniences and time saving devices, the pace of life and the demands of a modern lifestyle are making us all busier and more distracted. Family time, while still treasured by many well intentioned parents, is becoming a scarcer and scarcer commodity.

Most households do not have the luxury of having one parent stay at home full time with the kids. Even in those households with a stay at home parent, children often spend a few days a week in day care to insure that their child "learns socialization" and is not left out or abandoned by their peer group who are in full time day care.

Unless you are a stay at home parent who home schools you are looking at your child being out of the house 6 to 8 hours a day from infancy all the way until they move out on their own. In essence, a child is likely to spend more awake hours each school day with close friends then they will with their parents.

After school hours are rarely spent entirely at home. Many children enjoy extracurricular after school activities such as band, sports, or clubs. Other kids just like to play or socialize with friends. Add to this list the electronic devices networking them with friends or keeping them plugged in to their group or pop culture. This list would not be complete without adding the growing realm of interactive or personal gaming which often is done alone or with a peer.

Working parents, even part timers, often find that they are expected to do work or be available while at home necessitating being tethered to their cell phones. So, even when in the presence of their family, parents find themselves either distracted or at times completely removed from their child's world.

Parents and adolescents often find their energy and attention being hijacked by those not in their immediate environment as they respond to calls and texts. It is not unusual to see the majority of family members at a restaurant spending more time socializing on devices than interacting with each other in person.

When the children are very young, busy parents often find technology to be a great immediate babysitter. A whiny or hyper child who seems incapable of letting his parent cook, clean, or get some other household or business task done is often pacified by being entertained by a video game. After a while the child begins to be attached to such distractions and spends less time in the more physical activities and more and more time with technology. Often, parents later complain of the amount of time their child spends inactive passively looking at a screen or playing video games.

Years ago parents similarly complained about early TV as being the 'idiot box' and bewailed their child's tendency to watch for hours instead of going out and playing. Yet, oddly enough, the TV, radio, and even telephones were often the center of family life.

Even before the age of TV, families used to sit around and listen together to programs, stories, and music on the huge family radio in the living room. During the early years of TV, families would again sit around and watch together and talk about the programs during commercials or after the show was over. In many instances, TV and radio were the center of family time and inspired a good portion of family discussion of everything from news and current events to social issues, fashion, and the arts.

Most houses had only one radio, TV, and telephone and the use of each was far more of a public event than a private one. Engaging in these activities was seldom an individual event and more often a family one. The invention of the transistor radio started to personalize and individualize the experience, resulting in children and adults listening separately.

Many families in the 50's and 60's only had one car for the entire family. So, along with sitting in front of the TV, family trips were a venue for family conversation. Yet, as consumerism and technology advanced, families started to have more than one car, TV, telephone, radio, and computer. Over the last few decades family members have all become individual owners of these and additional technologies. The family and group activity has waned as the individual use of these has increased.

When there was one TV, car, and telephone it was a lot easier for parents to monitor and control the use of technology and the information and subject matter being exposed to the children. In today's consumer culture where products are small, personalized, and highly transportable, it becomes almost impossible to monitor and harder to use as a family activity.

So while children and adolescents are as impressionable, vulnerable, and exploitable as they were generations ago, our consumer society is placing in their hands information that requires adult decision making powers and maturity. Parenting today is far more challenging than ever before. Parents of the 21st century face unprecedented hurdles at protecting their children from exploitation, seduction, and the inculcation of values in opposition to those they want their children to adopt and internalize.

What's a Parent to Do?

What is a parent to do with technology, consumer culture, and work life nipping at their heels? How can we parent and establish a rewarding relationship with our children?

Probably the best thing is to be proactive. *Rather than spending most of your time warding off or trying to prohibit all dangers lurking about, your energy would be better spent doing fun things with your child while maintaining your high standards for mutual respect.*

Instead of trying to prohibit what games they shouldn't play, you could play the games with your child that you would like them to play. Earlier we noted that mammals and intelligent animals learn through play and that humans learn quickest and best when learning is fun and playful. Being a good and thoughtful parent does not preclude your being a fun parent who enjoys life and their children.

Video game manufacturers learned early on that kids will play and buy games that are fun, entertaining, and that quickly and routinely produce success for the player. Children loved when the game visually rewarded and **Praised** each success as they progressed from level to level. The quick and fairly continual **Praise** and reinforcement reduced children's tolerance for delayed gratification and increased their need for immediate success.

A child going outside to hit a baseball with a bat or throw the ball in a basket would seldom experience success as quickly as when playing the same game in a more exotic setting on the screen. If you were a child, which would you choose: swinging a bat and maybe hitting three out of a hundred, or playing ten minutes on a video baseball game and hitting homer after homer in a matter of minutes? Not a tough call is it?

Add the fact that a computer or video game is infinitely patient while a parent pitching the ball is seldom able to veil their frustration after a handful of misses, and you can easily see the attraction of video games. The video games also have better graphics than the back yard as well as entertaining cartoon characters cheering your child's every move and celebrating their every success.

While we can't compete with the cute characters and exotic graphics, parents have a huge advantage by being real. Our **Praise** and affection is far more rewarding than a video game. So, when it comes to the world of play, especially the gamers world, here are some things parents can do.

Activities With Your Child

1. *Play the games with your children on a big screen. Make yourself part of their fun experience, even if it is more to watch than participate. Try to incorporate video games into your relationship and family time with the children.*

2. *Get virtual interactive games that replicate physical events such as tennis, baseball, soccer, etc. There are many such games out there where you get an aerobic workout playing the video game. These types of games work very well even with older adolescents and are a great diversion from the sexual and violent games often the choice of teens.*

3. *When playing real sports and games with your children try to design the game in a way in which successes occur frequently. Quick and frequent success and competency are the surest way for your child to have fun at an activity and to look forward to playing it again in the future.*

The above discussion regarding video games also applies to many other areas of technology. Whenever possible try to balance individual use of specific technologies with family use or at least one-on-one time between parent and child. It is easier to adapt modern technologies to your shared life with your kids then to prohibit their use entirely.

Cultivating a strong interpersonal and highly interactive relationship with your child is the best and most efficient way of preventing them from misusing the technology, becoming the target of predators, or becoming an isolated and depressed techno-junkie.

It is advisable to find as many opportunities as possible to bring games and the most popular technologies into entire family or parent and child activities. Using the big screen over the small screen allows you access into your child's world and models fun as a shared and not a private or hidden activity.

While we are pointing out the benefits of taking small screen private technologies and making them shared large screen activities, we are not advising all parents to become lovers and users of every new technology. What we are **Advocating** is that you find and cultivate shared interests and activities strengthening your relationship with your child, while at the same time reducing the number of hours they are spending away from you and your ability to monitor outside influences. The more your child spends 'fun' time away from you or as part of a hidden society or club, the less you can secure their safety or monitor their value development.

It is important that you find opportunities to have fun with your children while remaining a good role model. *You don't want to lower your standards and have fun with them in a reckless, immature, or potentially destructive manner, but you also do not want to become a full time police officer whose hyper-vigilance lacks humor or pleasure.*

What we are **Advocating** is that you become and remain acquainted with your child's changing world. When they get involved in a new interest, activity, or technology let them give you a tour or provide a tutorial of their new world/gadget. Your child will not only find your interest in their world validating, but it strengthens your relationship with them.

Staying included and involved in their world also can alert you of any potential dangers or abuses that may lie ahead. Recent neurological studies validate what parents have long suspected, and, that is, that the rational decision portion of the brain does not reach full maturity till young adulthood (Siegel, 2013). Even older adolescents are biologically incapable of understanding the repercussions and the full impact of their actions. This means that while our children are becoming more mature and autonomous they still can benefit from our knowledge and wisdom, especially when it comes to things regarding their safety and security. Our children often have a particular blind spot when it involves attractive and potentially addictive habits which new technologies often present.

Building Family Relationships and Minimizing Unwanted Influences

In this chapter on *Parenting in the 21st Century* we've identified two interrelated areas posing a challenge to our success. One area involves the fast pace of life and the complexity of modern society. The second area centers on the potentially detrimental role outside influences play on the development of our children.

The majority of parents and their children lead busy lives. When you factor in work, school, obligations, and after school activities we are left with a precious few hours a day. If your child spends time in more than one household your time together is even more reduced.

The time our child spends away from us is dominated by outside influences including other adults, peers, and popular culture based social technology. So, in essence, our child spends far more time without us than with us, and, therefore, far more time influenced by others than ourselves.

Our antidote to these realities is two fold. *One, make the most out of the time you have with your child. Two, learn how to manage the outside influences through learning about them, engaging them, and helping your child organize and use their time in ways in which you are comfortable.*

As we noted earlier being at war with the outside world, becoming the influence police, or forcing your child to spend time with you are seldom effective. The best route to go is to share our interests and joys with them and share what gives them joy.

We can and should try to assist our children finding joy in productive and long term rewarding activities and interests. The following are some of the structures, routines, and strategies we can employ which gently guide our children in the right direction while maximizing the time and the relationship we have with them.

The following menu of ideas are recommendations which you might find useful; they are not to imply that you should try to incorporate all of them. The time you spend with your child is precious, and many parents find that the real world prevents them from being able to spend as much time with their child as they would choose. Many close parent and child **Relationships** have been forged despite a lack of free time or time together. No one should underestimate the importance of a parent's care, concern, and emotional investment.

Useful Ideas

1. **Quiet Time**: Establish a set time when the family congregates in a common area to engage in quiet tasks and interests such as doing homework, arts and crafts, reading, or research. This helps to insure that homework is done in the proper atmosphere as well as settling the home down.

   Today kids can quietly practice many instruments such as keyboards, guitar, bass, and even drums by wearing headphones. Parents can decide how much or little technology use is permitted during this hour. Often times social networking can reduce the family together feel of the hour, yet computers and held hand devices can be productive tools quite conducive to quiet hour.

2. **Peer and Family Groups**: This format can happen naturally or intentionally. Parents of young children often find or form a playgroup for their child. One can do so with the intention of finding a group of friends for your child whose parents have the same values as you regarding style of play, interests, and use of technology. In this manner parents can either directly supervise the children or be fairly confident that peer interactions will be of a beneficial nature.

   Since peer groups are seen as important and parents are often concerned about their influence on their child's interests and development, it is quite a relief for parents to see their children with peers they can trust. The forming or encouraging of peer alignments can occur at any age. Parents of older teens need to be sensitive to their child's wish for autonomy and therefore need to find ways of encouraging and assisting associations and not dictating them.

3. **Reward What You Prefer (Stacking the Deck)**: While consequences and restrictions can be very effective parenting tools, they can quickly become counterproductive when over used. Therefore, rewarding and incentivizing what you prefer is a far more effective strategy to use on a day-to-day basis.

   As an example, you could reward time spent with the family or acting responsibly and engaging in technologies shared and monitored by the family. While not forbidding personal texts or time away from the family, you could instead tie in treats, fun activities, and services you provide with family involvement. This might be accomplished by taking them shopping to buy a few things dependent on their joining in a family activity that precedes your going to the mall.

   One can limit individual, private, and secret use of technology by expanding family play and group technology participation. This idea of guiding your children to do things which you see as productive through **Praise**, recognition, and rewards leads us to the next tool.

4. **Devise Individual Activity Charts:** Design a weekly chart of target activities for each family member. Family members completing their weekly chart should get some form of tangible reward. You could base allowance, use of car, amount of time available with friends, curfew, and even choice of dinner menu on how much they accomplished on their chart.

Charts can include a wide array of goals and how often they plan on doing this activity during the week. The following are some possible areas which assist in making the chart diverse and challenging.

Activity Chart Suggestions

Here are some ideas for **Activity Charts** for your child (figure 21.1):

Activity Charts

- ✓ Art/craft/music: drawing, knitting, bass, piano, singing
- ✓ Physical activity/sport/exercise: walking, running, swimming, baseball, karate, dance
- ✓ Academic: reading, foreign language, spelling, vocabulary, writing, blogging
- ✓ Trades/hobbies: mechanics, woodworking
- ✓ Social/independent living skills: **Accepting Criticism**, volunteering, cooking

**figure 21.1*

Obviously your child's chart will probably involve some negotiation, tweaking, and clarification. Some kids will try to pass off making pop tarts for cooking. Yet, you will be able to define what is acceptable such as your child having to learn how to make actual entrees to be able to meet a cooking goal.

The beauty of the chart is that it encourages and rewards your kids for doing things that you feel are beneficial and wholesome. If you do incorporate a quiet time, the chart could give them plenty of things to do when they don't have homework. Also, every minute they are doing their targeted activities that you have agreed upon is a minute away from them engaging in activities you don't favor, such as endless texting or playing video games.

Later we will discuss the therapeutic benefits of **Replacing** unwanted behavior and habits with desired ones. **Replacing** behaviors stands in stark contrast to extinguishing or prohibiting undesired habits. **Activity Charts** can be a fun and gentle way of **Replacing** activities through encouraging new routines.

The fact that you will be supporting, encouraging, and rewarding your child for learning and mastering many new activities and talents can only strengthen the relationship you have with your child. Parents often find having a family reward for each individual member meeting their weekly goals is a great way to have the siblings support each other. As an example, let's say you have a family movie or game night scheduled when everyone meets their goals. If handled correctly, goal charts can be a great tool for relationship building and mutual support for each family member.

One final but very important potential benefit of goal and **Activity Charts** is that they help insure that your children are engaging in rewarding activities. Each goal is an opportunity for your child to feel increasingly successful and proud of their talents. The sense of personal development is vital to most kid's self-esteem and to have their efforts and progress recognized, supported, and **Praised** by parents and siblings is quite powerful.

A parent who is able to have their child be emotionally invested in life and proud of their skills is a very successful parent. If there is a common thread we've witnessed with the kids we have worked with in placements and facilities, it is in their level of boredom with life. A child who is bored and is not enthralled with their world is more likely to break the law, do self harm, get in trouble, abuse substances, or repeatedly engage in asocial behaviors.

This is not to say that activity alone is the answer, for one can be very busy and still be bored and unfulfilled. Some people's joys are more internal; they often involve acts of imagination, contemplation and observation. Such poets, philosophers, and spiritualists may look inactive, but their form of activity can be just as rewarding as that of the craftsman, tradesman, or musician.

The greatest gift we can give to our children is to help them find joy in what they do, pride in who they are, and meaning in what they experience. **Parenting in the 21st Century** presents its share of challenges and hurdles, yet it also provides many opportunities for rich **Relationships** and personal fulfillment.

Summary Parenting in the 21st Century

What it is:

The rapid pace of life and ever burgeoning technology present the **Parent of the 21st Century** with great challenges. The amount of time our children spend with peers, popular culture, and electronic devices can be far greater than they spend with us. This makes how we spend time with our children very important and makes it wise for us to take an interest in all the outside factors which influence our child.

Why do it:

We can learn to appreciate and incorporate much of what interests our child into a shared world. As parents we can incentivize and reward our children for time they spend with us as family, while supporting and praising the productive interests they engage in. As we noted above, *the greatest gift we can give to our children is to help them find joy in what they do, pride in who they are, and meaning in what they experience.*

Reframe, Replace, and Rewire:

Almost universally parents want their children to be healthy and happy while being good people and enjoying some measure of social success. Since parents have to make the tough choices and sometimes have to say no, children often feel that the adult's sole goal is to deny them having fun and to keep them from doing what they want. You will find your children more respectful to your wishes when you **Reframe** and focus on the joys and benefits of what you would like them to do, rather than on the deficits of engaging in what you don't want them to do. By identifying, cultivating, and sharing with them the interests which can make them happy, successful, and good people, you can **Replace** potentially harmful or useless activities and influences with ones promoting happiness and self-worth. In this manner, you can help them **Rewire** themselves in a way in which they will naturally gravitate towards beneficial activities and influences and away from harmful ones.

Parenting in the 21st Century Home Improvement Projects

1. New technologies are coming out on a daily basis. What technology, device or game does your child know more about than you? Ask them to teach it to you. If you fear your child will resist spending the time with you or will not want to teach you, then be prepared with an incentive for them.
2. Make a list of as many rewards and incentives as you can think of which might motivate your child. Divide this list (at least) into the following categories:
   - *Things you can purchase*
   - *Things you can do for them*
   - *Things you can do with them*

   Your goal in developing this list is to have a large variety in each category.
3. What kind of group could you form with other parents and kids your child's age?
4. What are the benefits of raising a child in the 21st century?
5. How can you maximize these benefits?

Change and Personal Development

Change and Personal Development

We will now enter our third main section of ***The Parental Tool Box*** dealing with the therapeutic aspects of change and personal development. Before doing so let's engage in a short conceptual review to see how we've gotten here.

The intended goal of this book is to be a comprehensive overview of therapeutic skills, strategies, formats, and perspectives to use as a resource guide to help you assemble your ***Parenting Tool Box*** and to help clinicians assist you. Much information is given in each chapter, so reading and rereading each section that interests you is highly recommended.

When we started, we imagined many parents picking up this book feeling frustrated, angry, and possibly defeated by their child's behavior and recent history. This is why we started with the **Power of Words**. We wanted you to know that though you may have felt lost and powerless, there are many things you can control and influence.

At the very beginning we pointed out that the words you speak and the words you say to yourself have an impact on how you feel about yourself and how your child responds to you. We offered suggestions on ways to **Frame** your words so your good intentions are heard by others and felt by you.

We provided many tools, skills, and formats allowing you to **Avoid Power Struggles** with your child while at the same time creating a harmonious and mutually respectful home environment. In many instances we noted that how a person says something is as important as what they say.

Throughout the second section on **Relationships**, we kept in mind that all people have both a desire to belong as well as to be recognized as a unique individual. In chapter after chapter we provided ways in which we can swathe our children in our care and concern while honoring their uniqueness and individuality. We discussed various strategies and activities we can employ to encourage our children to stay close to us and the family, while cultivating skills and interests which embody values that will help make their lives fulfilling and meaningful.

Now, in this section on **Change and Personal Development**, you will learn how to establish and implement long term goals for your child's growth and development. Having a vision for your child's path is beneficial for everyone.

The three sections can be broken down in the following manner.

As the parent:

1. Learn verbal strategies and discussion formats to help you avoid getting into arguments with your child by focusing on skill usage and not on topics.
2. Learn how to guide your child into healthy and caring **Relationships** with family and the outside world. Provide your child with appropriate outlets for feelings as well practical ways to address problems.
3. Learn how to create and implement a therapeutic treatment plan for your child which centers on a vision of how they can become the person they want to be. We can benefit by having a fairly **Clear** picture of the general direction our child is going in and how best to support it.

As the child:

1. Learn how to speak and act respectfully. See and experience the benefits of cooperation and compliance and how to express concerns and disagreements in a mature fashion.

2. Learn how to find a rewarding balance of **Relationships** with family, friends, and the global community. Learn how to properly collaborate with popular culture while cultivating personal interests and talents which can yield a deep sense of personal satisfaction.

3. Learn how to embrace change and take pride in having a long term plan for personal growth and development. Learn how to set realistic short and long term goals. Learn how to enjoy the day-to-day journey and process of living a rewarding life.

The original **Purpose** and major **Goal** of this book remains to insure that the underlying therapeutic thread of your child's treatment neither gets dropped nor broken. The intent of everything written is to help you and all the professionals stay on the same page and maintain therapeutic integrity wherever your child is on their treatment path.

It is our hope that this book will be helpful, if not vital, in cutting across differences in programmatic design, vernacular, and therapeutic ideologies that can arise when your child receives ongoing or intermittent treatment. We additionally aspire to have clinicians actively use this book as a resource to help bridge transitions and integrate treatment in such a manner as to allow and support the parents to interact with their children in a consistent manner.

Chapter Twenty Two

Appreciating and Valuing Change

Childhood is, by its very nature, a rapid time of physical and emotional growth. Progress can be rapid and challenging with all the inherent changes. Adolescence is known as a time of experimentation and risk taking and it is not a period usually associated with disciplined linear progress (Siegel, 2013). The exception, of course, is when an ambitious adolescent is dedicated to an art, sport, or manual skill that demands precise technique acquired through endless practice.

Difficult and stressful times can make a child or adolescent wary, cautious, and even resistant to change. In such circumstances, the fear of the unknown has one gravitate towards the familiar. The fear of imagined future failures is always scarier than the hardships through which one has already lived.

While success can make one very confident, difficult times and struggles can render one opposed to the introduction of anything new. Most kids who receive interventions are frequently required to change. In most cases, the change has not been their idea but rather is experienced as being imposed on them from the outside by adults, therapeutic professionals, and bureaucracies.

It is extremely advantageous to have your child become comfortable with change and view personal growth in a positive light. Change is inevitable and a child resistive to the new and unfamiliar is going to be in conflict with everything from school, to peers to themselves.

As a parent you usually have the benefit of knowing your child's history and can use this to pose some of the benefits of change. Reviewing the losses and gains ledger regarding the old and the new is an excellent way of slowly having your child see the benefits of change and of growing up.

You could start by talking about what your child enjoys during each season of the year. Let's say you start by asking what they like about the spring, and with your help they list everything from warmer weather and thunderstorms to longer days and more time outside. Then ask what they look forward to as summer approaches and they name school ending, family vacations, summer sports, staying up later, and watermelon and lemonade.

In review of this exercise you can point out that every change in the seasons involves the end of some joys and the beginning of others. You could add to this how each year they get older, new and better activities get added to their list, like long trips with friends, later curfews, having their own computer or TV, and driving a car.

It is not important to try to convince them that all change is great and life always gets better but rather that change always involves things that are lost and things that are gained. Yet, each change is an opportunity to add to their life and in many circumstances they can still do what they did before. You might mention that an old toy they still play with or that comforts them does not prevent them from playing with their new gadgets.

You can do this exercise with your child on any subject matter that involved change in their lives. Each year at school has involved new teachers, classmates, classes, and subject matter. After school activities, sports, and interests that have survived have all gone through an evolution containing desired change. Even if your child has been highly traumatized by their past they can usually identify freedoms and increased independence they have acquired by the sheer fact that they are bigger, stronger, and more mature.

The kind of reviews we are suggesting are an opportunity for your child to see growth and change in a balanced way and not just from a perspective of conflict, failure, and low self- esteem. It is also a chance for you as a parent to remember some of the good times which may have been lost in the chaos and intensity of the present. Additionally, it is an opportunity for you to work on your **Framing** skills to highlight the positive aspects of the road on which you and your child have been. Even **Framing** events as challenges or mistakes feels far different from **Framing** them as failures or nightmares or some other characterizations you've said to yourself or to your child.

Aligning Yourself with What Your Child Wants

Finding ways of having your child view change in a positive light is a noble goal and well worth the effort. It will not only make your child more open to the future but will also allow them to be more engaged in their own therapeutic progress and treatment. In this way they can guide and take the lead in their personal development rather than feeling attacked by the care of others or having the will of others imposed upon them.

When it comes down to basics, we all want the same thing. We want your child to be happy, healthy, and find life meaningful and rewarding. Even if they choose to be alone, we want them to be comfortable and cooperative with their contemporaries.

Often, the easiest and simplest way of engaging your child into the change process is to ask them their opinion on the matter. Questions such as, "*How do you want others to view or describe you?*" "*What kind of person do you want to be?*" or "*What qualities do you want to have?*" are all excellent ways to have you align yourself with your child.

If your child seems unsure of how to answer the question, it is useful to provide them with a basic menu of personality traits and qualities to choose from. The possible list is extensive. If you're at a computer just type in "list of personality traits" into a search engine and look through the lists offered for ideas. The list found this way will probably be too long and overwhelming, so just choose a dozen or so as a guide.

Such a list could be (figure 22.1):

As your child constructs a list of desired qualities to have, look for goals and habits which would help them cultivate these qualities. If they say, "*kind*," you could tie that into being respectful and calm in how they speak to and treat others. You then would commit to helping them reach their goals and suggest specific behaviors to master which would help them get where they want to be (voice tone, complimenting others, listening, volunteering, etc.).

Your child's descriptions of how they want others to see them

Personality Traits

- funny
- compassionate
- resourceful
- loyal
- friendly
- caring
- brave
- determined
- dynamic
- kind
- passionate
- charming

**figure 22.1*

or who they want to be can easily be adapted and **Framed** into typical therapeutic goals. Seldom have we not found ways to tie in the basic skills of cooperation and mutual trust (see **Accepting Criticism**, **Respectfully Disagreeing**) into their chosen qualities. Certainly, many of the components can be used such as calmly moving on, eye contact, saying OK, or statements of understanding.

In essence, you are finding ways to **Frame** and translate their goals and desires into skills of self-development and social sensitivity. So rather than these goals being agents of control imposed from the outside, they become means of assisting your child in becoming the person they want to be or in how they want to be perceived by others.

If during this exercise your child's list does not give you an opportunity to tie in areas that you feel are vital, such as **Accepting No** or **Accepting Criticism**, then blend in one of your goals with two of theirs. Let's say that they wanted to be brave and loyal, and they could not see how **Accepting Criticism** is being brave and loyal. You could convert loyalty into a target of being complimentary or not gossiping and bravery into doing the right thing even if it is unpopular. You then could suggest adding the third goal of **Accepting Criticism** to assist in making sure that they do not resist your criticisms regarding when they are acting in a disloyal or cowardly manner.

While it may be tempting to maximize the opportunity of your child giving you permission to help them meet their goals through self-improvement, it is important to not start with more than two or three targets. *When it comes to self-improvement and skill mastery, less is better.* This allows them and you an opportunity to focus attention on a manageable task while keeping things **Clear** and **Specific**.

Whenever you agree upon the first set of goals, you should give a few examples and do a couple of practices of what your support, guidance and monitoring will look and sound like. Be sure to give examples of compliments for using the skill, instances of when they missed an opportunity to show the desired trait, or times in which they acted or spoke in ways contrary to how they want to be viewed.

As an example, when talking about loyalty you may say things like,"*When you tell someone they have a good point, it shows loyalty,*" or "*When you didn't laugh at the insult of George he could see how loyal you were.*" Likewise, you could point out that when he didn't invite George to the game, George might feel upset.

Along with letting them know how it will look, let them know that it takes a lot of practice to make a quality into a habit. Let them know that you plan on looking for every opportunity you can to point out when they are or could be using the desired personality trait or skill. Encourage them to point out to you anytime they exhibited the trait and you missed it.

As we mentioned earlier, people learn best when it is fun. The more you can make these skills of self-improvement into a playful fun game the better. Even skills of compliance can become fun to teach and learn when your child is invested in learning and mastering the skill and you are giving compliments and criticisms in a supportive and upbeat manner.

Previously we also noted that video games and advanced technology have decreased our children's threshold for failure and delayed gratification. With this in mind, coupled with any lack of success our child has experienced of late, it becomes increasingly important that our children feel a quick sense of progress and success. While complete mastery of these traits and skills may take quite a while, make sure that you are identifying and celebrating any accomplishments.

If you are working on **Accepting Criticism**, celebrate any step or portion of the skill mastered such as if they are saying, "*OK*," a majority of the time. When it comes to an accomplishment, please maximize and emphasize its occurrence and not minimize any gain.

If your child goes through a rough patch, try not to label their behavior as a regression. Instead, internally pose and **Frame** their behavior in terms of a temporary set back and as a growing pain based on stressors or fears and not as a return to the past. In terms of the words you say to your child, avoid all explanations; focus on remaining supportive as you continue to state your belief in their abilities. When it comes to individual events, remain steadfast in **Being Clear** and **Specific** while reminding them of how proud you are of how far they have come.

Once a skill is considered mastered, try not to reassign them the same skill again. If similar problems reoccur, find another target name with similar components which sufficiently address the issue. As an example, a child who has previously mastered **Accepting Criticism** but is once again arguing with you could receive a target such as cooperation or teamwork.

The important thing is for you and your child to feel and celebrate any growth, and to put all current difficulties into perspective. As much as possible we want to **Frame** and experience whatever happens as part of the **Personal Growth** and **Development** process which is never a straight line but full of twists and turns.

Having your child keep the same goal for more than three months is more often than not counterproductive, frequently resulting in both you and your child feeling frustrated and defeated. Keep in mind and possibly share with your child that studies on human behavior show that it takes at least 4-6 weeks to master a new skill and behavior (Repetition and Learning, 2018).

In Sibling and Family Harmony we discussed the mechanics of **Verbal Contracts** and **Safety Plans. Verbal Contracts** and **Safety Plans** can be very valuable tools in having your child emotionally invest in the process. The following is a partial list of potential benefits of using **Verbal Contracts** and **Safety Plans** as a means of having your child appreciate and value change (figure 22.2).

Verbal Contracts

- ✓ A verbal commitment has them invest in making the change
- ✓ Verbal agreements give you permission to assist
- ✓ These agreements put you into a supportive **Advocate** role

**figure 22.2*

Summary of Appreciating and Valuing Change

What it is:

This chapter offers suggestions in how you can have your child view change in a positive light. A child who is more comfortable with change is less likely to be resistive or opposed to the idea of personal growth and development. The resultant goal is for your child to take a more active role in identifying what qualities and skills they want to work on and improve.

Why do it:

A good portion of resistance is removed when we elicit our child's permission and personal investment and when they accept our assistance in becoming the person they want to become. Instead of their feeling controlled or pressured into doing something others want, they are able to feel your support and see that you are on their side. The more the child feels an equal partner in their therapeutic treatment, the more trusting and aligned they feel with everyone's care and concern for their welfare.

Reframe, Replace, and Rewire:

When you ask and help your child identify the admirable qualities they would aspire to (such as being kind, loyal, smart, etc.), it is easy to tie in all your goals and expectations into their goals. In this manner you can **Reframe** desired behaviors and skills from demanding what you want and expect into supporting them in achieving their goals. When you are supporting and guiding them to be the person they want to be, you are **Replacing** imposing your values and wishes on them with helping them become the person they yearn to be. Over time this will **Rewire** your child into becoming more autonomous, taking pride in engaging in actions and skills which improve their self-esteem and social functioning.

Appreciating and Valuing Change Home Improvement Projects

1. What has changed in your relationship with your child over the past year?
2. What are some of the gains and losses of this change?
3. Pick **one** or **two** habits you would like your child to change, such as pouting, interrupting or arguing. Start to notice when there are opportunities to **Praise** improvement in reducing these habits rather than pointing out when they are doing it wrong.
4. In what ways are you willing to change to strengthen the relationship with your child?
5. What support do you need to make these changes?
6. How will you make sure you get this support?

Chapter Twenty Three

Maximizing Therapeutic Growth

In this book we have discussed and outlined many tools you can use to effect desired change in your child. We've talked of **The Power of Words** you chose to say to yourself and your child and how you **Frame** them. We've outlined many interactive formats for discussion of feelings and problem solving. We've explored ways to identify and enhance your child's value system and how to improve their self-esteem. We've discussed how to promote the mastery of skills increasing your child's sense of cooperation and mutual respect, as well as how to improve your relationship with your child and how you relate to them.

All of the tools, strategies, perspectives, skills, and formats have been provided with two simple goals in mind, and they are to *help you create a more harmonious home environment and to tangibly affect desired changes in your child.* We have strived to accomplish these goals with the maximum care and concern and therapeutic integrity.

Often, the most important changes our child makes have more to do with intangible things such as improved self-esteem, values clarification, and talk therapy designed to resolve long standing psychological issues. Yet, all of these abstract areas of growth show up in the day-to-day improvement in the words and actions of our child. In this chapter we will focus on the way you as a parent can work in the most tangible ways to assist your child in making lasting improvements in their words and actions. We will now attempt to outline a concise but complete framework to use as a guide to foster lasting positive change in your child's words and actions. We will do this by investigating the importance and function of the following areas:

✓ *Quantity and Frequency of Teaching*

- ✓ *Teaching Affect and Mechanics*
- ✓ *The Three Dimensions of Change*
- ✓ Replacing *versus Extinguishing*

Quantity and Frequency of Teaching

All skills, habits, and talents we develop are mastered through practice and repetition. It matters little if the skill is physical, such as walking or playing piano, or social such as saying, "*Excuse me*," or singing a song. If a baby only tried to walk once a week we would still likely be falling down at the age of ten.

Social skills, like **Accepting No**, **Following Instructions**, or **Respectfully Disagreeing** are no different. The more you practice them the more natural and reflexive they become, establishing themselves deep in our body memory. A child who has been taught to say, "*Please*," when asking for something was coached and corrected by mom hundreds of times before it became a habit. Similarly we want our children to learn more sophisticated social skills and make them habitual in the same way where they just say,"*OK*," without even thinking about it.

The need for repetition becomes even stronger when one desires to **Replace** an old habit with a new one. A child who has the habit of getting defensive every time they receive criticism has to unlearn the old habit as they learn the new one. The old practiced defensive responses need to be **Replaced** by giving eye contact, saying, "*OK*," and calmly moving on.

Parents are often reluctant to teach to the skills with great frequency for fear of irritating their child by verbally drawing attention to their behavior. This is self defeating on two levels. First, your child will not get enough practice and repetition to make a new habit. He will stop thinking of the new practice and fall back into the old habit (body memory). Second, you the parent then will only point out the bad habit when you can't take it any more, showing anger and frustration in your correction.

If you are teaching frequently you can find numerous times

when they are doing the skill correctly or, at least, not doing it incorrectly. As an example maybe your child didn't say, "*OK*," when you told them not to hold the knife in front of them, but they didn't argue and they did point the knife down as they carried it to the sink.

During the day there are dozens of opportunities for you to identify their usage of basic skills such as **Following Instructions** and **Accepting Criticism**. The more they hear **Praise** and **Prompts** the easier it will be for them to master the skill. A prompt is when you give your child a visual or **Auditory Cue** or signal to use the skill.

As an example, let's say your child sometimes forgets to say, "*OK*," when you've given them a directive or feedback. Instead of going into a thorough description of their forgetfulness you just pull on your ear which is a pre-arranged signal you both previously agreed upon using. Many kids, even older adolescents, prefer simple visual **Cues** to verbal ones to help remind them to use their skills. Again, if done with an air of support and humor, many kids will respond to the **Prompts** as a fun game as long as it is done in a way that doesn't embarrass them in front of their peers.

The more relaxed and fun you make your feedback, **Praise**, and support the easier it will be for them to accept the frequency and quantity of instruction needed to insure skill mastery. How much should you teach and practice skill use? Well, the more the better. Mastery does not mean perfection, but rather that a new habit has **Replaced** an old undesirable one.

Teaching Affect and Mechanics

On numerous occasions we've suggested that how you say something is often as important as what you say. No matter how descriptive, insightful or frequent your teaching, it is often wasted or resisted if said in a tone of anger or frustration. A parent whose voice tone implies, "*Now I got you*," or "*You see what I'm talking about*," is not going to be perceived by their child as being on their side or caring. In fact, your child will often feel challenged or attacked and not supported. We strongly caution you to avoid making skill instruction into a contest to demonstrate to your child how bad they are behaving.

Teaching done with a poor or belligerent affect will usually only enflame resistance and not be successful at inspiring your child to master a skill, comply, or listen to what you say. Yet, it would be totally unrealistic for us to expect that a parent who has been living in an emotional war zone with their child is going to instantly adopt a calm and supportive voice tone in each verbal interchange. You will be learning how to **Give Criticism** while your child is learning how to **Accept Criticism**.

Giving Criticism

Here are some suggested steps for you to master. Across from each step we've included some guidance or a caution (figure 23.1).

Giving Criticism

- Eye Contact - Speak to and not at your child, avoid glaring
- Voice Tone - Firm, yet calm and supportive
- Be Descriptive - **Be Specific** without labeling, insulting, or judging
- Interact - Avoid ranting or lecturing
- Thank them for listening - This is the first step to making learning fun

**figure 23.1*

Just as it will take time and frequent practice for your child to master skills of **Respect** *and* **Cooperation**, *it will take you time and frequent practice to master the art of* **Giving Criticism**. The more you give feedback, whether it be positive or corrective, the quicker you will master it. Giving an abundance of feedback will instill the skill into your body memory and will not be dependent on your conscious awareness. This will make it easier for you to use the skill when you are frustrated or your child is falling into his old habits of challenge and resistance.

When you do react and yell or engage in a power struggle, rather than focus on describing the behavior in the manner above, it would be better to halt the interaction and compose yourself. Talking to your child later about your struggles to master **Giving Criticism** may help them be patient and appreciative of your efforts. Each successful interaction you have with your child helps both of you deal with the times where skills are temporarily forgotten.

In a previous chapter we mentioned that encouraging your child to point out when you missed their proper use of a skill was a good idea. This often motivates your child into using the skill so that they can catch you not paying attention and recognizing their efforts.

A child pointing out that you missed an opportunity to identify or **Praise** their use of a skill is accomplishing two things. One, your child is demonstrating that they are vigilantly looking at their behavior, and trying to master the skill. Two, it is helping you get better at identifying opportunities to teach and support.

If you do not encourage your child to help you see their good behavior they may hold your missed observations against you. We've known many kids who avoid looking at their own behavior by convincing themselves that their parents only see or focus on their bad behavior. A child of a parent who does not teach very often is more likely to deflect the teaching when it does occur as being more about their parent's bad mood than their behavior. A child taught too infrequently often concludes that learning the skill isn't really necessary or that the parent only teaches when they are in a bad mood.

The main thing to remember is a child who is being yelled at is not prone to listen or be motivated to please you. Learning how to give feedback in a supportive fashion opens their ears and makes learning into a positive and fun experience.

A parent who teaches in an angry or volatile manner often turns the tools in this book into weapons rather than a means of creating mutual respect. When a parent falls prey to anger they often make their teaching into a contest and a battle of wills. In such a circumstance the parent's goal is to be right and to win, but if the parent wins doesn't the child lose?

The tools in this book are about care and concern and getting on the same team as your child and not about defeating them. *Always keep in mind that goal number one is to help you create a relationship with your child based on mutual respect. A child whose parent enjoys teaching is more likely to enjoy learning.*

The Three Dimensions of Change

The more specific and complete you are in addressing an undesired behavior or perspective, the better the chance of success. When your goal is to successfully change behavior in a meaningful and lasting manner, it is usually best to honor and address the following three aspects of behavior:

Three Dimensions of Change

We can breakdown the ways people change into the following categories (figure 23.2):

How We Change

1. Behavioral and/or habit
2. Psychological and/or emotional
3. Biochemical and/or neurological

**figure 23.2*

While an awareness of the interplay of all three components is not usually necessary to successfully **Replace** an old habit with a new skill, it does usually speed up the process. Honoring the psychological/ emotional and biochemical/neurological while involving them in the

Replacement process reduces resistance to change and makes changes gained more lasting.

By definition something is a habit because we do it more often than any alternative. It makes sense that we have an emotional or psychological attachment to the habit for it is the familiar and is our preferred behavior. A habit is formed because it serves a purpose, and we get something from it. Therefore, one can usually find psychological and emotional elements which are invested in the behavior being continued and resistive to any alternative (**Replacement**) which neglects or conflicts with these factors.

Some kids exaggerate, tell stories, or lie in order to be viewed by others as interesting or talented. Others interrupt conversations to feel some sense of control or to make sure that they are not being overlooked or taken for granted. Our success at finding **Replacements** for these behaviors becomes easier when we find ways for their emotional and psychological needs to be met either through the **Replacement** behaviors themselves or through some other skill or activity we add to their lives.

Likewise, our body has also become used to the biochemical state the habit induced or unleashed through its occurrence. While not all biochemical dependencies result in addictions, the body often does become accustomed to a certain chemical economy and reacts poorly when that economy is disturbed. Anyone who is used to a general amount of caffeine understands how their body responds if they do not get their daily dosage.

Brain studies demonstrate that specific neural pathways are often created by the kind of repetition necessary to form a habit. Therefore, we should realize that the learning of a new habit will take time due to a new pathway being formed (Siegel, 2012).

We have worked with hundreds of children on helping them change and **Replace** behaviors and habits which were negatively affecting their quality of life, interpersonal **Relationships**, and their ability to successfully function in society. *Their ability to successfully* **Replace** *old behavioral and verbal habits was greatly increased when their new behaviors honored and replicated the psychological, emotional and biochemical components of the old behavior.* These concepts are equally true in overcoming addictions.

Usually the new behavior was not able to completely replicate or satisfy all the needs and roles of the old behavior. Yet, in almost every case one could add a few other rituals that complemented the new behavior and sufficiently tended to the previous needs, thereby removing the resistance.

As an example, many of the children who frequently lied or stole were resistive to **Replacement** behaviors even when we made sure that they got more and had more fun when they were honest and respectful of other's belongings. This was often due to emotional and psychological pay-offs they received when engaging in the negative behavior, such as pride in their ability to lie or steal and their sense of control, or the thrill they got by the challenge of not getting caught. The emotional thrill they got was accompanied by a biochemical rush.

The resistance to the **Replacement** behaviors fell away once we found other outlets for their sense of control and pride, as well as finding activities for them to engage in with a sense of excitement, whether that be skateboarding, competition, or acting.

Replacing old habits, attitudes, and routines often demand a blend of insight and functional repetition of the new habit. Behavior repetition without insight is often blind to our needs, and insight without pragmatic skills lacks the means of bringing that understanding into your moment-to-moment existence.

> *When one* "**incorporates**" *a skill, it literally means giving that skill a body, to have the skill become part of the habit body.*

The following is a list of some psychological and emotional factors which sustain and motivate behavior (figure 23.3):

Behavioral Motivations

- A sense of control one gets by familiar behavior
- Pride in a skill harbored by the behavior
- A sense of protection
- A sense of retaliation
- Self-nurturance
- Release of anger, frustration, irritation, etc.
- A sense of excitement or thrill contained in the behavior
- Loyalty to parent, loved one, or respected person
- A sense of identity, or authenticity

**figure 23.3*

Here is a list of some of the ways the old habits can impact your biochemical/neurological economy which will show up in your heart rate, energy level, and perceptual awareness (figure 23.4):

Biochemical Impacts of Habits

- The old behavior gives you an adrenaline rush
- It can make you giddy
- It can numb you or works as an anesthesia
- It will amp you up and has your body feel strong and powerful
- It relieves emotional or physical pain

**figure 23.4*

Many parents reading this will either be intimidated or overwhelmed by the prospect of having to identify their child's emotional, psychological, or biochemical payoffs underlying asocial behaviors. While some of you will be quite confident in your ability to gain insight into your child's motives, others might find your child's behavior quite a mystery.

While ascertaining the emotional, psychological, or biochemical underpinning of your children's undesirable habits is helpful, it isn't necessary. If you feel completely in the dark about these matters it would be good to consult with clinicians, therapists, or specialists in the area of child and adolescent behavior who might aid you in your search for clues.

Yet, every parent reading this section can benefit by having a greater understanding of how complex effectively **Replacing** a behavior can be. This will help you to be patient in realizing that while your child has made some improvements, mastery is difficult to achieve.

When you are feeling defeated or that you've run into a brick wall, you may want to look at the above lists and make some adjustments that focus on a factor which could be at the source of your child's continued resistance. While one size does not fit all, there are a couple of factors which seem to benefit many children and adolescents in treatment.

Generally, finding ways to increase your child's sense of competence, power, and control often reduces resistance. Likewise, activities that boost their ego through recognition of talents and skills is helpful. When it comes to the biochemical, increased fun and exercise has a high success rate, as does either a rise in comforting or exciting behavior dependening on underlying depression, anxiety, or general metabolism.

The important thing to remember is that your child's behavior is often fueled by the factors being discussed here. When **Replacing** a behavior, try to be mindful of what your child gets from the behavior or what effect that behavior has on their emotions and body. Finding appropriate ways to continue getting those needs met will go a long way towards melting away their resistance and improving their consistency.

Replacing Over Extinguishing

Extinguishing a behavior means that we simply prohibit or demand someone stop doing a specific behavior. **Replacing** a behavior means instead of doing one thing, we suggest you do another. We have made a strong case for **Replacing** not only a behavior but the psychological, emotional, and biochemical elements underlying the behavior as well.

Forbidding someone to do something often just increases their willful desire to do what is being prohibited. Yet, when an option isn't offered it is also natural for the mind to have a hard time moving on. A person demanded to not think about bears will almost instantaneously start thinking about bears. From the brain's perspective, if you don't want a person to think about bears you could start talking about cats or dogs. The alternative animals become a **Replacement** for thoughts about bears.

A child told not to argue is going to at least think about arguing, whereas a child asked to say, "*OK*," is given an option, an alternative. Prohibiting or trying to extinguish power struggles often just places more focus and will on power struggles. Focusing on a **Replacement** skill, such as **Accepting Criticism** or saying, "*OK*," puts those **Replacement** concepts into their minds.

Let's take a look at a specific case history which demonstrates the benefits of **Replacing** a behavior over attempts to extinguish the behavior.

Mathew was 12 years old and had been in various placements and hospitalizations since the age of 8. One of his many diagnosis was nyctophobia (fear of the night). Matt's fear of the night was steeped in traumas he experienced at night at the family home. These traumas resulted in his being diagnosed with PTSD (Post Traumatic Stress Disorder). At night his home was frequently the site of violent acts and emotional fights between his parents. Both he and his brother were physically abused and the police came to the house numerous times after midnight.

Every evening at the group home Matt's behavior would escalate with his anxiety. He would get defiant, argue with the other kids, get into fights, and generally draw all attention to himself. Even after he settled down, he remained highly vigilant through the night and despite his medications found it hard to sleep.

Matt had come to us after "failing" at numerous other placements that tried to control and extinguish his difficult behavior with harsh consequences and various medications. Play therapy and family therapy were not enough to help him manage his fear of the night. Understanding that his nighttime explosions had served practical and emotional roles in his life, we decided to help him experience and see the night in a different manner.

Our success with Matt was not instantaneous but came over a span of time in which we were able to create new habits and perspectives (**Framing**). One new goal was to have Matt see that he was safe and secure. Another was to have him look forward to the night by scheduling some of this favorite activities beginning in the early evening.

We found bedtime rituals that not only decreased his anxiety but gave him joy. We played board games, watched TV, read stories, and had some quiet time. Matt found a night time shower relaxing and realized he was able to sleep if he went to bed listening to relaxing music. Without ever having a need to talk about the possible reasons for his fear of the night, we slowly created, through a host of rewarding routines, a new perspective of the night.

Taking a look at how the change in Matt's nighttime routine (**Habits**) affected the quality of his life we could note the following:

1. *Matt's fear of the night put him in an anxious self-preservation mode in which he felt a need to attack and control his environment (*Psychological*);*
2. *The new rituals (*Behavioral*) gave him the control (*Emotional*) he sought without having him distance, hurt and alienate all those around him;*
3. *His new* Behaviors *gave him a means of becoming more at home and comfortable with the night (*Biochemical, Neurological, *and* Emotional*); and*

4. *His new* Behavior *improved his* Relationships *with his peers and had him feel better about himself* (Psychological*).*

Summary of Maximizing Therapeutic Growth

What it is:

In this chapter we noted that frequent teaching executed in a positive and supportive manner is internalized quickly and meets with the least resistance from your child. We also noted that it can be extremely beneficial to identify and honor the emotional, psychological, biochemical, and neurological elements which often accompany or result from the undesired behavior.

Why do it:

Staying sensitive to the reasons and payoffs inherent in your child's asocial behavior can go a long way towards making the **Replacement** process less foreign or jolting. In this way, the successes they experience both socially and personally through the mastery of new skills are not being hindered by any lingering emotional and physical needs which were previously satisfied through the old behaviors.

Reframe, Replace, and Rewire:

The more adept you become at **Reframing**, **Replacing**, and **Rewiring** the more you **Maximize Therapeutic Growth**. You are **Reframing** when you identify the behavior to be changed and convert it into a skill to be mastered. The better you understand the psychological and emotional components which sustain the undesired behavior, the easier it becomes to **Replace** the old behavior with one that takes those motives into consideration. The better your understanding of the biochemical and neurological forces involved in the old behavior, the easier it becomes for you to **Rewire** your child through finding new behaviors and activities which **Replace** the old behavior, thereby, **Maximizing Therapeutic Growth**.

Maximizing Therapeutic Growth
Home Improvement Projects

1. Making lasting changes takes time, effort, and consistency. As parents our children need us to dedicate our time and effort in consistently teaching them skills to help them lead happy and productive lives. In what ways are you willing to increase your time, effort, and consistency in teaching your child? **(Be Specific)**
2. Refer to the **Giving Criticism** guidelines and develop a **Script** of criticism you can give to your child.
3. Take a deep breath and remind yourself of your **Personal Values** before starting this next exercise. Record (audio or video) yourself practicing the skill of **Giving Criticism**. Listen to the recording and **Praise** the areas you think are well done. **Be Specific** on what you want to change, then maybe practice it again or role play with some one you trust.
4. What are some of the **Psychological** or **Emotional** components which sustain and motivate your child's behavior?
5. What are some of the *Biochemical* and *Neurological* effects your child experiences in relation to their undesired behaviors?

Chapter Twenty-Four

Generalization of Skills

The goal of most parents is for their child to use a skill such as **Accepting Criticism** or **Following Instructions** on a full time basis. Very few parents are satisfied when their child is cooperative and respectful for only part of the day, or in certain circumstances. The expectation is that once our child has mastered a skill they will use it consistently and in any situation. If they make an error, then we want them to respond quickly to any **Prompts** or requests to "use their skills."

Generalization of Skills refers to this ability to use the target skill in all situations and environments. Though we are very happy when our child learns how to cooperate and respect us, we still are not satisfied if he continues to get in trouble at school each day for arguing with teachers or peers. Our desire is for respect and maturity to become part of their personality and not just a performance for a few people.

The more artful you become in giving criticism or in teaching any social skill, the quicker your child will learn and the more receptive they will be to making the new skill a habit. Yet, at some point your child needs to understand that they are totally responsible for their constant use and mastery of the skill.

In order for the skill to be truly mastered its successful usage cannot depend on the maturity level, personality, or style of the person with whom they are interacting. One needs to be mature, polite, and respectful despite the ill manners or disrespectful behavior of others. While we as parents may not be happy with the style of some adults, we do not let our child use the way others talk or act as an excuse for them not to use their skills.

Parental expectations of the public usage of skills showing

respect are often higher than what we expect in the home. Many parents do not expect older adolescents to say please and thank you at every meal or interaction inside the home. Yet, even parents who accept informal respect inside the home often expect higher and more formal levels of politeness when with strangers or in public.

If your child is having particular difficulty generalizing and using the skill in specific environments or with certain personality types, it is often helpful to spend some time supportively teaching them how to succeed in those situations. This can be accomplished through recreating the problem situations through **Dress Rehearsals** and **Role Plays** and practicing some realistic **Scripts** to promote their success while using the desired skills.

When parents begin to teach formal skills they are often amazed at how often opportunities to identify and teach to a social skill such as **Following Directions** or **Accepting No** occur. Within weeks they are almost overwhelmed by the dozens of opportunities they missed to **Praise** or correct. This experience helps us all be a little more patient and understanding of our child's difficulty in generalizing their usage of the skills they are mastering.

A child prone to arguments will sometimes not recognize that an opportunity to use a skill of cooperation is occurring. Often what started out as a pleasant conversation soon turns into a battle with the child feeling frustrated and as angry with themselves as they are with the person with whom they are in conflict.

Our frequent pointing out of opportunities to use the skill will help our child begin to see opportunities as well. Sometimes it's a good exercise to go to a public place where adults and kids are interacting and just have your child observe and recognize when the kids he's listening to could have used a skill of respect or cooperation.

Due to their importance we have focused on the generalization of basic skills regarding respect and cooperation such as **Following Instructions**, **Accepting No**, **Accepting Criticism**, and **Respectfully Disagreeing**. Yet, the generalization of any skill you want your child to master is equally valuable whether that be attentive listening, asking for assistance, appropriate humor, patience, or any other area you feel would help your child in being more successful, happy, and confident.

Many children, especially younger ones, are thrown off track when a directive or criticism is given in the form of a request or question. Examples of a directive and criticism done in this fashion would include questions like, "*Could you please double space your essay?*" or "*Would you mind not talking so loud?*" In such circumstances our children need to be taught how to focus on the goal and intention of the speaker and act accordingly.

The ability to use a desired behavior in all situations available is the ideal and the goal of skill mastery. Yet, ideals always have to adapt to reality. In most cases any troubles our children have with generalization can be tended to by education and practice and as they learn how to separate their skills from the personality and teaching style of others.

A person gifted at generalization easily sees **Relationships** between things and how that same relationship or pattern appears again and again in various situations and settings. The ability to generalize can be very uneven and a person skilled at seeing patterns in one area may not see **Relationships** and similarities that the majority of people see in another. A mechanic sees patterns in machines that many miss, and the psychologist sees patterns of behavior that aren't necessarily apparent to a dentist.

Generalization and Neural Processing

It is popular today to point out that there are various learning styles. Some people learn best by memorization, others by hearing, some manually, others by seeking patterns, etc. The field of education has identified various deficits referred to as learning disabilities. Psychologists often categorize the types as visual, auditory, tactile (kinesthetic) learning styles (Nichols, Moravcik & Tetenbaum, 2009).

As a whole, learning disabilities are often viewed as being steeped in how a person's brain processes and organizes information. There are many recognized forms of neural processing which affect how one learns and discerns information (including Autism Spectrum Disorder) which often have a profound impact on one's ability to read social and **Emotional Cues**.

While we sometimes teach organizational, study, and manual skills (such as keeping one's living area clean), the vast majority of the skills we teach our kids are social skills. Our children's ability to master and generalize these skills in a host of social settings is negatively impacted if they have a deficit in reading and understanding social interactions.

In the case of Autism Spectrum Disorder (ASD) this deficit regarding the ability to read emotional and **Social Cues** often presents a real hurdle for children to overcome and is not indicative of their overall intelligence. Many people with neural processing issues restricting their ability to read emotions and **Social Cues** score very high on many intelligence tests such as IQ. High performance on intelligence tests often reflects an ability to "read" or recognize visual, spatial, or sequential patterns. In the realm of ASD Level 1 (Aspergers Disorder) it is not unusual for someone to be considered at genius level intelligence while struggling to be able to identify when someone they are talking to is happy, confused, or making a joke.

A child with neural processing issues which impact their innate ability to read **Social Cues** or understand the meaning of another's emotions and facial expression is not necessarily prohibited from being able to successfully generalize social skills. What it does mean is that those of us teaching these children social skills need to be both patient and extremely specific in our instruction (Nichols, Moravcik & Tetenbaum, 2009).

In essence, we are teaching a child with such neural processing issues a new (foreign) language. This language expresses the intent and meaning behind gesture, look, innuendo, humor, body language, and all of the other social conventions that the rest of us just get and take for granted. A child can only use the skill of **Accepting Criticism** or asking for assistance if they recognize when the opportunity arises by understanding the situation they are in and the internal world and intentions of the person with whom they are interacting.

Playing games such as "*Name that Emotion*" in which you adopt a stance and facial expression and the child identifies it can be very helpful. Another exercise which has proved helpful is to watch a recorded TV show with your child that involves many interactions and humor between the characters. After a few minutes of viewing stop the show and ask questions such as, "*Why did everyone laugh when Tom said he didn't know where Sharon was?*" or "*Why did Tom walk out of the room after Bill said hello?*"

Obviously such games are only to be played if your child has significant neurological processing issues which impair their ability to read and understand social situations. If we are to have our children with social deficits based in neurology become socially comfortable and successful, such exercises may be quite important.

It is important not to assume that a skill our child has mastered in our presence is going to be generalized with everyone and in all situations. Two of the factors we have covered which can hinder our child's ability to successfully generalize a mastered social skill are:

1. *our child's lack of being able to read others and*
2. *if they are highly reactive to certain personality types or ways of being addressed.*

If our child is reactive to adults they view as controlling, sarcastic, or unsupportive it is important that we encourage them to use their skills and not rely on these perceptions as an excuse to be disrespectful or combative. Whether our child's lack of generalization is due to being reactive or structured in difficulties reading **Social Cues**, the solution is to patiently engage in practices and exercises which support and challenge our children. A steady diet of observation, practice, repetition, and identification involving numerous situations, settings, and styles is the surest way of having your child successfully generalize a mastered skill.

Generalization of Skills Summary

What it is:

A skill is considered to be generalized when it is used consistently in a variety of settings, situations, and environments. A mastered **Generalized Skill** will be exhibited by our child regardless of the personality, approach, or attitude of the people with whom they are interacting.

Why use it:

A skill that is generalized (not being dependent on the maturity of others) allows your child to be successful in even the most adverse of situations. **Generalized Skills** are durable and seldom, if ever, deteriorate through any extended period of nonuse.

Reframe, Replace, and Rewire:

Every time your child is able to identify a situation in which they can use a skill that you are having them master, it helps them **Generalize the Skill**. Each time they recognize the opportunity to use a skill in a new situation they are **Framing** and relating the event to the desired skill. The more often they seize upon the opportunity to use a skill they are learning, the easier it will be for them to **Replace** their old habits with the new skill being mastered. The mastering of the new skill allows it to be generalized, and its reflexive natural use demonstrates that they have **Rewired** this skill into their body and brain.

Generalization of Skills Home Improvement Projects

1. What are some skills your child has generalized over their lifetime?
2. What are some parenting skills you have generalized?
3. What are some ways you can **Praise** or *Celebrate* the skills both you and your child have generalized?
4. Our educational system uses report cards as a way to give feedback on a student's performance. In a **Family Meeting** or as an activity ask your child to help you develop a **Parent Report Card**. You can find examples of these on the internet to give you some ideas.
5. Ask your child to complete the **Parent Report Card** and to discuss it with you.

Chapter Twenty-Five

Parenting the Non-Responsive or Implosive Child

The fight or flight response is thought of as being natural for people or animals when they feel threatened or imperiled. In most of this book we have focused on children whose standard response to conflict, confrontation, control, or even criticism is to fight or engage in a power struggle.

There are a number of children who rather than openly battle or argue with their parents, instead take flight from the situation. While few literally run and bolt out of the room, a sizable number of children freeze, stare, curl up into the fetal position, or mentally shut down and become totally unresponsive, often for great lengths of time (McCurry, 2009).

Parents who freely express their feelings of hurt and anger are often baffled and frustrated by having to deal with a child who shuts down and refuses to act or speak. Since you are not getting any clues on how to respond, it is often puzzling how to continue when children retreat into themselves while you are trying to teach, critique, or give them a directive.

We will start by going over a general menu of frequent reasons and possible motivations underlying a child becoming non-responsive, retreating, or shutting down. Following this we will offer some suggestions regarding strategies, teaching styles, and interventions you can employ which have proven successful with non-responsive youth.

While in most cases there is no cause for alarm at the prospect of dealing with a non-responsive child, there do are situations in which severe or prolonged non-responsive behavior indicates a need for professional guidance and assistance. When it comes to insuring your child's physical, emotional, and psychological well being, extreme caution is warranted.

If your child demonstrates a sudden relatively unprovoked withdrawal in which they have no memory of the episode or of events immediately preceding or following their withdrawal, this could be a sign of a neurological or psychological crisis needing professional assessment or evaluation. The more withdrawn and internalized your child, the more difficult it is for you to track or predict their behavior. This makes it all but impossible to ascertain if your child is potentially a threat to themselves or others. A child who withdraws or isolates themselves for great periods of time should definitely be evaluated by a mental health professional.

It is wise to address such apprehensions quickly to see if a professional assessment or evaluation validates or eases your concerns. A parent who frequently worries that their child is fragile or potentially dangerous is apt to form habits which could unintentionally reinforce their child's tendency to withdraw and shut down.

Since your child is not being communicative it is often difficult to identify the source of their retreating or freezing. A parent can be confused by what specific event led to your child's withdrawal or why they chose to withdraw. The following is very abbreviated list of some of the reasons that children adopt withdrawal as a habit:

- *To wear a parent down, assuming the parent will get tired or bored and just walk away*
- *A common survival mechanism of feeling overmatched by the will of another*
- *An expression of poor self-esteem in which they just implode*
- *To avoid taking responsibility by internally "digging in their heels" and stubbornly being noncompliant through staying mute*
- *To avoid conflict*
- *A means to frustrate or irritate their parent (passive-*

aggressive control)

Keep in mind that a a behavior becomes a habit due to its filling some role in a person's life. A child who freezes feels that being non-responsive is the best option available to them at that moment. As is the case of **Replacing** any behavior, we need to offer them alternatives that work better while meeting their emotional, psychological, and biochemical needs (see **Three Dimensions of Change** in chapter entitled **Maximizing Therapeutic Growth**).

A parent who becomes fearful that their child may hurt themselves or that their child's emotional fragility renders them incapable of meeting basic expectations of respect and daily functioning is unintentionally validating their child's non-responsive behavior. On one level a parent could be validating the child's poor self-concept and feeling of incompetence. On another level a parent could be letting their child know that they will back down from expectations, doing everything for their child when they appear fragile.

The goal of working with the non-responsive child is to reach a balance between being compassionate and supportive while remaining firm in your belief in their capabilities. We want to develop verbal strategies that patiently support and encourage without lowering expectations and standards. As parents, we do not want to enable our child's feelings of incompetence by speaking for or doing everything for them.

When your child withdraws and goes mute it is difficult to avoid the temptation to fill in the empty space by asking them many questions to ascertain what they are feeling and thinking. In most cases, when a parent does this, the child ends up learning more about the thoughts and feelings of their parent than the parent learns about what is going on with the child. Even when a child graces us with some shrugs and nods, it is still only our interpretation and hunch as to what they are responding. We have no idea if the nod relates to their actual thoughts, or they are just somewhat randomly selecting from the menu we are offering.

While asking a probing question is not always a mistake, a safer and more reliable route is to offer your child descriptive statements of what you see them doing. Follow this with encouraging and patient statements of belief in their ultimate ability to successfully work through the situation. A parent doing this may note, "*Your head is down and your body looks rigid, in the past it has helped when you've taken a few deep breaths. Go ahead and take a few deep breaths.*"

A parent who describes what they see their child doing, or how they look from the outside, is engaging their child without analyzing, hypothesizing, judging, demanding, or insulting. A supportive and encouraging voice tone reaffirms their safety and affirms your care and concern without its having to be expressed by either removing all expectation or promising to do things for them.

Speaking for your child and telling them what you think they are feeling or thinking may at times have you feel good and speed up the process, but it does nothing to keep this habit from reoccurring. It is making the reappearance of the habit all the more likely. If speaking and feeling for your child is the source of their success, then why would they not become non-responsive in similar future situations?

Statements of belief and encouragement can be followed with silent spaces allowing them time to process and to show them your resolve to be patient and not give in or do their work for them. Withdrawals are often a form of silent tantrum in which your child is expecting you to finally fold and give up, give in, or give them what they want. This strategy is very similar to the child crying at the grocery store register in an attempt to outlast the parent who is initially refusing to buy them candy. Yet, even when not an intentional tantrum, your child's non-responsive behavior will only be changed by developing skills that can effectively **Replace** this style of dealing with stress, conflict, or pressure.

Responding to a Non-Responsive Child

Here's a short summary list of recommended paths to take with a non-responsive child:

1. **Remain Patient and Supportive,** use a calm but not fearful or

pitying voice tone. Make sure that your voice does not convey to them that you might fold, negotiate, or bail them out.

2. **Get On the Child's Level** (do not tower over them). If they curl up on the floor, get on the floor with them. While an occasional pat or caring touch can be beneficial, prolonged physical contact such as hugging or cradling may be counterproductive in being too reinforcing and not leading to the adopting of new self-reliant behavior in the future.

3. **Avoid Lecturing or Engaging in a Monologue** consisting of questions, observations, or insights.

4. **Stay Calm, Optimistic, and Comfortable with Long Silences.**

5. **Let Them Know They Are Safe and Secure.**

6. **Explain How You Are Showing Your Care and Concern** for them by staying firm in your belief that they can meet expectations. Let them know that your desire for them to be self reliant is because you care for and love them.

7. **Occasionally Describe What You Observe.** Note and **Praise** any positive occurrences such as raising their head up, a deep sigh, speaking, body movement, etc.

8. **Provide Frequent Statements of Belief and Encouragement.** Reviewing past successes they have had speaking and working through their feelings can be helpful.

9. **Provide a Road Map** of how they can take the next step. Let them know what they need to do, but make sure that they are the one doing the work to get there.

10. **Use "When/Then," Statements** as both a motivator and limit setter. "*When you let me know what you're feeling and demonstrate that you are safe, then we can go to the store.*"

If your child has a long history of becoming quiet and withdrawn to activate others' assistance and sympathy by arousing fears, they may use this to control or influence their environment. They may derive a certain sense of power by being able to get people to worry about them and give them special considerations and accommodations. The power and control they acquire through being fragile or a victim may be very seductive to them. They may use this influence to make sure things go their way or to be excused from doing something they don't want to do.

When your patience, encouragement, and support lead to your child taking action, expressing themselves, and becoming functional again, make sure you **Reward** and **Praise** this behavior. Their desire to **Replace** non-responsiveness with self-responsibility will only take place through your **Praise** and their feelings of success. The key is for your child to feel more success through speaking and doing for themselves than they did by withdrawing and getting other's sympathy or active assistance.

Often times assigning your child social skill goals such as *Asking for Assistance* or *Self-Responsibility* can assist in having your child see and feel the benefits of acquiring more mature and confident ways of accessing people's support and care. The mastery of such skills can build up your child's self-esteem while providing you with many opportunities to reward their emerging and much desired self-reliance **(Replace)**.

While you always want to monitor your child to make sure they are safe and to demonstrate your care, you don't want a non-responsive child to consume all of your time and attention or find your undivided attention too reinforcing. If your attention is too reinforcing they might become non-responsive anytime they are starved for attention or want your complete attention.

If your child appears safe and under control and you have spent a sufficient amount of time expressing your care, support, and encouragement, you can use a "**When/Then**," **Statement** to let them know what they need to do to move on. You might say something like, *"I am confident that you will let me know when you are ready to move on. In the meantime I will be (sewing, reading, making calls, cooking, etc.) while sitting here waiting for you to let me know when you're ready to talk."* If the task you are going to do requires you to leave the immediate area, let them know that you will be checking in with them every few minutes, but that they could call for you or come and get you anytime they are ready.

Your general "**When/Then**," model **Statement** with a non-responsive child is, "*When you do speak or do such and such, then we can move on.*" When issuing the statement try to make sure that your expectations are realistic and will not have to be modified. If you modify your expectation of what they need to say or do, they may conclude that their non-responsiveness succeeded at getting you to lower your expectations.

"When/Then," Statements used correctly provide realistic limits and expectations while providing the structure, safety, and security non-responsive children crave. In this way **"When/Then," Statements** can be both an effective verbal strategy and a bridge away from non-responsiveness to self-responsibility. **"When/Then," Statements** are also great tools for providing your non-responsive child with a practical road map of how to move forward while maintaining your expectations and having them do the work.

Delayed Acting Out of Non-Responsive Children

While the behaviors identified in the next paragraph can be engaged in by openly combative children as well as non-responsive children, it is important to point out that some non-responsive children act out in a delayed manner. Non-responsive children who keep their feelings underground often find risky or self-harmful outlets for these feelings hours or days after shutting down during your time with them.

A child who "represses" their feelings often have them "seep out" later when by themselves or with peers. These delayed behaviors could include self-harming actions such as cutting or self-mutilation, running from home, suicide gestures, substance abuse, engaging in risky dare devil activity, or behaving in a way to incite or goad their peers into hurting, bullying, or publicly humiliating them. We will address how to deal with such behaviors in a future chapter entitled **Liking Your Own Skin**.

Generally, you will be using a different set of tools to **Replace** self-harming behavior than those you use to **Replace** non-responsiveness. The tools and strategies offered in this chapter are specifically designed to help you successfully have a non-responsive child become more self-reliant and self-functioning.

> *The non-responsive child requires a blend of patient support and encouragement with remaining firm in your realistic expectations that they speak, express, and act on their own.*

This is the most efficient means of **Replacing** withdrawal with social interaction and integration.

A non-responsive child often benefits from pro-active planning of what to do instead of withdrawing into themselves or taking things underground (see **Verbal Contracts** and **Safety Plans** in **An Ounce of Prevention**). In this manner a parent often can reach a child and have them become responsive by reminding them of their previous commitment or of the steps available to them in their **Safety Plan**.

Summary of Parenting the Non-Responsive or Implosive Child

What it is:

A non-responsive child is one who routinely shuts down, withdraws, goes mute, or freezes when they are being confronted, questioned, or being asked to do something they do not want to do. In such a situation, it is important that we remain patient and understanding while not lowering our expectations or doing everything for them.

Why do it:

A non-responsive child will have difficulties succeeding or even functioning in any environment where expectations might become overwhelming such as school, a job, or any activity involving a skill or social performance. A child learning how to work through conflicts or feelings without freezing or withdrawing will be better equipped to function socially without drawing undue attention to themselves. A child who is less dependent on others is more confident and capable of dealing with the day-to-day challenges of life without panicking or shutting down.

Reframe, Replace, and Rewire:

The methods and strategies used to engage the non-responsive child are often different than those used with a defiant child. Understanding how to approach the implosive child helps you **Reframe** the situation and use tools which are more successful with that personality type. The use of such techniques will help the parent **Replace** acts showing frustration, anger, or fear with that of patience, understanding, and confidence. Approaching the non-responsive child with patience and confidence while maintaining your high standards and belief in your child's abilities will **Rewire** them as they **Attune** to your calm and strength.

Parenting the Non-Responsive or Implosive Child Home Improvement Projects

1. How do you react when someone responds to you in a non-responsive manner?

2. Are there times you react in a non-responsive or implosive manner?

3. In what ways does your child exhibit the behavior of a non-responsive or implosive child?

4. What can you do to respond in these situations which will support the intentionality of your **Personal Values**?

5. We have stressed the importance of spending quality family time with your child. Studies show consistently how critical **Family Meals** are in building positive bonds with your child and improving overall **Relationships**. At a **Family Meal**, **Family Meeting**, or as an activity together decide on a receptacle to hold **Conversation Topic Ideas**. This could be a family heirloom bowl or a box you decorate together, whatever works for you and your family and is age appropriate. Together and independently come up with **Conversation Topic Ideas** to put in the bowl/box. There are games which have these already made up and ideas also on the internet. Eventually, personalize the ideas for your family.

Chapter Twenty-Six

Effective Tool Use

The basic purpose of any tool is to allow you to do a task and to get the job done. A tool is considered to be a good tool when it helps you complete the task relatively quickly and efficiently. *The goal of* ***The Parental Tool Box*** *is to help you do your job as a parent in a way which eases your burden while maximizing the growth of your child and the harmony of your home.*

As we mentioned earlier in the book, tools misused could do more damage than assist. Therefore, we want to take a moment to review a few basic principles of ***The Parental Tool Box*** which will help you be a successful and generally happier parent.

Goals of The Parental Tool Box

1. *Have teaching your child be* Strength Based.
2. *Ensuring your child gets more when cooperating than when not cooperating.*
3. *Ensuring consequences have a positive goal.*

Have Your Teaching Be Strength Based

Strength Based means focusing your attention on success and skill usage rather than on errors. We want you to celebrate the good times, and use the not so good times as teaching opportunities rather than as a chance to lecture, threaten, or punish.

A **Strength Based** parent is one who is proactive in setting up and recognizing skill usage and mastery and not reactive and feeding into their child's attempts to engage in an argument or power struggle. The effective use of all the skills and strategies of fostering cooperation involves:

- Catching Our Child Being Good; *and*
- Praising *and reinforcing their good times which motivates them to comply and give their best effort during times of conflict or emotional tension.*

Strength Based means you want to build new skills while **Replacing** old behavior rather than attempt to extinguish, destroy, or prohibit. Frequent and consistent teaching is also **Strength Based** because it emphasizes the importance of learning the skill and decreases the emphasis on the importance of any specific topic or event.

The more often you teach a skill the quicker your child can learn it and make it into a new habit.

Make Sure Your Child Gets More When Cooperating

Often times children feel that they get more through lying, stealing, arguing, and manipulating than when they behave and are cooperative. Even when they get in trouble they often get more of a parent's attention than when they listen and obey.

So, for many kids misbehaving is a win/win proposition. They get more when misbehaving than when they are good. Even when in trouble they are getting either all your attention or more of it than their siblings who are being good. We have known many siblings who have spent years being the good one feeling resentful and then finally deciding to join in bad asocial behavior just to get some attention.

It is understandable that a parent would focus their energy on dealing with problems and crisis and take the good times for granted or as a moment of personal respite. Yet, it is also understandable for a child who gets more by being selfish, argumentative, and not following the rules to choose that route over being cooperative. While both perspectives are logical, they are not beneficial or necessary.

We've heard many parents state that they felt that good behavior is to be expected and not be rewarded. Rewarding good behavior is viewed by some parents as a form of bribery and is an indication that their child has a faulty or impoverished value system. Being good and doing the right thing, it is often noted, should be its own reward.

While we agree that good behavior and life affirming values should not depend on bribery or heavy reward, we would add that not many children are born compassionate, polite, and ethically sound. Most children have to be taught how to share, consider others feelings, and to do the right thing. The question then becomes how do we teach these values.

Rewarding your child does not necessarily mean giving them money, extra deserts, or other such tangible objects. Often times their reward involves your smiles, words of pride and appreciation, and your willingness to do something they want to do as recognition for their efforts and good decisions. Most people find fun more rewarding than hardship, but they also find feeling good about themselves very rewarding. When our external **Praise** and physical rewards become internalized, our child's doing the right thing becomes its own reward.

We live in a very competitive consumer based society in which our children can find many ways to access rewards and creature comforts while not doing what we want them to do. While getting desired things through cheating or manipulating destroys the self-concept and is not as fulfilling as getting something earned, it is still often chosen over not getting anything at all. We have previously discussed how lying and stealing can become areas of a certain sense of pride and control. Yet even in the most extreme cases we can usually find ways to make earning things more rewarding and fulfilling.

A parent who routinely rewards their children with **Praise**, pride, affection, and personal gifts is often able to give their child more than they can get through any other means. Your attention, especially your positive and fun based attention, is very, very important to your child even if they don't show it.

A child who is amply rewarded can feel and see the benefits of using desired skills and being respectful. Yet, the longer they have found rewards through asocial and selfish means, the more they will have to be convinced that doing the right thing is worth all the effort.

Make Sure Consequences Have a Positive Goal

- *As an opportunity for learning*
- *Monetary, emotional, or functional restitution/amends*
- *As a means to earn back your trust and heal the relationship*

Above we mentioned the importance of making sure that your child gets more when they cooperate than when they don't. One way you can accomplish this is to make sure they get less when they do not act in a respectful or socially acceptable manner. Consequences are one way in which you can make sure they are getting less by giving them assignments occupying their time or using restrictions which limit their access to things they desire. Let's take a more detailed look at the three possible uses of consequences listed above and how they can be positive consequences.

A positive usage of consequences is to have your child learn something that relates to their misbehavior. If they are caught lying about something very important, have them write a paragraph about how they felt when they were lied to by a friend and how it affected their relationship. *Make sure to discuss what they write to help cement the "moral" of the story.* If your child was excessively rude and disrespectful in how they treated you, they could be required to write a paragraph on the benefits and importance of respect.

Whenever you make a written assignment it is usually important to follow it up with a discussion to insure that they took the assignment seriously and that they are internalizing its content. If your child doesn't give their best effort, then give them an additional story or article to read that pertains to the topic at hand. One of the beauties of the internet is that you can type in a few key words like "stories and fables about hurtful words" and a slew of potential resources instantly pop up for you to select.

It is hard to imagine any moral or topic on which you won't be able to find some articles, fables, and even short videos on the internet teaching to the subject. Consistent use of the technique of giving your child additional assignments until they give a strong effort will eventually motivate your child to try their best on the first assignment so that their consequence can end quickly.

While we focused on written assignments, you can use any medium at your disposal to have your child learn how to do or say things better the next time. A child who took too long to do a chore such as sweeping the floor, might be given an additional chore to do and be given a reasonable amount of time to complete it. Once done, you can emphasize the importance of doing a task quickly so that the flow of the home is not hindered or disturbed. At the close of the discussion get a verbal commitment by your child to be more on task the next time they sweep the kitchen floor.

A final story of how to use teaching consequences involves a volatile but sensitive older adolescent named Keith who lived in a group home. The female houseparent (who was seven months pregnant) was in the room when Keith went into a verbal tirade. The male houseparent dealt with Keith's tantrum and the pregnant house parent left the area.

When Keith was calm, the male houseparent educated Keith on the effects his shouting could have had on the baby's nervous system. While reassuring him that babies are resilient Keith was also informed that studies showed babies can tell the difference in speakers, and it would be good if he could reassure the baby that everything was all right.

Keith was quite remorseful and wanted to make amends. When Keith said he was ready, the female house parent was brought back in the room so he could let the baby hear that everything was all right. When Keith asked the pregnant houseparent if there was anything he could do, she suggested he read the baby a bedtime story and although he was a little embarrassed, he did. The lesson seemed well learned as Keith did not have another major blow out the remainder of his stay.

The story of Keith involves both a learning consequence and an opportunity to make amends. If a child has done something mean they can always be assigned an act of kindness as a way of emotional restitution. If they have acted irresponsibly they can be given a responsibility, such as walking the dog each night for a week or taking the garbage out each night. If they stole something they could find a way to return it and either do an act of charity or give away something they own.

If your child has broken or stole something (that cannot be returned), then monetary restitution is often a good choice. If your child has broken a window or broke some furniture then have them work it off through various chores done around the house for a few dollars an hour.

When a child has violated your trust or abused your relationship with them, your consequence will deal with earning back your trust and restoring the relationship. A parent who has lost trust in their child can keep them on a very short leash and restrict and monitor their movement. While this often involves a child "being grounded," it can also involve numerous check-ins via phone calls made to parents, bosses, teachers, etc., who can track their movement and provide you with updates.

Let your child know that the more they accept and comply with the restrictions and check-ins, the quicker trust in them will be restored and the sooner they will be able to enjoy their old freedoms and autonomy. Often times children need to be reminded that trust, freedom, free time, and fun time with you, the family, and their friends is earned and not a basic right. Generally, the more responsibility one can successfully and maturely handle, the more that freedom and autonomy are given. This applies to not only home life, but at a job, school, or any organized social group.

In the chapter **Cooperation and Avoiding Power Struggles** under the subsection **Consequences that Promote Good Behavior**, we discussed the benefits of making sure a child receiving a hefty or long term consequence can shorten and lighten it through complying and giving a good effort. When a child is given no incentive to comply and behave, they often treat the consequence as a jail sentence and decide to spend much of their energy punishing their jailer as they merely serve their time. Please refer to that chapter for a more thorough explanation.

Parents who give long punishing consequences with no light at the end of the tunnel often end up being more punished by the consequence than their child. It is very important that you do not give consequences to your child which are brutal or emotionally draining for you to enforce.

> *Consequences with positive goals such as a lesson being learned, restitution being made, and trust and* Relationships *being restored are easier to manage, less punishing on the parent, and less apt to become mired in perpetual power struggles and hissy fits.*

A child can meet and counter a parent's anger with their own, and the resulting battle often has the child feel justified in their venom. Soon in their mind the issue isn't what they did or said, but is their parent's hateful and bad attitude through which they have to suffer. Most angry punishing consequences end with almost nothing learned by the child except a solid personal conviction that they are the victim of the situation.

While it is often easy for children to deflect or battle a parent's anger, it likely is harder for them to avoid a parent talking about the emotions that lie behind their anger. Most parents who are angry with their children are also deeply disappointed in their child's words and behavior and feel hurt as well. It is unrealistic to expect parents to not be angry at their child or not have it seep into the conversations that accompany the administering of a consequence. Yet, it is quite feasible for parents to (at least towards the conclusion of the discussion) state and emphasize how disappointed or hurt they were by their child's actions requiring the consequence.

Parents of older adolescents often complain that their children are too old to truly have any aspect of their life restricted for any length of time; making harsh consequences almost impossible to design, let alone implement. We would generally agree with this viewpoint and say that any parenting strategy heavily laden with long and hefty restriction-based consequences has little chance of producing good results, even if they are enforceable. Such situations often become adversarial and an all out battle for control.

When the majority of consequences are relatively short and not extremely emotionally intense, our child can see the underlying care and concern in our efforts to have them act and speak in a suitable manner. *Positive consequences designed to teach and make amends are easier for our child to perceive as an act of care and often strengthen their bond with us.* It is upon this caring instructive relationship that your child's acceptance of highly restrictive consequences are based, as will be their appreciation that they have crossed a very important line.

While modern technologies make it harder and harder to enforce highly restrictive consequences which isolate your child, there are still ways you can have your child feel a tad exiled until they learn, make amends, or earn back your trust. Even with older children one can always make continued services you provide them contingent on their engaging in respectful and socially acceptable behavior. A menu of such services would include things like use of car, monetary assistance, access to home based technologies, payment of phone bills, cooking their meals, washing their clothes, or any number of independent living skills they are not usually required to do. As mentioned earlier, hefty consequences could also stress important social aspects in and out of the home such as privacy, autonomy, and use of free time.

We want to stress again that consequences with positive goals generally fair much better than highly restrictive consequences. Highly restrictive or harsh consequences work best when used sparingly. We also want to remind parents that care and effort need to be put in the design of consequences to insure that you are not being restricted or punished by the implementation of the consequence.

Summary of Effective Tool Use

What it is:

We outlined three basic principles to help insure proper and effective use of the parenting tools presented in this book. One is to have your teaching be **Strength Based**; another is to make sure your child gets more when they are respectful and cooperate; and the third is to that your consequences have a positive goal.

Why use it:

The principles discussed help assure that your child accepts, internalizes, and implements what you are teaching them. No matter how good your tools, if they are not used correctly "your results may vary," usually in the negative.

Reframe, Replace, and Rewire:

Using the tools in your tool box in a **Strength Based** manner allows you to **Reframe** your child's behavior in a positive light. By focusing on and emphasizing their respectful attitude and cooperative actions, you can begin to **Replace** the conflictual and tense atmosphere of your home with one that is calm and supportive. The mutually reinforcing interactions of parent and child will result in **Rewiring** all family members to look forward to spending more time with each other and having the family be a source of comfort and support.

The effective use of the skills and strategies contained in ***The Parental Toolbox*** results in comfortable and successful interactions and experiences with our children. Each warm, comfortable feeling and caring, successful thought we have has its corresponding biochemistry and neurology. *What we think and feel is what we become, and through the frequent use of effective tools we* **Rewire** *ourselves and our children into compassionate, respectful, and loving individuals.*

Effective Tool Use
Home Improvement Projects

1. List some ways you can start **Catching Your Child Being Good**. How will you remind yourself to do this?

2. List some ways you can start **Catching Yourself Being Good**. How can you reinforce your effective use of ***The Parental Tool Box***?

3. Psychology teaches us the importance of stating positives each day. Get or make a blank journal for the family, and every night at dinner have each person write down (or write it for them if your child is not able) **3 positive things in their life**. Or, if every night seems too daunting a task, try for once a week or on the first Monday of each month. This ca become an established **Family Ritual**.

4. List some ways you can reinforce the good times in your family which are age appropriate for your child.

5. Write a **Script** of something you want to say to your child. Have someone you trust read this **Script** to you. How did you feel in your body as this **Script** was read to you? What was effective and comfortable? What was less effective and less comfortable?

Chapter Twenty-Seven

Visual Guides, Aids, and Documentation

In this chapter we'll give an overview of tangible ways to track where your child has been, where they're going, and how to get there. While you may be familiar with many of the tangible and visual ways to document, track, and motivate, it is always good to review ideas that can be updated or reused.

What we are about to cover is therapeutic in the widest sense since it will mainly deal with your child's day-to-day successful functioning in all areas of life including academic, social and the interpersonal. We will only scratch the surface of the potential applications of many of these mediums and leave it to you to adapt it to your and your child's specific goals and needs.

Diaries and Journals

Personal **Diaries** have been a favorite of adolescents (especially females) for centuries. While some personal **Diaries** can be useful, many are often little more than a safe place to complain about peers, parents, and any other pet peeve a child may have.

We are **Advocating** the use of **Diaries** and **Journals** as venues for personal growth, insight, goal setting, and progress tracking; a source for conversation and processing with you; as well as a means of personal expression. The frequency, goal, and style of the journal or **Diary** is something that can be negotiated between you and your child.

The subject matter of a **Diary** or **Journal** can be wide ranged or very specific and its topics can stay the same or change as often as each day. A parent could occasionally, or frequently, assign specific topics to be explored or give a potential menu of suitable topics for their child to choose from each day.

Your child is always free to have a personal **Diary** or **Journal**, but a therapeutic one is a source for conversation and dialogue. This means the therapeutic journal is something you are given permission to read or at least its subject matter is to be openly discussed. It is often a good idea to promise that the information shared from the **Diary** or **Journal** will remain confidential among your child and parenting adults, unless the information shared by your child shows her to be a danger to herself or others. In the therapeutic world safety always takes precedence over confidentiality, but in all other cases confidentiality is honored.

There are literally hundreds, if not thousands, of ways in which you can structure and use the **Diary** or **Journal** format. Before moving on we'll quickly mention a couple of problem solving and strength based **Diary** models.

Therapeutic Diary and Journal Ideas

1. Gratitude Journal - *Your child could write three things each day for which they are grateful or thankful. This type of journal helps reinforce their positive feelings.*
2. Angry Feelings Journal - *If your child is emotionally reactive, you could have them create an anger management journal in which they document when they felt angry and how they dealt with or expressed those feelings. When processing their anger issues, it is often helpful to have them* Reframe *statements of blame towards others to statements of what they did and how they could have responded differently.*
3. Goal Setting Diary - *Your child could keep a goal setting* Diary *in which each evening before going to sleep, they write down their goals for the next day while reviewing how they did on the goals they set the previous night.*
4. Success Journal - *Your child could keep a success journal in which each day they list their*

accomplishments.

5. **Skill Journal** - *Another version of this is where your child keeps track of all the times they used a skill that they are trying to master, tracking both successes and missed opportunities.*
6. **Food Diary** - *Your child could keep a food intake journal to help them maintain a healthy diet (please seek professional guidance on how to implement this journal if your child exhibits any tendency towards an eating disorder).*

Notebooks

The main difference between **Notebooks** and **Diaries** or **Journals** is that **Notebooks** are not written in a narrative form. **Notebooks** are typically a collection of pictures, facts, data, or examples organized according to sections. While the old spiral notebook is the general model, notebooks can be on computers, handheld devices, or in any format where information can be added and placed in its corresponding section.

Notebooks are a great way for your child to organize and keep track of an ever expanding or evolving subject matter. In many cases the information could be stored in separate folders inside of a larger notebook. In essence, **Notebooks** are a centrally located tangible resource to help guide, remind, and be available for review.

Notebooks are great tools for creating a master resource file for academics. One can have a vocabulary or spelling master list. One could also construct an ongoing math master file of formulas and model problems for everything from fractions and decimals to solving quadratic equations or problems with more than one variable.

Your child could construct a **Notebook** portfolio of their drawings, photos, or visual directions on how to draw specific objects. **Notebooks** could also be constructed of study and memorization skills, organizational tips, or reminders and exercises as to how to deal with transitions, calm oneself down, or any other number of social skill tools.

Other areas ripe for **Notebooks** would be a master list of social skills and their components, or a list of household chore cards and "how to do" instructions for anything from lawn mower and car maintenance to recipes and cooking instructions. Such **Notebooks** can be physically tangible and kept in binders, or they can be on a computer, earmarked websites, or apps on devices. The important thing is for them to be user friendly and frequently reviewed and used.

Charts and Calendars

It is the rare home in which no one is in need of gentle reminders to do all the tasks they've been assigned. Visual reminders in the form of **Charts and Calendars** are for many individuals a necessary element in being able to complete all their goals for a day, week, or month.

We've already discussed the beauty of **Chore Cards** in which **Clear** and **Specific Instructions** are written down allowing for even the most forgetful child to meet expectations when doing a routine task or chore. Similarly, in the subsection **Building Family Relationships** and **Minimizing Unwanted Influences** included in the chapter on **Parenting in the 21st Century**, we gave examples of **Weekly Activity Charts** and **Calendars** which guide your children into identifying and developing wide areas of interests. Such charts can be very therapeutic in their design and goals as well as a great and fun means for your child to feel productive, engaged, and talented.

Attaching familial recognition with the fulfillment of doing all assigned tasks is a wonderful way of creating support and teamwork. This is especially true if there is a group reward for the family, such as a special outing, when everyone has completed their goals and assigned tasks.

Goal Oriented Charts can involve anything from tasks to complete or social skills to master. **Family Goals** could be posted, such as being complimentary or patient, as a gentle reminder to promote **Family** cohesion and **Harmony**.

Ceremonies and Rites

Ceremonies and **Rites of Passage** have played an important role in tribes, communities, and societies as a means of insuring shared values and recognizing personal accomplishments. While your family may already celebrate religious and national holidays as well as partake in religious, social, and ethnic ceremonies, there are many opportunities to start your own traditions and formal rites of passage or recognition.

There are hundreds of things you could celebrate or recognize which can unite the family or have the spot light placed on one of its members. Graduation, academic accomplishment, mastery of a skill, progress in music, sport or art, or the acquiring of a new job are all moments to celebrate and savor.

Ceremonies are a great way to mark the end of one stage of life and usher in the new. **Rituals** can be used to motivate, excite, applaud, or fill one with pride. We can use **Rituals** to take a moment to appreciate the good times or as a time to recommit oneself to a goal or a desired path.

While many **Rituals** can be traditions which involve milestones that every family member will one day accomplish such as graduation or a first job, there are numerous **Rituals** you can create which are specific to the unique personality or needs of an individual child. Many times these individual **Rituals** can be designed to tend to a therapeutic issue of personal importance which might be celebrated with just the parents or one-on-one.

An individual child might be recognized for overcoming a specific fear, or working on a sensitive issue. A child who has a tendency to hoard could have a weekly or monthly **Ceremony** in which they choose a few items to throw away. A child whose sense of guilt makes it important that they are able to "*clean the slate*," and start anew may have a weekly **Ritual** in which they write down all the wrongs they think they have done, and then you either bury or burn the list with them.

Family Nights can often be a very fun and rewarding family **Ritual**. A movie night is a great time to enjoy shared laughter, some affection, and favorite treats. While movies can be rewarding just in the shared time together, they also can serve a therapeutic purpose while remaining very entertaining. You can find movies which are inspirational, moving, and motivating with a specific subject matter that speaks to either one child or to the entire family.

The Art and Artifacts of Family

Many families decorate their walls and end tables with family photos of important events, accomplishments and vacations. Likewise, works of art, achievements, and awards of family members are often posted on the refrigerator or are prominently displayed throughout the home. These recognitions of family members create a sense of warmth and connection to friends, pets, and relatives while showing pride in each member of the family unit.

Each photo, souvenir, or piece of memorabilia you display that commemorates an individual accomplishment or captures familial intimacy is an opportunity to further solidify family bonds of love and care. The more purposeful attention you give to the what and how of the placement of your treasured memories the more impact they can have. Sometimes even the most powerful memories can be weakened by the photo being placed in the same spot too long where it no longer stands out or attracts anyones attention.

You could use your creativity to do family projects and activities which show or document family unity, goals, and accomplishments. Some families make a family coat of arms or construct a small totem pole which represent their shared values, history, and traits. Doing videos, audio tapes, or written interviews of grandparents, or other dear relative's life stories also add to a family's sense of pride and cohesion. Family trees are another great exploratory resource which can be documented on paper and lovingly displayed in the home. Making yearly calendars from family pictures and art work is another great way to show pride.

While the possibilities are endless we'll close with a couple of musical suggestions. A family could find a song with sentimental or nostalgic ties which they adopt as their theme song. The family tune could be the song that both parents or even grandparents remember as being "their song." It could also be a song which the entire family remembers being played during a particularly nice time, like at a wedding, vacation, or graduation ceremony. On another note (pun intended) a family could invent their own lyrics for an old song or write their own family song. A family could keep the same song for years, or maybe vote on new songs during a **Family Meeting** each year.

Summary of Visual Guides, Aids, and Documentation

What it is:

In this chapter we discussed the benefits and beauty of having visual aids to assist in the smooth functioning of the home and as a means of documenting and celebrating the bonds of the family as well as the individual accomplishments of its members. Many tangible and visual mediums were hinted at and a few explored included the use of **Diaries**, **Journals**, **Notebooks**, **Charts**, and **Calendars**. We also discussed the role and power of cultural and ethnic **Rituals**, **Traditions**, and **Rites** as well as the possibility of your family inventing their own ways of recognizing, celebrating, and documenting the importance of family.

Why Use It:

Many people are more visually oriented than auditory when it comes to learning and processing their experiences. A family home that provides many types of visual assistance, recognition, and documentation of family history is more likely to function smoothly while being able to celebrate and appreciate the importance of familial intimacy.

Reframe, Replace, and Rewire:

Charts and **Visual Aids** are not only vital tools for visual learners but also a great way to document, motivate, and regulate progress. **Visual Aids Frame** things in a way making misinterpretations or misunderstanding of goals and performance nearly impossible. The documentation aspects of visual aids and charts make it easy to **Replace** unproductive or empty time with concrete beneficial activities. **Activity Charts** as well as any other **Visual Aids** which encourage, measure, and celebrate growth and success are an excellent means of ensuring that a sufficient amount of repetition occurs allowing the biochemical and neurological **Rewiring** to take place.

Visual Guides, Aids and Documentation Home Improvement Projects

1. Which of the **Diaries**, **Journals** or **Notebooks** are appropriate for you?
2. In a **Family Meeting** introduce the topic of **Diaries**, **Journals**, and **Notebooks** and have each family member commit to trying one for the next month. Reevaluate after one month the pros and cons of doing this.
3. Making **Activity Charts** or **Skill Based Growth Charts** for each family member normalizes the function of learning and valuing change. Although each member can make their own, it is a wonderful way to build family unity by giving input and helping each other identify goals and make them together. Finding a place to post them side by side is a great way to reinforce the daily use of the charts.
4. What are the **Ceremonies** and Rites particular to your family?
5. In a **Family Meeting** discuss some new **Ceremonies** and **Rites** which you would like to adopt as a family.
6. What are some ways in which you could honor your family using **Arts** and **Artifacts**?

Chapter Twenty-Eight

Liking Your Own Skin

When it comes to therapeutic growth and learning skills your body is a very important player. A person who does not physically feel good or has a very low energy level often finds it hard to act their best. We all know what kind of hurdle it is when you're uncomfortable, irritable, or in pain, and how difficult it can then be for you to be polite, respectful, or considerate of other's feelings. A person who does not physically feel good often finds it hard to feel good about themselves mentally.

In the chapter, **Give What You've Got** we talked about the benefits of taking care of yourself and pointed out the simple reality that a parent can only give what they have. We emphasized that a parent needed to take time for themselves to recharge their batteries and feel good about their lives. Without a bit of self-pampering most parents would have a hard time being a good role model or be able to maintain a positive attitude.

While it is extremely important for parents to feel good in their own skin, it is also just as important that their child is generally rested, healthy, physically comfortable, and pain free. It is normal for any active child to have scratches, bumps, and bruises that come along with doing an occasional activity to excess. Yet, a child who feels good physically has an easier time feeling good mentally, and a child with a healthy self-concept who feels good mentally has a much easier time being happy and respectful.

Exercise, Laughter, and Play

Clinical studies, questionnaires, and personal interviews all seem to indicate that **Laughter**, **Play**, and **Exercise** are good for your physical and mental health as well as lifting depression and enhancing one's mood. While perfect health is an ideal that few, if any, people attain, people who **Laugh** frequently, **Play**, and **Exercise** are generally healthier people. As it turns out, from a mental and physical health perspective, fun and enjoyment are definitely not a waste of time.

While we have never heard of someone laughing to excess, we have known people to take play and exercise to harmful extremes. Therefore, while **Exercise** and **Play** are highly beneficial and can be a boon to therapeutic growth, it is important to monitor them so that they do not become structured in compulsions and addictions.

We noted in an earlier chapter that most higher animals, humans included, learn much of their skill set through **Play**. While infants learn most of their skills through **Play**, even preschool and early elementary school children learn most quickly when information is associated with a dance, song, or game.

Studies have shown that high school students who engage in physical activity shortly before taking a test or doing an assignment scored better, often dramatically so, than students who hadn't **Exercised**. So, not only does a child who **Exercises** feel better but they also perform better in academic settings (Ratey, 2008).

Many of the tools mentioned in this book have to do with your child learning and mastering basic social skills. We also noted that your child would be less resistive to learning the skills and would master them quicker if you made your instruction fun or into a game. Another great example of this comes from working at group homes. A house of nine adolescent boys was not doing very well with most of the boys resisting being respectful and cooperative. The house parent took the boys outside and played "skill catch" with them. Each time the ball was thrown it was accompanied by an **Instruction, Criticism**, an opportunity to **Accept No** or **Respectfully Disagree**, or some other social skill the boys were working on. Within a few minutes all the boys were having fun with the game and began using the skills with smiles on their faces. This activity soon became a house favorite and all the boys in the cottage mastered the skills in short order.

You can encourage and build play and exercise into much of what you do with your kids. Whether it be through the development of activity or **Goal Charts** or by parking at the opposite end of the mall where you plan to shop, you can create a growing appreciation of exercise.

Baby steps of increasing exercise works better than ambitious attempts to drastically increase your child's level of activity. Many forms of Play are not particularly physically challenging, and many parents find **Play** easier to introduce than **Exercise**. Yet, the more fun your child is having with you, the more open they will be to adding a little **Exercise** to the **Play** and good times.

While one cannot always plan **Laughter**, it often accompanies **Play**. If we play and are playful, then **Laughter** is sure to follow. Watching comedy movies the entire family can enjoy is a way to schedule fun and **Laughter**. A parent on the look out for **Laughter** can usually find it in humorous plays, TV shows, books, or situations.

No Body's Perfect, but...

While aerobic **Exercise**, sports, and games are a great way to improve one's spirits and make a body healthier and more stress free, it surely isn't the only way to attain these benefits. Improvements in diet can add energy, reduce anxiety and nervousness, and strengthen one's immune system.

Since each person's metabolism and body are different, there is no one diet which is best for everyone. While we can make some general statements about the benefits of avoiding massive amounts of sugar, fats, and highly processed foods as well as the benefits of a daily intake of vegetables, proteins, and vitamins, there is no "one size fits all" when it comes to food intake.

When it comes to your child's diet, the best a parent can do is to observe the effects specific foods have on their energy level, mood, and weight. Often times a problem can be not so much in what your child eats, but when they choose to eat it. Many foods eaten in the morning which may actually benefit their performance at school may prevent them from going to sleep if eaten right before bedtime.

About the only constant in an adolescents life is that they are in constant change. Between growth spurts, hormonal floods, and puberty every aspect of their body and brain are in a state of flux. Even if an ideal diet did exist for your twelve year old, it would not be the ideal diet when they are fourteen. Therefore, changes in your child's diet are to be expected, and their weight, energy level, and over all health should help guide you to what adjustments you can and should make.

Since our knowledge of diet is ever expanding, it is always good to read articles or books on the subject. If ever in complete doubt one should consult a pediatrician or a dietician for guidance.

When doctors and health care professionals talk about how best you can help your child be and feel healthy and function at their maximum, they usually put sleep on the same level as diet and **Exercise**. All the physical, emotional, and psychological changes of adolescence require and use up a great deal of energy. While food provides the fuel and **Exercise** keeps the system running smoothly, sleep insures that your child can function at their maximum when they are awake. A sleep deprived child is one who has difficulty concentrating and learning which weakens their immune system making them more vulnerable to stress and disease.

Lack of Joy and Enjoyment

It is extremely rare to find a child who is in placement, therapy, or some form of therapeutic intervention whose sense of joy and enjoyment doesn't increase when they master skills or begin to reach their clinical goals. Similarly, most children who find **Joy** and **Enjoyment** in their life most of the time, and who also are showing respect for themselves and others most of the time, are not usually in need of therapeutic interventions.

A person who is frequently in pain and discomfort has a difficult time finding **Joy** in their moment-to-moment existence. Individuals whose skin always itches, have frequent headaches, stomach aches, gastrointestinal issues, or colds is seldom a happy and content individual. Likewise, people who have sensorial sensitivities to bright light, loud sounds, and strong smells and yet are made to spend a great deal of time in such environments have a difficult time maintaining good behavior.

Our body's health and comfort plays a huge role in our general mood and how much joy and enjoyment we glean from our experiences.

Trying to focus on our child's behavior or psychology while ignoring the body is often self-defeating. Skill development, education, and insight offer great therapeutic potential, but their benefits are greatly reduced if the body remains pained, uncomfortable, or physically ill.

> *So, while therapeutic, social, and personal success can have a person feel better and be open to* Joy, *the body still needs to get rest,* Exercise, *and have a diet which increases overall health, energy, and comfort levels.*

Improvements in your child's level of **Joy** and **Enjoyment** is a very good indication that you are going in the right therapeutic direction. While we are emphasizing the importance of the body's health, we do not want to underestimate the impact that a positive **Frame** of mind can have on how the body feels.

> *A parent's* Praise, *affection, and assistance at having your child be successful socially and interpersonally will go a long way to having them be comfortable in their body and like being in their skin.*

Yet, just as injurious to one's sense of enjoyment as body discomfort can be, a sense of being unaware of the body or being absent from one's sensorial experience can also be harmful. We have worked with many children who for one clinical reason or another are absent or not present in their body. These are the children who cannot tell you what they had to eat fifteen minutes after dinner. Due to fears, anxieties, compulsions, attention deficits, or some form of mental preoccupation they are just not present in their bodies (Ogden, Fisher, 2015).

With such children their lack of being aware of their own bodies or present in sensorial experience makes it hard to assess if they are fleeing their skin due to pain and discomfort or if it's an act of the mind. In many therapeutic placements the percentage of children who are absent to the majority of their sensorial experiences can be quite high.

With such children getting them to be present and a part of

their sensorial experience is just as high a priority as the mastery of any social skill. In fact, sensory awareness if often one of the first skills they are asked to learn and master. Years of working with such children seems to indicate that their ability to feel **Joy** and find **Enjoyment** in life is greatly enhanced when they learn how to appreciate their own experience. Being in their body and aware of their surroundings is often the first step in their ability to like and appreciate themselves and establish compassionate **Relationships** with others.

Parents of children who are unaware of their sensorial experience can find fun ways to quiz their children on their environment and what they are physically feeling, seeing, and hearing as a way to have their child derive pleasure and **Joy** from their experiences.

Sensory games could include having your child close their eyes and identify things put in their mouth, or play name that tune, what's that smell, or what is that texture? You could also have them do a number of different physical activities and have them become increasingly aware of the changes in their heart rate, breathing, and body temperature that each activity induces.

Yet, most children who are absent are not present for a reason, plus they are comfortable and familiar with this habit. You will likely meet some resistance when asking your child to be aware and in their body, so be patient and make the exercises fun and enjoyable. If resistance persists or increases it probably would be a good idea to seek professional assistance to help assess the possible deep seated need your child has to distance themselves from their body and their experience.

Probably the most common reason that adolescent children miss an opportunity for **Joy** and **Enjoyment** is because they "are bored." Boredom is almost certainly the most common experience and complaint of children in placement and therapy. It should not be surprising that unhappy or discontented children have difficulty engaging or investing themselves in what they are doing. The most frequent solution to this problem is usually just increasing your child's social and relationship skill levels and that will engender success. With success will come their **Enjoyment** and emotional investment in what they are doing.

Indirect or Self-Destructive Joys

Children with poor self-esteem often seem to be happiest when they are being mean, irritating others, or doing damage to or defacing public or private property. Anyone who has worked with these children quickly understands that this is not authentic **Joy**, but is a perverse and usually a retaliatory one. The **Joy** is fleeting and its source is just in the ability to incite in others anger, pain, or frustration.

Some children find a form of solace and a release of tension through being a bully or when engaging in mean, disrespectful, or irritating behavior. A part of this **Joy** is often in the sense of power and control they acquire through getting people to react or be afraid of them. There are a number of children who get a sense of power or at least a sense of validation of their poor self-esteem by goading others into shunning, hurting, or exploiting them. Such children often deem themselves as damaged goods, and those abusing them only prove that their view of themselves is accurate.

Whether the underlying source of their temporary **Joy** is solace, power, release of stress, or validation of their being a victim or unloveable, their repeated use of these indirect means of getting **Joy** become habitual. So, while these means are very ineffective, they can become a child's preferred way of acting and responding.

In the chapter on **Parenting the Non-Responsive Child**, we mentioned other self-destructive behaviors a child can engage in which can be used for solace, a release of tension, or as a delayed means of acting out. These behaviors include running away, suicidal gestures, substance abuse, scapegoating, and cutting or self-mutilation. In this context the scapegoating usually involves a child who goads others into abusing, humiliating, or hurting him.

Replacing Harmful Joy with Healthy Joy

Children can be quite resourceful in their efforts to deflect, relieve, or act out their physical, emotional, or psychological pain. In many cases these often risky, harmful, or self-injurious behaviors can become habitual or addictive. It is for this reason that, though they are a very ineffective means of experiencing **Joy**, the child will be resistive to **Replacing** these behaviors with more efficient and healthy means of **Enjoyment**.

We've already covered the benefits of **Exercise**, **Laughter**, and **Play** and the role they can have in creating **Joy** and **Enjoyment**. Likewise, we've discussed the benefits of rest and a good diet for helping someone feel good in their own skin. We've also pointed out numerous times that the success of any **Replacement** behavior is greatly increased if it is presented in a fun and **Enjoyable** manner and if its positive effects occur frequently.

In the subsection **Three Dimensions of Change** in the chapter **Maximizing Therapeutic Growth**, we explained the benefits of making sure your **Replacement** behaviors deal with the **Emotional**, **Psychological**, and **Biochemical** payoffs of the old behavior. So once again, we see the importance of this as we strive to create **Joy** and **Enjoyment**, or when we try to **Replace** old self-harming behaviors that harbor an addictive quality.

The introduction of fun and productive activities is one of the best ways to **Replace** *the biochemical component of resistive self-destructive or risky behaviors*. The **Activity Charts** which we have discussed on a few occasions have proven themselves to be very good at both engaging kids and getting them to find **Joy** and **Enjoyment** in healthy ways. **These Charts** are a great way for children to overcome their boredom; get in touch with their bodies; or **Replace** the biochemistry of risk taking, self-harm, and even substance abuse in a healthy manner.

It is somewhat counterintuitive to try to **Replace** cutting, substance abuse, and risky or self-destructive behavior with activities geared towards the experience of **Joy** and **Enjoyment**. The normal response we have to destructive, mean, and self-destructive behavior is to try to control and extinguish it. In any crisis and emergency a certain amount of control may be necessary to insure everyone's safety. Once safety is assured, resistances to the adoption of new skills and rewarding interests is best accomplished through **Play** and **Enjoyment**. *Learning*, we've noted often, *happens quickest and lasts the longest when it is fun and playful.*

Environmental Sensitivities

Some children, especially those on the Autism Spectrum, have notable and persistent sensitivities to specific sounds, lighting, textures, tastes, or smells. Parents of children and adolescents with such sensitivities need to do their best to honor these preferences by making changes in the home which help keep your child calm and comfortable. Likewise, parents need to inform and educate schools and other social environments of your child's needs.

Experience shows that improvements in diet, exercise, and social success can reduce some of the sensitivities. Any improvement you can make in your child's comfort level within their own skin will help in their tolerance of environments which they find challenging to their senses. Let's now look at an expanded list of activities a parent might consider to help their child be more comfortable in their own bodies.

Activities to Help Feel Comfortable in Your Body

Here are some activities you may find help you get comfortable in your own body (figure 28.1):

Body Enriching Activities

- Massage
- Meditation
- Yoga
- Martial arts
- Dance and movement
- Acupuncture
- Chiropractic
- Neurofeedback
- Bubble baths

**figure 28.1*

In this book we have tried to remain cognizant of the fact that many parents do not have infinite financial resources. With this in mind, we've tried to insure that most of our tools, suggestions, and strategies are not reliant on your spending much money. Yet, the list above contains some suggestions which could be quite expensive. This list is by no means essential, but may prove helpful in many situations.

Summary of Liking Your Own Skin

What it is:

Being comfortable in your own skin is accomplished when we are healthy, rested, and get sufficient exercise.

Why do it:

Children who are comfortable in their own skin experience **Joy** and treat themselves and others with respect.

Reframe, Replace, and Rewire:

A person in pain, tired, or physically uncomfortable has a difficult time feeling good about themselves or functioning at their best. **Liking Your Own Skin** is a **Strength Based Frame** of the desire to have one functioning at their best. A person comfortable in their body is able to **Replace** irritation, anger, and defiance with confidence, **Joy**, **Cooperation**, and kindness. The biochemistry and neurology of a person in pain is drastically different from a person who is comfortable and content. Each and every moment a person likes their own skin they are **Rewiring** themselves to feel that way more often.

Liking Your Own Skin Home Improvement Projects

1. What are three ways you can add more **Laughter**, humor, and **Joy** to your life?
2. What are three ways you can add more **Laughter**, humor and **Joy** to your relationship with your child?
3. What are the environmental sensitivities for each member of your family?
4. Getting a good night's rest begins with establishing healthy night time **Rituals**. Watching TV, being on the computer, or using devises right before bedtime stimulates the brain rather than calming it down. How can you reinforce healthy, age appropriate, bedtime **Rituals** without it turning into a power struggle?
5. Are there any items on the **Activities to Help Being Comfortable in Your Body** list which you are willing to start with your child?

Twenty-Nine

The Big Picture Part 1: Designing a Long Term Plan

There are few things in life that can be as exhausting and gratifying as being a parent. The role of parent is many things including a responsibility, challenge, opportunity, and gift. Infants grow into children, who grow into preteens, to teenagers, and then young adults. So while our goal as a parent is to always do the right thing and hit the bullseye, the reality of the situation is that we're aiming at a moving target.

Adapting to the continual changes in our children's mental capabilities, interests, and emotional maturity is a full time job. In this chapter we will talk about ways in which you can use knowledge of your child's basic character and personality to come up with longer term plans and goals. This master plan will help you prioritize your parenting goals including what needs and skills to address and in what order.

In a clinical setting such a master plan is often referred to as a **Therapeutic Treatment Plan**. We will use this format as a basic model to help you construct your own master plan for your child.

Master Treatment Plans

Many of you reading this have attended treatment team meetings for, or with, your child in which clinicians, therapists, social workers, program and/or school staff, and maybe an **Advocate** review your child's progress and come up with future goals. The meeting is based on a **Master Treatment Plan** which often gets amended and updated during the meeting with all participants signing off on goals and decisions made.

Master Treatment Plans are based on various documents such as interviews with parents, psychological evaluations, and social, medical, and academic histories. The frequency of treatment team meetings varies due to funding source guidelines and policies, as well as agency standards. **The Long Term Goals** of a therapeutic treatment plan may change little, but short term goals usually evolve with your child.

It might prove helpful if we take a look inside the structure of a **Master Treatment Plan**. After a short adjustment period allowing your child to get acclimated, the first set of goals focus on having your child be respectful and compliant with the adults with whom they interact. This is very logical for one can only teach and assist a child who is listening to and respecting the adults in charge of monitoring and documenting their progress.

Once a child has demonstrated a willingness to accept the help being offered them, they are assigned a second set of goals, skills, or target behaviors. These focus on their developing healthy and age appropriate **Relationships** with peers. If a child is very passive the goals will include skills such as standing up for ones rights, getting assistance, expressing opinions, and helping others. A child who is forceful may be asked to respect others privacy, develop boundaries, and to let others speak freely.

A child who is able to work and interact harmoniously with adults and peers is then assigned skills that focus on their own personal development and improvement. These skills may focus on resolving long standing personality or character tendencies which hamper their self-esteem or make it difficult for them to function successfully in society. All of these goals are geared towards improving the child's self-concept and quality of life helping them find ways of feeling engaged and connected while taking pride in their unique gifts and talents.

All goals are decided upon by a combination of observation and the various documentation mentioned above. Goals are assigned only when they are challenging, but attainable. Each set of goals is designed to build up the ego strength and positive feelings needed to be able to meet the next set of challenging goals.

Developing A Master Plan For Your Child

Many of you reading this have children who already have a treatment plan of some kind either for special education, treatment interventions, or as a part of out-of-home care. In such a case, your increased knowledge of the workings and goals of treatment planning may make it easier to support, enact, and monitor the plan as well as increase your ability to have input into its future evolution.

For those of you whose child does not have a therapeutic treatment plan, we will look at the potential reasons for creating a formal master plan. The job description of the average parent includes guiding and supporting your child. *The writing of a* **Master Treatment Plan** *allows you to guide and support your child in a very organized and intentional way.*

We all want our children to be healthy, happy, and comfortable with themselves and other people. In an organized plan we can express our hopes and dreams for our child regarding how they feel about themselves and interact with others. In essence, this is what most parents think about, and often act on, but most do not write it down and make it official.

The design and implementation of a formal master plan is based on the unique personality of your child. It involves the development of their interests and mastering important social skills which can bring them personal **Joy** and interpersonal success.

Such master plans are not a good idea if their goal is to control and force your child down a specific path that you need them to follow. In such circumstances, a master plan would be potentially injurious to your child's self-esteem and sense of individuality.

Let's take a brief moment to consider your qualifications for designing and writing a **Master Treatment Plan** for your child. As we mentioned at the beginning of this chapter, professionals construct therapeutic treatment plans based on a combination of tests, personal and social history of the child, interviews with the child and family, and clinical observation. So, unless you've been an estranged parent who has spent years away from your child you have the knowledge of their personal and social history.

The time you have recently spent with your child and plan to spend in the future allows you plenty of observation time. If you read this book thoroughly you will have a good idea of what to watch for to insure that your observations are clinically based. If you read additional parenting books and articles on how to deal with your child's feelings and behaviors you will also be able to insure that your master plan is focused on the best interests of your child and not on your own personal agenda.

In fact, the construction of a larger plan allows you an opportunity to wisely select some realistic and attainable initial skills and goals for your child to begin to learn and master. A formal plan allows you to monitor and document their progress helping you determine if you need to seek professional help in assessing and evaluating your child through tests and interviews.

We've stated on numerous occasions the importance of your developing a mutually respectful relationship with your child. The mastery of skills of cooperation contributes to the establishment of a harmonious environment. We've thoroughly outlined and have gone over the components of four basic social skills: **Accepting Criticism**; **Accepting No**; **Following Instructions**; and **Respectfully Disagreeing**. The learning and mastery of these basic skills would fit in with the initial skills that most therapeutic settings emphasize allowing for a child to be open to therapeutic assistance and guidance.

A very important qualification is your emotional investment in your child and a long history of care and concern for their success and happiness. Couple this with your intimate first hand knowledge of your child and the accompanying insights into their personality and habits, and your qualifications to construct an effective master plan seem quite sufficient.

Designing A Strength Based Master Plan

In a **Strength Based Master Plan** you have an excellent opportunity to articulate a shared vision of the type of person your child will become. In the chapter on **Appreciating and Valuing Change** under the subsection **Aligning Yourself With Your Child**, we outlined ways to include your child's wishes and goals into the skills we select for them to master. One of the tools discussed involved having your child choose from a menu of desired qualities such as funny, loyal, smart, kind, compassionate, friendly, determined, passionate, resourceful, caring, dynamic, charming, and brave. As we mentioned before, extensive lists of potential personality traits can be found on the internet to help your child in choosing the qualities they would like to possess.

In the chapter entitled **Personal and Family Values**, we referred you to lists of values which could be used to help you in coming up with **Long Term Goals** for your master plan. Using lists of personality traits and values, you will be able to find fitting goals upon which both you and your child can agree. While having your child's agreement on the master plans goals and objectives is not necessary, it surely is highly preferable.

A **Strength Based**, as opposed to a problem based, **Plan** is able to be optimistic and more attractive to your child. Rather than emphasizing what is wrong or a problem, *a* **Strength Based Plan** *begins with one's dreams and goals and then articulates a realistic way of attaining those goals.* This does not mean that you ignore or deny deficits or misused skills, but rather you address these weaknesses by focusing on the desired skill to be mastered.

In a **Strength Based** *format you design positive goals based on desired values and traits. You then convert those desired traits into skills to be mastered.* The mastery of the skill is then a way to have their desired quality built into their actions and become an integral part of their personality. By frequently identifying times when your child showed the quality by using the skill or when they missed an opportunity to use the skill, your child begins to understand what it takes to have others view them as loyal, kind, or as exhibiting whatever trait they desire to have.

We do not want the master plan to be experienced by your child as a force imposed from the outside, but as a guide to assist them with the challenges that they face and as a vehicle for their personal development. The more **Strength Based** you make your plan the more likely your child is going to emotionally and practically endorse it.

No matter what your child and you decide are the **Long Term Goals**, it is strongly recommended that your first set of goals deal with the mastery of skills having to do with respect and cooperation. As we've stated on numerous occasions, until you and your child are listening to each other and talking to each other in a respectful manner it will be difficult for any sophisticated or individualized instruction to take place.

The sets of skills to be assigned and mastered will be dictated by the goals and traits upon which you and your child agreed. If your child wants to be more assertive then you can have goals such as *Asking for Assistance, Expressing Feelings and Opinions*, and *Planning.* If they want to be kind you could go in the direction of *Volunteering, Supporting Others*, and *Compassion.*

If your child is persistent in choosing a quality with which you are uncomfortable making into a formal goal, you can use your ability to **Reframe** and choose a more suitable word of similar meaning. If they are adamant at "wanting to be the best" you could state that one becomes the best through "discipline" or "leadership" and then come up with skills and actions which foster discipline or leadership to help them accomplish their goals.

Your Child's Master Plan and Their Mental Health Diagnoses

Many of you reading this manual will be parents of children with one or more diagnoses. In the next chapter we will explore some of the ramifications your child's diagnoses can have on the way you approach skill instruction. Yet, at this moment you may be wondering how you rectify a diagnosis with a **Strength Based Master Plan**.

Many of your children with a diagnosis already have an active treatment plan for you to help implement and monitor. It would be counterproductive for you to design a master plan while one is already in use. Your personal **Strength Based** plan could be designed as part of a transition or termination phase of treatment to insure that the therapeutic thread does not get dropped or broken.

Yet, let's consider what a diagnosis is to help you assess how it can fit in with your **Strength Based Plan**. A diagnosis is a name given to a general constellation of behaviors which indicate a certain way of reacting to and being in the world. It is a useful shorthand and gives clinicians a common perspective from which to begin. Diagnoses are not life sentences but a starting point for all psychotherapy, cognitive behavioral, or medicinal interventions .

In essence your use of a diagnosis lies in the behaviors, attitudes, and perceptions that led to the diagnosis being assigned to your child. The questions you ask are what skills does a child with anxiety or an adolescent with bipolar disorder need to learn and master to be successful and happy?

Generally diagnoses are not **Framed** in **Strength Based** language and are instead laden with sickness and deficit terminology. There are many reasons for that, such as the use of the medical model which stresses disease and pathology and the need to state things as a problem to get funding for treatment.

Many may find it odd that we've remained silent on the role of pharmaceuticals in your child's treatment plan. This omission may seem more exaggerated when we've emphasized the need to tend to the biochemical as well as psychological components of a behavior when mastering and **Replacing** a behavior.

There is little debate that prescription medications can be a valuable and in some cases an essential intervention. There is also little debate on the fact that many pharmaceuticals are over prescribed. It is not for us, nor are we qualified, to either promote or dissuade you from making prescription medications a part of your child's therapeutic care. In this book we've been focusing on the ways you can stimulate and effect the biochemical economy naturally through activity and eliciting positive emotional responses.

In the following chapter we will move from designing to implementing a **Master Plan**.

Summary of Designing a Long Term Plan

What it is:

When you document your **Long Term Goals** for your child, that is considered to be a master plan. A **Strength Based Master Plan** involves the identification of a couple of desired personality traits or values your child would like to incorporate. The **Master Plan** is then used to identify and assign skills to master which help your child accomplish becoming the person they desire to be.

Why do it:

A **Master Plan** is a great way of giving direction to your parental teaching and support. The identification of **Long Term Goals** allows your child to see the purpose and benefit of mastering the skills as a way of helping them get where they want to go.

Reframe, Replace, and Rewire:

Long Term Plans are a great way to house and **Reframe Long Term Objectives** in a concrete and agreed upon manner. Often times **Long Term Plans** are a way to **Replace** impatience, urgency, crisis, and pressure with perspective, patience, and a recognizable path for all to work towards. **Long Term Goals** and plans can provide a consistency of vision and practice which foster the ability to **Rewire** one's personal and social path.

Designing a Long Term Plan Home Improvement Projects

1. What desired personality traits or values do you want to include in your child's **Long Term Plan/Master Treatment Plan**? Are they **Strength Based**?

2. Here are some interview questions to ask your child in helping you **Design** their **Long Term Plan**:

   ✓ *"What kind of person do you want to become?"*

   ✓ *"How do you want to be described by others?"*

   ✓ *"What traits or habits do you want to change?"*

3. What goals do you have for your child to achieve one year from now?

4. What goals do you have for your child to achieve five years from now?

5. Find a way to have a conversation with your child so you can let them know the goals you have developed. This might be best accomplished in the company of their therapist. Then, give them a chance to state their goals for the next year and five years.

Chapter Thirty

The Big Picture Part 2: Implementing Strength Based Plans

Let's look at an abbreviated list of some of the things you may want to consider in the design and implementation of a **Strength Based Individualized Plan** for your child. Most of the suggestions outlined will be a review of essential teaching tools as well as a sprinkling of a few new ideas to obtain a comprehensive view of important master plan considerations and guidelines.

1. Values and Personality Traits

While you are free to come up with your own completely original ideas for the major goals of your **Long Term Plan**, we suggest using lists of **Values** and personality traits as a menu from which to choose. While these lists are quite extensive, we will cite a few examples of possible goal plans you could design, such as: *Having a Career* and *Living on One's Own*; *Being Happy and Creative*; *Fame and Fortune*; *Influential and Helpful*; *Calm and Insightful*; or *Athletic and Healthy*.

These **Long Term Goals** will basically function as two word conceptual headings to give direction in helping you decide what type of skills to assign your child to master. If your child's goals are to have a career and be on their own, then the majority of your skills should focus on independent living skills and autonomy. If your child chose influential and helpful, you would choose targets such as leadership, teamwork, or critical thinking.

2. Respect and Cooperation

As we've mentioned numerous times, typically your first set of goals will deal with **Respect and Cooperation**. The most common skills in this area are **Following Instructions**, **Accepting No**, **Accepting Criticism**, and **Respectfully Disagreeing**, yet you could also have others such as attentive listening and cooperation.

Most children do best when they are only working on two or three goals at a time, so you might want to start with **Following Instructions**, **Respectfully Disagreeing**, and either **Accepting No** or **Accepting Criticism**. Try to make sure you include their strongest of these skills in the first batch so that they can experience some success.

3. Frequent Praise

It takes a lot of practice to **Replace** one habit with a new one. So when teaching a new skill make sure you identify and **Praise** the desired skill frequently. Remember *quantity and frequency plus supportiveness equals mastery*. A child may be given the skill of how to get someone's attention (which is a **Replacement** for interrupting or talking over others) when they typically begin a conversation by shouting for you from a few rooms away. Therefore, it could take much practice for them to get in the habit of seeking you out and making eye contact (first step) and saying excuse me before beginning a conversation with you.

In a **Strength Based Model** you would **Praise** the proper use of the skill and when possible address the misuse as a missed opportunity rather than as "misbehaving" or being difficult. This positive style reduces resistance and power struggles. **Replacing** *a behavior is more about learning a new skill* *and not so much about extinguishing an old habit.*

Yet, even in a **Strength Based** approach one should remain firm in expectations. When your child has a tantrum or takes an inordinate amount of time to use the skill, do not argue with them, get angry, or lecture. Instead, remain calm and patient and encourage them to use the skill. When the tantrum is over you could have them do some form of time "restitution" where they either do a task or have to wait for you to do the tasks that you couldn't get to during their tantrum.

4. Practice Patience

Be patient with yourself as well as your child. Don't expect to be perfect; it's okay for you to make mistakes. Any time you react poorly (such as entering into a debate or a power struggle with your child), just stop your reaction when you can, compose yourself, and go back to focusing on encouraging your child to use the skill. This would also require you to stop debating the topic or arguing over whose perceptions are right and whose are wrong. Likewise, do not panic when you realize that you missed an opportunity to **Praise** skill usage or that you didn't address an old habit you are trying to change. You can always go back and **Praise** a past event and thank your child for their efforts. Any bad habit you missed identifying in the moment, if it truly is a habit, will provide you with many opportunities to address and teach to it in the future.

5. Focus on the Positive and Set Your Child Up for Success

When assigning skills to your child make sure that you start easy and work towards more challenging or sensitive issues. Every improvement made and skill mastered will build up your child's confidence and self-esteem. Often times this increased ego strength is essential in their having the courage and determination to deal with a deeper seeded behavioral pattern or an emotionally sensitive skill area. It is always wise to reach first for the attainable and slowly build on that as a foundation.

While being respectful may not be the easiest issue to work on, it usually is a smoke screen for other more important clinical issues. Your child's mastery of skills showing respect will help them be willing to listen, increase their trust in you, and see you as being on their side. Once your child views you as a support, they will be more willing to follow your lead into areas that they previously made taboo from discussion. The more your teaching leads to their success, the easier it will be for them to feel safe in your care and concern and trust in your judgment of what they should work on next.

Focusing on the positive often involves emphasizing what you want your child to do and not on what you want them to avoid doing. In other words you are actively **Replacing** undesirable habits and reactions with new personally and socially beneficial ones. **Cues** and **Prompts** signal what your child is to do or become aware of in a positive way and any pre-arranged agreements (see **Verbal Contracts** and **Safety Plans)** give your child a positive **Frame** or physical **Script** to engage in which sets them up to be safe and succeed.

6. Work with Your Child

Always work with your child, not against them. The goal of a **Strength Based Plan** is to maximize your child's natural tendencies and personality, it is not to change them. There is no ideal or perfect personality type, and each personality has strengths and potential drawbacks. Our goal, therefore, is to enhance and develop our child's strengths and to have them find attainable alternatives to the aspects of their habits which either minimize their joy or cause problems with others.

While being introverted may make it difficult for your child to have their voice be heard, they can learn skills of how to **Advocate** for themselves without the need to become aggressive or a socialite. Likewise, an extroverted child may have poor boundaries and not respect the privacy of others. They can learn how to respect and listen to others without necessarily becoming withdrawn or meek.

In a **Strength Based Approach** you are always looking to accomplish something rather than just having an absence of an unwanted behavior. As an example, you would focus on your child being calm rather than extinguishing their anxiety, or you would encourage their being friendly rather than just forbidding their belligerence.

7. Respect Your Child's Basic Nature

When teaching to a skill always keep your child's basic nature in mind. Children can engage in the same general behavior for entirely different reasons. Your approach to teaching a child who has trouble **Following Instructions** because of attention deficits would be different than teaching to a child who is defiant. In the anxious or hyperactive child you are supporting the child in developing organization and focus oriented skills along with calming techniques. With the defiant child you patiently, but firmly, have them focus on being respectful and being cooperative, while you avoid debate and power struggles. With the defiant child there is little dialogue and just a focus on skill use. With the anxious child you provide ample verbal support and encouragement.

Interventions that work with a child's basic nature are more successful and meet with less resistance. Often times long standing problems can almost instantly melt away when we find the right approach. It is for this reason that we have provided many tools with varying strategies and perspectives. If you are patient and search long enough, you will be able to find the tool for any given parental need you may require.

Summary of Implementing Strength Based Plans

What is it:

The implementation of **Strength Based Plans** involves identifying a series of skills which will have your child reach their **Long Term Goals**. A **Strength Based Approach** focuses on creating and identifying successful skill use as it happens and then to build on that success. The self-confidence generated by each mastered skill becomes the springboard providing the ego strength required to master the next challenging skill.

Why do it:

Long Term Strength Based Plans provide a shared vision of your child's future giving meaning and incentive to all the skills you are teaching and monitoring. A child who sees the practical value of the skills being suggested is more motivated to learn and master them.

Reframe, Replace, and Rewire:

Strength Based Plans are by their very nature a positive **Reframing** of our **Long Term Goals** for our children. **Strength Based Plans Replace** fear based or rigid goals with those endorsed and valued by your child. The positive nature of **Strength Based Goals** has your child focus on what to do, rather than what not to do, and thereby **Rewires** them by keeping their vision **Clear** and relatively anxiety free.

Implementing Strength Based Plans Home Improvement Projects

1. How important are the values of *respect and cooperation* in your relationship with your child?
2. Now that you have almost completed this book, which **Values** are the most important to you as a parent?
3. Think of **three** things you could **Praise** your child for today.
4. Name **three** ways you could practice patience with yourself as a parent.

Chapter Thirty-One

Bringing Out the Best In You

In the beginning of this book we stated that our intent was to write a comprehensive resource guide for parents of children with challenging mental health and/or behavioral issues. We wanted to help insure that the therapeutic thread was neither dropped or broken during transitions. These transitions could be from a high level of care to a lower level of care; a transition from placement to home; or from one facility to another.

We have taken great care to make the book very thorough while remaining concise. This book could easily have been hundreds of pages longer, especially considering the amount and wide range of information it covers. Due to the density of important and valuable information, we strongly suggest you read and reread many of the sections until you feel you've mastered how to use the tools and strategies outlined.

The activities were created as a way to supplement and expand on the basic ideas of the chapters, allowing us to present examples and provide exercises to help with your practical use of the strategies, skills, and perspectives. In this manner we were able to keep the main flow concise without sacrificing any practical assistance.

Just as your child will learn and master skills through their frequent identification and practice, so will you master the tools in this book through frequent use and practice. **Repetition** *is at the base of all learning and mastery.* A person becomes whatever they do on a daily basis; a person who paints each day will one day become a painter, just as a person who enjoys life every day becomes a happy person.

At first you will probably have to put a great deal of thought into the use of many of the skills in this book. Yet, if you continue to remind yourself to use these strategies they will one day become second nature and you will no longer have to think before using them. If you persevere you will one day become the master of any of the tools in this book you desire to make part of your parenting.

We have emphasized the importance of creating a relationship with your child based on mutual respect. In line with this thinking we've stressed the importance of having your child master skills of respect and cooperation. Many of the reasons and benefits of this preference have already been covered in this book, but let's take a moment to highlight two of them.

When children in placement are asked why they feel they are in placement they usually state it is due to some diagnosis (oppositional defiant, depression, bipolar, etc.) or because, "*My parents stuck me here.*" The fact of the matter is there are literally millions of children with the same diagnosis who are not in placement. So, what is the reason children end up in placement?

It is our experience that children generally end up in placement due to their severely or persistently angering or frightening those who have to mange or deal with them (parents, teachers, or therapists). Children can anger or frighten adults by being violent and aggressive or self-harming and fragile. A child who is 'outstanding' in this arena is the most likely candidate for placement.

A child who routinely **Accepts Criticism**, **Respectfully Disagrees**, **Accepts No**, and **Follows Instructions** is almost never considered a candidate for out-of-home placement. While there are exceptions, it would appear that having your child master skills of compliance is the surest way of not being identified as needing to be removed from home. So, with this in mind, there is no mystery as to why we've stressed their importance.

Another reason we've emphasized making cooperation skills into a centerpiece of parenting is its benefits for you. The reduction of stress and improvements in the quality of life for parents of children who are respectful is usually quite significant. The value of having a harmonious home environment is hard to overstate. Many parents are so satisfied when their children master respectfulness that they see no reason to go on to teaching any other skills. While we feel that respect is just the beginning and many joys lie ahead, we understand and appreciate the feeling of completion that such mastery can engender.

Expectation and Opportunity

In this book we have presented many strategies and perspectives from which you can choose, as well as many techniques and skills for you to adopt and hone. Our intent in doing this was to give you a chance to find the parent and relationship building tools you want to use with your child. All the resources in this book are designed to **Bring Out the Best in You** as a parent and as a person, as well as helping you **Bring Out the Best in Your Children**.

We have all known poorly skilled children who have gone on to become successful and socially competent adults. Many of us ourselves were obnoxious children who have gone on to become functioning, healthy, and successful adults. This fact should make it very **Clear** that your use of this manual is not a necessity, duty or expectation. Each perspective, strategy, technique, and skill are just an opportunity to make your job as a parent a little less stressful and more rewarding.

The title of this section is **Bringing Out the Best in You**, and that pretty much sums up our goal and intention. This entire book is a gift of tools for you to consider using which have helped thousands of parents and children become closer and more harmonious. It is a ***Parental Tool Box*** for you to look inside and choose from one of the many tools available whenever the need arises. Whatever the parenting task you can use this resource to help guide you in a potentially fruitful direction.

While being perfect is impossible, being better at something is inevitable if you put in the time and practice. So, while our goal has never been for you to be or become the perfect parent, our purpose has been to provide you with the tools to help you become a better parent. Do not expect any miracles or place unrealistic demands on yourself, your spouse, or child, yet use the tools and give yourself the opportunity to become better each and every week (remembering we all have our bad days).

Enjoying the Journey

We realize that many of you reading this have been through some very difficult, exhausting, and painful times with your child. We are aware that some of you have experienced fear and even dread at the prospect of your next interaction with your child. We do not want to deny or even minimize what you have been through. Yet, we will not support a conclusion that your parenting, child, or life is beyond improvement or being healed.

When we ask you to enjoy the journey we are not being idealistic or blind to the realities of many of your personal histories. We are in the business of hearing the all too often horrific stories of parents and families. Yet, we also are in the business of seeing the positive side of personal change and development.

In many respects we've come full circle in this book. We started by empathizing with your situation and possible feelings of total frustration, powerlessness, and resignation and by pointing out you are in control of how you choose to **Frame** your world. The words you say to yourself and to others, we observed, have a very profound affect on how you experience life and the direction in which it will go.

Using many of the verbal strategies in this book, you now can avoid many battles and power struggles by **Framing** your child's disrespect as an opportunity to use a skill rather than fight over a topic. You can **Frame** your interventions as an act of care and concern rather than as a desire to control or out will your child. Hurtful blaming statements of others can be **Reframed** as **"I," Statements**. **"I Feel," Statements** or **"When/Then," Statements** can **Replace** ultimatums and threats.

Frames, as we stated earlier, are not illusions or denials of reality but a choice of perspective. A parent who feels defeated and powerless typically **Frames** all possible options as being hopeless and silly. Yet, the same parent using some of the strategies in this book will start to focus on success and build on each positive use of a skill. Soon they will be **Framing** their child's behavior in terms of growth and progress instead of only pointing out errors and opposition.

The **Verbal Strategies**, **Relationship Techniques**, **Social Skills**, and therapeutic perspectives give you the option of seeing and reacting to your child in a new and improved manner. Your usage of these skills have the potential of adding greatly to your level of happiness and satisfaction as a person and as a parent. Your child's usage of the verbal and social skills outlined in this book could greatly improve their social functioning and self-concept.

This all opens up the possibility and the **Frame** of **Enjoying the Journey**. Parents and children who feel that they are a team working towards the same goal are generally more appreciative of each other and their relationship.

A parent who observes and describes what they see is able to be honest without being insulting or judgmental. **Framing** things as descriptions of individual events prevents a parent from using categorical language that labels or judges. *Stating how someone's actions are not matching their words is quite different from calling someone a liar.* One is about a skill of honesty and the other **Frame** is one of labeling someone's basic character. The skills of being **Clear** and **Specific** emphasize the here and now and avoid the tendency of language to be categorical and historical.

Another concept we mentioned early on is the basic need for every human being to both belong and feel connected while at the same time being recognized and appreciated as a separate unique human being. So even as your child is more appreciative of you and your relationship with them, they will still need to separate and become more autonomous. The more you recognize and respect that basic ambivalence, the easier it is to **Frame** and experience their thrust towards autonomy as something to celebrate and not as a form of rejection.

The relationship of parent and child is one of the most amazing and complex journeys available in human life. Due to the intense nature of this relationship, its powers of destruction and beauty are almost unmatched. We hope we've given you a reason to see and feel the journey as something to savor and celebrate. ***The Parental Tool Box*** has been dedicated to exploring ways to make your parent/child journey more comforting and rewarding. We sincerely hope you find a way to use it which makes your journey a little more enjoyable.

Summary of Bringing Out the Best In You

What is it:

The Parental Tool Box provides you with ample skills and strategies to **Bring Out the Best in You** and your child. **Bringing out the Best in You** is being a supportive and caring parent while maintaining high expectations for yourself and your child.

Why do it:

It is easier to remain patient and confident in your parenting when you feel that you are able to access the right tool for the job. **In Bringing About the Best in You** the goal is not to be the perfect parent or have the perfect child but rather to create a harmonious home environment where being a parent is an enjoyable and rewarding experience.

Reframe, Replace, and Rewire:

While it is true that being a parent is a huge responsibility, it is also true that parenting is an incredible opportunity to provide your life with joy and meaning. ***The Parental Tool Box* Reframes** the task of parenting from one of a need to be perfect and always do the right thing to a rewarding life long project of building an enjoyable and rewarding relationship with your child. When using the right tools both you and your child can **Replace** conflict and hurt with joy and self-appreciation. Through accenting the positive and limiting the troublesome, one **Rewires** the entire family thereby creating a happy and harmonious living environment making both parenthood and childhood a positive experience.

Bringing Out the Best in You Home Improvement Projects

1. Focusing on the positives in your family, make **Certificates of Achievement** for each family member to acknowledge something accomplished. Give these out at a **Family Meeting**.
2. What tools in ***The Parental Tool Box*** were the most helpful for you?
3. What tools in the ***The Parental Tool Box*** make you feel more hopeful?
4. One of the best ways to learn something is to teach it. Which skills learned in this book are you willing to share and teach to another parent?
5. What are your favorite memories of being a parent?
6. What skills are you most excited to use? Prioritize these skills in order of importance.

About the Authors

Dayna Guido, MSW, LCSW, ACSW is a psychotherapist, clinical supervisor, consultant, educator, and trainer. She has a private practice in Asheville, NC and specializes in providing clinical supervision. She has been teaching graduate school for over 20 years as an Adjunct Instructor for the University of North Carolina at Chapel Hill School of Social Work; Lenoir-Rhyne University, Clinical Mental Health Counseling; and East Tennessee State University, Department of Social Work. Dayna provides clinical trainings and is the author of *Creative Ways to Learn Ethics: An Experiential Training Manual for Helping Professionals.*

Jim Guido is a consultant, trainer, writer, educator and musician. Over the last forty years he has worked with children, young adults, and their families in a variety of therapeutic, educational, and recreational settings. He has designed, developed, and implemented programs for both private and public agencies in educational and therapeutic realms. In writing ***The Parental Tool Box***, Jim draws from diverse roles as a direct care provider and supervisor in residential facilities and alternative schools; parent trainer; in-home interventionist; coach; and tutor.

daynaguido.com
jimguido.art
globalheartgroup.com

The Global Heart Group is dedicated to improve and sustain the quality of life for all of the earth's inhabitants. Our mission is to promote and support literary and artistic works exploring the art of living in a life affirming manner.

References

American Psychiatric Association. (2013). *Diagnostic and Statistical Manual of Mental Disorders, Fifth Edition. Washington*, DC: American Psychiatric Association.

Barkley, Russell A. (1997). *Defiant Children: A Clinician's Manual for Assessment and Parent Training, Second Edition.* New York: The Guilford Press.

Baker, Jed, PhD. (2008). *No More Meltdowns.* Arlington, TX: Future Horizons.

Basco, Monica Ramirez, PhD. (2006). *The Bipolar Workbook: Tips for Controlling Mood Swings.* New York: The Guilford Press.

Bloomquist, Michael L. (1996). *Skills Training for Children with Behavior Disorders: A Parent and Therapist Guidebook.* New York: The Guilford Press.

Bourne, Edmund J. PhD. (2005). *The Anxiety and Phobia Workbook, Fourth Edition.* Oakland, CA: New Harbinger Publications, Inc.

Bronson, P. & Merryman. (2009). *Nurture Shock - New Thinking About Children.* New York: Hatchett Book Group.

Burnett, B. & Evans, D. (2016). *Designing Your Life: How to Build a Well-Lived, Joyful Life.* New York: Alfred A. Knopf.

Butcher, K. (2013). *Becoming a responsive parent through attunement – Part 2.* http://msue.anr.msu.edu/news/becoming_a_responsive_parent_through_attunement.

Cline, Foster & Fay, Jim. (2006). *Parenting with Love and Logic (Updated & Expanded).* CO: NavPress.

Coloroso , B. (2002). *Kids Are Worth It! Giving Your Child the Gift of Inner Discipline, Revised Ed.* New York: HarperColins, Publishers, Inc.

Dewar, G. Ph.D. (2014). *The cognitive benefits of play: Effects on the learning brain.* https://www.parentingscience.com/benefits-of-play.html.

Dowd, Czyz, O'Kane & Elofson. (1994). *Effective Skills for Child-Care Workers: A Training Manual from Boys Town.* NE: Boys Town Press.

Faber & Mazlish (2012). *How to Talk So Kids Will Listen & Listen So Kids Will Talk*. New York: Scribner.

Faherty, Catherine. (2000). *What Does It Mean To Me? A workbook explaining self awareness and life lessons to the child or youth with High Functioning Autism or Aspergers*. Arlington, TX: Future Horizons, Inc.

Gottman, John. (2011). *Raising an Emotionally Intelligent Child*. New York: Simon & Schuster.

Greene, Ross, PhD. (2001). *The Explosive Child*. New York: HarperCollins.

Greene, Ross W., PhD. and J. Stuart Ablon, PhD. (2006). *Treating Explosive Kids: The Collaborative Problem Solving Approach*. New York: The Guilford Press.

Grandin, Temple, Ph.D, & Moore, Debra, Ph.D. (2016). *The Loving Push: How Parents and Professionals Can Help Spectrum Kids Become Successful Adults*. Arlington, Tx: Future Horizons, Inc.

Hanson, Rick, Ph.D. (2013). *Hardwiring Happiness: The New Brain Science of Contentment, Calm, and Confidence*. New York: Random House.

Harmon, K. (2010). *How Important Is Physical Contact with Your Infant?* https://www.scientificamerican.com/article/infant-touch/.

Hughes, D. (1998). *Facilitating the Bonds of Attachment*. Northvale, NJ: J. Aronson.

Hughes, Daniel A. (1997). *Facilitating Developmental Attachment: The Road to Emotional Recovery and Behavioral Change in Foster and Adopted Children*. Northvale, NJ: Jason Aronson, Inc.

Kaufman, Gershen, Ph.D. (1992). *Shame: The Power of Caring, Third Edition, Revised and Expanded*. Rochester, Vermont: Schenkman Books, Inc.

Kranowitz, Carol Stock, M.A. (1998). *The Out-of-Sync Child: Recognizing and Coping with Sensory Integration Dysfunction*. New York: The Berkley Publishing Group.

Kuczaj, S. A., & Eskelinen, H. C. (2014). *Why do dolphins play?* Animal Behavior and Cognition, 1(2), 113-127. doi: 10.12966/abc.05.03.2014.

Lally, P.,Van Jaarsveld, Potts, and Wardle (2010). *How are habits formed: Modelling habit formation in the real world*. European Journal of Social Psychology 40, 998–1009. Published online 16 July 2009 in Wiley Online Library (wileyonlinelibrary.com) DOI: 10.1002/ejsp.674.

Lipsky, Deborah & Richards, Will. (2009). *Managing Meltdowns: Using the S.C.A.R.E.D.*

Calming Technique with Children & Adults with Autism. London: Jessica Kingsley Publishers.

Lynn, George T. M.A., M.P.A., C.M.H.C. (2000). *Survival Strategies for Parenting Children with Bipolar Disorder.* London: Jessica Kingsley Publishers.

Lythcott-Haines, J. (2015). *How to Raise an Adult: Break Free of the Over Parenting Trap and Prepare Your Kid for Success.* NY: Henry Holt & Co.

McCurry, C., Ph.D. (2009). *Parenting Your Anxious Child with Mindfulness and Acceptance.* CA: New Harbinger Publications, Inc.

Myles, Brenda Smith and Jack Southwick. (1999). *Asperger Syndrome and Difficult Moments: Practical Solutions for Tantrums, Rage and Meltdowns.* Shawnee Mission, Kansas: Autism Publishing Co.

Nichols, S.; Moravcik & Tetenbaum. (2009). *Girls Growing Up on the Autism Spectrum: What Parents and Professionals Should Know About the Pre-Teen and Teenage Years.* London: Jessica Kingsley Publishers.

Ogden, P. & Fisher, J. (2015). *Sensorimotor Psychotherapy: Interventions for Trauma and Attachment.* New York: W.W. Norton & Company.

Pozatek, C. (2011). *The Parallel Process: Growing Alongside Your Adolescent or Young Adult Child in Treatment.* New York: Lantern Books.

Ratey, John J., MD. (2008). *Spark: The Revolutionary New Science of Exercise and the Brain.* New York, NY: Little Brown and Company.

Reedy, Brad M., Ph.D. (2015). *The Journey of the Heroic Parent: Your Child's Struggle and the Road Home.* New York: Regan Arts.

"Repetition and Learning." *Learning and Memory.* Encyclopedia.com. 3 Jan. 2018 <http://www.encyclopedia.com>.

Siegel, Daniel, M.D. (2013). *Brainstorm: The Power and Purpose of the Teenage Brain.* New York: Penguin.

Siegel, Daniel., M.D. & Bryson, Tina P. (2014). *No-Drama Discipline: The Whole-Brain Way to Calm the Chaos and Nurture Your Child's Developing Mind.* New York: Bantam.

Siegel, Daniel, M.D. (2012). *The Developing Mind: How Relationships and the Brain Interact to Shape Who We Are, 2nd Edition.* New York: The Guilford Press.

Siegel, Daniel., M.D. & Bryson, Tina P. (2011). *The Whole-Brain Child: 12 Revolutionary Stratagies to Nurture Your Child's Developing Mind.* New York: Bantam.

Sohn, A. & Grayson, C. (2005). *Parenting Your Asperger Child: Individualized Solutions for Teaching Your Child Practical Skills.* New York: Penguin Group.

Stallard, P. (2002). *Think Good - Feel Good: A Cognitive Behavior Therapy Workbook for Children and Young People.* England: John Wiley & Sons, LTD.

Thayne, Tim, Ph.D. (2013). *Not By Chance.* SC: Advantage.

Townshend, John PhD. (2006). *Boundaries with Teens: When to Say Yes How to Say No.* Grand Rapids, MI: Zondervan.

Vorrath, Harry & Brendtro, Larry. (1974). *Positive Peer Culture.* Chicago, IL: Aldine Publishing Co.

Index of Terms

A

B

C

D

E

F

G

H

I

J

L

M

N

O

P

Q

R

S

T

U

V

W

ACKNOWLEDGMENTS

I cannot fail to say "thank you" to my sweet hubby, Andrew, who endured untold hours in coffee shops to sit with me while I worked on this novel and spent many a Saturday afternoon sitting in the library where I met with my local writer's group.

"Thank you, Felty Tribe, for your patience with requests like, "Hey, can you read this and tell me what you think?"

Hats off and warm hugs to my awesome editor, Lourdes, and my incredible team of beta readers.

It truly takes a "village" to write a book these days.

All the characters in this book are fictitious. Any resemblance to actual persons, living or deceased, is purely coincidental.